Formative Assessment for 3D Science Learning

Formative Assessment for 3D Science Learning

Supporting Ambitious and Equitable Instruction

Erin Marie Furtak

Foreword by Lorrie A. Shepard

TEACHERS COLLEGE PRESS
TEACHERS COLLEGE | COLUMBIA UNIVERSITY
NEW YORK AND LONDON

Published by Teachers College Press,® 1234 Amsterdam Avenue, New York, NY 10027

Copyright © 2023 by Teachers College, Columbia University

Front cover image by Sven King via Unsplash.

All rights reserved. No part of this publication may be reproduced or transmitted in any form or by any means, electronic or mechanical, including photocopy, or any information storage and retrieval system, without permission from the publisher. For reprint permission and other subsidiary rights requests, please contact Teachers College Press, Rights Dept.: tcpressrights@tc.columbia.edu

Library of Congress Cataloging-in-Publication Data

Names: Furtak, Erin Marie, author.
Title: Formative assessment for 3D science learning : supporting ambitious and equitable instruction / Erin Marie Furtak.
Other titles: Formative assessment for three-dimensional science learning
Description: New York, NY : Teachers College Press, [2023] | Includes bibliographical references and index. | Summary: "This comprehensive book provides a framework for designing and enacting 3D science assessments that center students' interests and support rigorous and equitable instruction (K-12)"—Provided by publisher.
Identifiers: LCCN 2023003443 (print) | LCCN 2023003444 (ebook) | ISBN 9780807768594 (hardcover) | ISBN 9780807768587 (paperback) | ISBN 9780807781845 (ebook)
Subjects: LCSH: Science—Study and teaching—Evaluation. | Science—Study and teaching—United States. | Educational tests and measurements—United States. | Educational equalization—United States.
Classification: LCC LB1585.3 .F87 2023 (print) | LCC LB1585.3 (ebook) | DDC 372.35—dc23/eng/20230301
LC record available at https://lccn.loc.gov/2023003443
LC ebook record available at https://lccn.loc.gov/2023003444

ISBN 978-0-8077-6858-7 (paper)
ISBN 978-0-8077-6859-4 (hardcover)
ISBN 978-0-8077-8184-5 (ebook)

Printed on acid-free paper
Manufactured in the United States of America

For Dave, Maia, and Aidan

Contents

Foreword Lorrie A. Shepard	xiii
Preface	xv
My History in Science and Formative Assessment	xvi
Why I Wrote This Book	xvii
Scope	xviii
To Whom This Book Is Directed	xviii
Acknowledgments	xxi

PART I: FRAMING

1. It's Time to Rethink Formative Assessment in Science Education	**3**
What Is Formative Assessment in Science?	4
New Understandings About Learning That Influence Curriculum, Instruction, and Assessment	5
Formative Assessment for Ambitious and Equitable 3D Science Learning	11
Initial Drawings	15
Family Activity	15
How to Read This Book	16
2. Broadening Our View of Science Formative Assessment	**19**
Formative Assessment in a System of Classroom Activity	21

Defining Elements of a Formative Assessment
Activity System 23

How Activity Systems Work to Support Learning Through
Formative Assessment 33

Looking Ahead 38

3. **Formative Assessment as a Vehicle for Equity and Justice
in Science Learning** 39

Structural Influences on Science Formative Assessment 40

Constraints on Formative Assessment 43

Formative Assessment as a Vehicle for Equity
and Justice 45

Self-Reflection for Ambitious and Equitable Teaching 47

Centering Equity and Justice in Formative Assessment:
Examples 49

Equity and Justice: Connective Threads for Formative
Assessment Design and Enactment 53

PART II: TASKS AND PRACTICES

4. **Questions Worth Answering: The Role of Phenomena in
Formative Assessment** 57

Considerations for Phenomena 58

Types of Phenomena for Formative Assessment 63

How Different Phenomena Support Formative Assessment
Across an Instructional Unit 66

Resources for Identifying Phenomena for Formative
Assessment 69

Putting It All Together: Framing Formative Assessment
Tasks With Phenomena 69

5. **Formative Assessment Tasks: Artifacts and Material
Representations of Student Thinking** 71

What Do We Mean by "Tasks"? 72

	The Role of Formative Assessment Tasks	73
	Integrating the Three Dimensions in Formative Assessment Tasks	75
	Elements of Multicomponent Formative Assessment Task Design: Supporting Learners to Show What They Know	81
	Putting It All Together: Redesigning a Multicomponent Formative Assessment Task	92
	Beyond Paper and Pencil: Technology-Assisted Formative Assessment Tasks	100
	Looking Ahead: The Importance of Practices and Feedback	103
6.	**Norms, Routines, and Community: Classroom Enactment of Formative Assessment**	**105**
	What Do We Mean by "Enactment"?	105
	Participation Structures	106
	Norms and Routines	111
	Talk Moves: Essential Elements of Formative Assessment Classroom Practices	118
	Putting It All Together: A Formative Assessment Conversation to Support the Development of Student Thinking	119
7.	**Feedback**	**125**
	Feedback to Support Science Learning	126
	A Model of Feedback	127
	Medium Cycles	138

PART III: BEYOND THE CLASSROOM

8.	**Tools and Routines for Professional Learning: Collaborative Formative Assessment Design**	**143**
	Teacher Professional Learning Through Formative Assessment Design	144

Steps for Collaborative Formative Assessment Design	145
Increasing Opportunities for Teachers to Learn Through Collaboration and Formative Assessment Co-Design	159

9. Learning Progressions: Tools for Formative Assessment — 161

Defining Learning Progressions	161
Learning Progressions for Three-Dimensional Assessment	163
Three Functions for Learning Progressions in Formative Assessment	164
Features of Learning Progressions That Support Formative Assessment	174
Potential to Guide Formative Assessment, With Caution	176

10. Conclusion: Formative Assessment for Ambitious and Equitable Science Learning: Toward a New Horizon — 177

Main Arguments	177
What Can We Do?	178
Closing	179

Appendix A. Phenomenon Planner	181
Appendix B. Heated Cup Task	183
Appendix C. Formative Assessment Task Design Checklist	185
Appendix D. Weather in Three Places Task	187
Appendix E. Snowmelt Task	189
Appendix F. High-Elevation Task	191
Appendix G. Enactment Planning Guide	197
Appendix H. Skateboarder Modeling Task	199
Appendix I. Sample Meeting Agendas for Collaborative Formative Assessment Design	201

Appendix J. Learning Progression Unit Planner	**203**
References	**205**
Index	**221**
About the Author	**227**

Foreword

By writing *Formative Assessment for 3D Science Learning: Supporting Ambitious and Equitable Instruction*, Professor Furtak has provided a generous resource for science teachers and school leaders. Teaching was never simple, but today's teachers face a seemingly insurmountable number of demands—including administrative trivia alongside the emotionally charged needs of their students, plus multiple reform initiatives that are often uncoordinated and sometimes at cross-purposes. This book is powerful because it weaves together and brings coherence to multiple initiatives, not only the three dimensions of the Next Generation Science Standards but also formative assessment, ambitious instructional practices, and equitable learning environments. This weaving together is especially important for the integration of 3D science reform with diversity, equity, and inclusion (DEI). DEI initiatives are everywhere, but too often they are undertaken separate from subject matter learning. This makes them feel inauthentic for students, when nothing changes in how they are taught in their history or language arts or science class.

This book is both deeply theoretical and immensely practical. To be of the greatest practical use, only the first two chapters focus on theory. But these clear explanations of sociocultural theory and classroom activity systems are important. They help us see how 3D science reforms—especially participation in disciplinary practices—come from the same research and theory that underpin formative assessment practices designed to elicit and respond to student thinking. Sociocultural theory also provides the evidence and arguments as to why responding to students' identities and life experiences is critical for meaningful learning. Theoretical insights, thus, tie things together in a way that makes profound improvements in teaching and learning possible.

Abundant examples in the remaining eight chapters show us how these ambitious practices can be enacted. Most science teachers have heard reform rhetoric, for example, about drawing on students' "funds of knowledge" as a resource for teaching or moving beyond right/wrong interpretations of students' answers. But they may not know yet the specifics of what these and other 3D science slogans could mean in the context of their own practice. Professor Furtak's examples—about centering equity, resources for identifying phenomena, attending to culture and language without "watering down" expectations, and feedback strategies that draw out and extend student thinking—are a gift because they help us see that next level of detail, showing us how theoretical intentions can be brought to life.

Professor Furtak is also generous with her care about teacher learning. She is honest and thoughtful about lessons from her own experiences as a high school Biology teacher, and she acknowledges challenges, like the risks and surprises of opening up to students' ideas. In the closing chapters of the book, Professor Furtak addresses the resources and supports teachers need to take up formative assessment as an integral tool for enactment of ambitious and equitable science learning. One personal example of a crucial resource was the importance of convincing a high school principal to allow one class period when no biology was taught so that teachers could meet to collaborate within the bounds of the regular school day. Throughout the book, Professor Furtak emphasizes the importance of collaboration and shows great respect for the teacher teams with whom she has partnered. Again, she provides specific examples suggesting how willing teachers can find collaborators, even in rural schools, and she offers tools that help teachers get the most out of joint efforts, including ways to deepen our own understanding of the science we want to teach, ways to learn together by reviewing an individual student's work, and even respectful norms for watching a video together.

For me, the best chapter of all was Chapter 6, "Norms, Routines, and Community: Classroom Enactment of Formative Assessment," because it made me think, of course, that "we teach *everything*" that our children come to know and are able to do. If you want students to be able to think, you have to teach thinking. If you want them to treat each other with respect, teach that. Teaching includes modeling, sometimes telling, but always it means allowing for practice with ways of doing and being. By being explicit about how classrooms are organized around formative assessment tasks, Professor Furtak suggests that we can purposefully design for equity, making sure that there is space for all students to contribute their ideas. Together with students, we can develop norms and routines making it customary for students to share ideas in low-risk pairs before whole-class discussion, to draw initial models with the understanding that they will be revised as we learn more, and to listen with respect to each other's ideas.

Professor Furtak lets us see how the theory works. What a wonderful and empowering professional gift.

—Lorrie A. Shepard

Preface

It's an exciting time full of possibility for science learning and classroom assessment. Nearly a century of science education reform efforts have culminated in a three-dimensional vision for science learning in which students learn the disciplinary core ideas of science by engaging in the practices of scientists and applying concepts that cut across the science disciplines (Board on Science Education, 2012). This approach to science education reform grew out of larger shifts in how we conceptualize learning as changes in participation in disciplinary practices over time (e.g., Ford & Forman, 2006; National Academies of Science, Engineering and Medicine, 2018). These shifts have necessitated ambitious instruction that engages students in interactive, authentic tasks; challenges students intellectually; and supports students in developing in-depth understandings (Smith et al., 2001; Smylie & Wenzel, 2006; Windschitl et al., 2018).

Our efforts in science education reform center learning experiences on the resources and ideas that learners bring to the classroom, and particularly the interests and identities of students often left behind in schools (National Academies of Sciences, Engineering, and Medicine, 2022). U.S. classrooms are increasingly populated by students with a rich diversity of racial identities, gender expression, linguistic backgrounds, ways of learning, and socioeconomic status. As we move ahead with three-dimensional science education reforms, we seek not just to bridge but to intertwine students' multiple identities, experiences, and interests with their science learning (Bang et al., 2012; Tzou et al., 2019). We seek to engage learners' stories and questions, to break down the walls between the school and students' everyday lives and experiences, and to make science classrooms a space where students can have opportunities to make sense of the world with the support of their peers, their teacher, and other resources.

Classroom assessment should stand in the service of these monumental shifts in science learning, learning theory, and promoting equity. While educational assessment is often seen as a gatekeeper, this book will explore how it can be repositioned as a tool for promoting equity in our increasingly diverse classroom settings. My specific focus will be on formative assessment, or the assessment conducted by teachers and students to surface and work with student thinking while learning is in progress. Since formative assessment happens every day in routine teaching and learning interactions, it is ideally positioned to support the new three-dimensional vision of science learning. Formative assessment that promotes more equitable engagement in science learning. Formative assessment that supports ambitious science instruction.

MY HISTORY IN SCIENCE AND FORMATIVE ASSESSMENT

I come to writing this book as the daughter of a scientist and an elementary school teacher. I was raised in a home where my parents talked about learning and the contexts of schools and organizations over the dinner table every night. I visited my father's lab and saw what science looked like on a day-in, day-out basis. I also joined my mother in her elementary classroom on the weekends, helping her set up instructional materials and organize for learning. After studying biology as an undergraduate, I became a public high school science teacher. I sought to co-design assessments with my students and to provide feedback that would support their learning. I was puzzled, however, by how my assessment tasks could be of greater interest to my students. This led me to graduate and postdoctoral studies in science teaching reforms, classroom, and formative assessment. I had the chance to visit and learn from teachers enacting formative assessment across the United States. Later, I learned to speak German and studied science teaching in international schools with multilingual learners in Berlin.

As I carried these experiences forward into my own career as a professor and an educational researcher, it became clear to me that formative assessment is inherently tied up with the identities and experiences of those involved. As a classroom teacher, I had not been aware of my own role in tacitly, yet actively, maintaining existing power structures and hierarchies through what I viewed as the simple act of assessing what students knew about science. As a researcher, I could see how students who were multilingual were positioned as "lesser" than monolingual English speakers. Students of color were often clustered in lower-track classes, where curricula were more didactic and assessments were focused on basic skills and knowledge. In some cases, teachers dedicated large amounts of class time to allow students time to talk about their ideas, and then moved on without taking up those ideas or making connections (Furtak, 2006). In other instances, formative assessments became a more efficient way of drawing out ideas that were then identified as "misconceptions," and teachers encouraged students away from those ideas (Furtak, 2012). My team's efforts to design and enact better formative assessments to support student learning were intertwined with school policies and teacher perceptions that limited, rather than broadened, access to science learning for many students.

Yet I still saw the promise of formative assessment as a transformative teaching practice. I witnessed interactions in which students took ownership of their questions, making sense of observable events as they thought together and with their teacher about the science they were learning. Consistent with other studies examining the efficacy of formative assessment in science education, I found that it could support both teacher and student learning (Furtak et al., 2008; Furtak, Kiemer, et al., 2016). I also identified the ways in which teachers' own understandings of student ideas, their classroom practices, and their ways of describing the science they were teaching developed as they collaborated with their colleagues around formative assessment task design (Furtak, Kiemer, et al., 2016; Furtak & Heredia, 2014). These shifts were supported not only through small interventions with individual teachers from schools, or through long-term professional learning, but also in sustained partnership with school district leaders.

WHY I WROTE THIS BOOK

In the context of the new wave of science education reforms, formative assessment is once again at the forefront. But unless it moves ahead with the reforms—unless it shifts to a different plane, so to speak—it unfortunately has the potential to snap the teaching of science backward to match outdated forms of instruction that are disconnected from students' lives and have little hope of increasing their opportunity to learn.

This book represents my best effort to synthesize across multiple literatures—from educational theory, science education philosophy and reform, classroom assessment and educational measurement, among others. I integrate research I've conducted with an incredible cohort of current and former graduate students, teachers, school district leaders, and colleagues to provide evidence for different approaches, as well as rich examples. I hope that I have created a synthesis that weaves together literatures to push the conversation in science formative assessment to a new place.

SCOPE

This book focuses on the design and enactment of science formative assessment in K–12 classrooms. It establishes theoretical foundations for taking a broad look at formative assessment that serves the purposes of educational equity in the context of three-dimensional science learning. It explores the design of formative assessment tasks embedded in authentic, everyday phenomena, and how to enact those tasks with learners through a variety of interactive strategies that challenge student thinking. In particular, the book explores how the design of formative assessment tasks, and the ways we use those tasks with learners, can promote more access and opportunity to learn science. It also explores how to plan for and provide feedback to student responses that moves learners forward. Finally, the book describes how teachers can work together to plan for, create, and reflect on formative assessment in ways that support teacher and student learning.

The book is organized into three sections: a framing, the design and enactment of tasks in the classroom, and professional learning. Within these sections, chapters are framed by the concept of a system of classroom activity (Engeström, 1987, 2001; Moss, 2008). Each of the substantive chapters includes framing and definitions of an element of the activity system, such as a formative assessment task, samples from practice, and in many cases, quotations and transcriptions of classroom conversations. I have drawn examples from across multiple sources of science curricula and assessments spanning different science disciplines and grade levels K–12.

TO WHOM THIS BOOK IS DIRECTED

I hope this book will serve as a foundational resource for those aiming to broaden student access to and participation in science learning through formative assessment. Teachers will find accessible descriptions of elements of a classroom activity system, how these elements interact, and concrete guides to planning and enacting assessment, providing students with helpful feedback to advance their learning and suggestions for collaborating with colleagues. Science curriculum leaders will find examples of how formative assessment can be enacted across classrooms and create opportunities to coordinate practice at a larger scale.

At the same time, I have articulated a clear theoretical foundation to organize the approach of the book that researchers and graduate students studying science teaching and classroom assessment will find useful. I hope that the synthesis of literature across multiple areas will also provide helpful starting points for those wanting to better understand ambitious science teaching (Shepard, 2021; Windschitl et al., 2018), three-dimensional approaches to science education reform (Board on Science Education, 2012; National Academies of Sciences, Engineering, and Medicine, 2022), sociocultural foundations of assessment (Gee, 2008a; Moss, 2008; Shepard, 2000), and transforming assessment for justice and equity (Kang et al., 2022; Kang & Furtak, 2021; Randall, 2021).

Acknowledgments

This book represents many ongoing conversations as I have learned with and from a wide range of colleagues and collaborators going back to my work as a classroom teacher. I am grateful to all the teachers and students whose stories are represented here, as well as the district and state leaders with whom I have worked. Thank you for your stories, your candor, and your trust.

I am grateful to Emily Spangler, my editor, for reaching out and inviting me to write a new book on formative assessment in 2017. Thank you for continuing to believe that I could write this forward-looking book, and for your critical and constructive feedback over the 5 years it took from our first conversation to delivering the manuscript. Kathy Schultz, thank you for the Starbucks conversation in 2019 that led me to reach back out to Emily and actually start writing the book.

I am so fortunate to have learned from Lorrie Shepard for the past 15 years. Thank you for hiring me, Lorrie, which set me on the trajectory that prepared me to write this book. Co-teaching with you was among the honors of my professional career, and our conversations have pushed me into a new frame of theorizing assessment. Thank you for reading and providing feedback to chapters (and many more ideas) in this book.

Many researcher colleagues have supported my learning in bringing a critical stance to formative assessment, including Hosun Kang, Christopher Wright, Rasheda Likely, Aneesha Badrinarayan, Carrie Tzou, and Jennifer Randall. Melissa Braaten was a key thought partner in thinking through a better version of a task than I was able to write as a student teacher and encouraged me to own the term "ambitious" for the work included here. Okhee Lee—thank you for your colleagueship, and for telling me to stop apologizing and just do the good work. Meggin McIntosh, thank you for encouragement, and for believing I could write two books at once (still figuring that part out).

To my research team alumni Jason Buell, Kelsey Tayne, Kate Henson, Deb Morrison, and Sara Heredia: it has been a joy and privilege to work and learn with you over so many years. Jason, Kate, and Sara—thank you for reading and helping to improve elements of this manuscript. Caitlin Fine encouraged me into a new, more critical space as a scholar of formative assessment, and I continue to learn from her. My current students Clarissa Deverel-Rico and Keelin O'Connor read and provided feedback on the entire manuscript—thanks for being my safe space as I prepared to launch these ideas into the universe. Clarissa, thank you for so many hours of conversations, writing, and planning as we have dived into a new frame for formative assessment. I'm so glad we're continuing to learn together.

To my parents, Tom and Kay Furtak, whose abiding love involved knowing to almost never ask how the book was going. To my family Dave, Maia, and Aidan Suss—thank you for seeing the writer in me. Your love is imbued in every page of this manuscript. I love you all.

Formative Assessment for 3D Science Learning

Part I

FRAMING

CHAPTER 1

It's Time to Rethink Formative Assessment in Science Education

Courteney is a Mexican American who comes from a Spanish-speaking family in the Pacific Southwest of the United States (see the full description of the case in the original article by Kang et al., 2022). While she liked science, she was not fond of chemistry and physics, as she linked them with mathematics, where she had not been successful in school. Several of her family members worked in or were pursuing careers in the medical field, and someday she hoped to be an anesthesiologist or a nurse. She had learned a lot at home about the human body from her mother, a surgical scheduler.

When Courteney took physics in the 11th grade she was initially afraid, as she had heard the class involved a lot of math. But her teacher had been working with his colleagues to develop curriculum-embedded assessments that expanded what it means to be "good" at science for students like Courteney and her classmates, who overwhelmingly identified as Hispanic, received free or reduced-price lunch, and two-thirds of whom were multilingual. The unit—and its embedded assessments—were deliberately designed to invite students to bring their experiences, concerns about the people whom they cared about, home languages, and ideas into processes of doing science.

During the unit, Courteney and other students in her class had opportunities to learn about momentum by developing and using models, building explanations, and engaging in argumentation from evidence. The unit was designed around a central question: "How are modern cars designed to keep you and your family safe in a collision?" Students had opportunities to show what they know on assessments in a variety of ways, including by drawing and frequently revising models, using online simulations, collecting and analyzing data, and talking with their teacher and peers. Students ultimately revised a car design to make it safe based on what they had learned, and then delivered a "sales pitch" for their design to a panel of judges who then gave them verbal and written feedback. Students also shared stories of a loved one they were keeping safe with their design, and wrote a letter to that loved one to share their dream design.

When reflecting on her experiences in the class, Courteney recalled that she had received a lot of support from her teacher in putting together ideas about her car design; she also took away that her experience learning physics was humanizing and "for the people" (p. 31). She contrasted the "claim-evidence-reasoning" assessment that had been taken as a norm of doing science at that time with writing a letter to a loved one about a dream car design for them.

> Courteney thought drawing the dream car for the loved one and writing a letter was "really good" because "it has you thinking about other people, instead of just yourself . . . I was thinking about [my mom's] safety and everyone in the car that would be with her." In this humanized learning context, Courteney thought she "actually learned more about cars, in a way, and how it would help me in the future with choosing a car." (Kang et al., 2022, p. 32)

Courteney's experience illustrates so much of what we hope to do in formative assessment in science. In recent years, educational theorists and researchers have started to fundamentally reframe how we think about learning, with enormous implications for how we think about formative assessment. We seek to engage students in the practices of scientists such as modeling, explanation, and argumentation as they learn core and crosscutting concepts in the science disciplines (Board on Science Education, 2012). We hope to support them through interactive experiences in which they share what they know in discussions and have opportunities to demonstrate not just memorizable pieces of knowledge but also their engagement in practices over time (Moss, 2008; National Academies of Science, Engineering and Medicine, 2018). We seek to deliberately design these assessments around the resources students like Courteney bring to school, including what they have learned at home, their family's relationship to the places they live, the languages they speak, and what they care about and are interested in (Kang & Furtak, 2021; Tzou et al., 2021).

WHAT IS FORMATIVE ASSESSMENT IN SCIENCE?

Formative assessment is traditionally defined by the process of finding out what students know and providing ongoing feedback and support to further student learning, while instruction is still in progress. This is usually contrasted with what we often call summative assessment, which happens at the end of learning sequences, and is also used to assign grades, or to find out information about what students are learning across educational systems. Formative assessment, instead, lives in classrooms and happens on a daily, ongoing basis. It is both formal and informal, happening at preplanned moments, and also spontaneously in conversations between students and teachers. It can even happen when students pause to reflect on their own processes of learning. In sum, formative assessment is a powerful process for teachers and students to increase science learning and has the potential to promote equitable participation in science learning (Black & Wiliam, 1998).

Formative assessment is often framed by three central questions: *Where are we going? Where are we now? How are we going to get there?* (Pellegrino et al., 2001). Responses to these questions form a central, three-step framework for formative assessment in science education: It begins with setting learning goals, usually drawn from standards documents. Then, teachers determine the status of students' current progress through some kind of activity that elicits student performance. The concluding step is some form of feedback that pushes students forward in their learning and tailors subsequent learning to meet students' needs.

Nice and simple, right? Yes . . . and there's a lot more to the story.

NEW UNDERSTANDINGS ABOUT LEARNING THAT INFLUENCE CURRICULUM, INSTRUCTION, AND ASSESSMENT

In order to support learning, curriculum, instruction, and assessment should be aligned with each other (Pellegrino et al., 2001; Shepard et al., 2018). This relationship can be represented as a triangle, where curriculum materials are developed to support teachers and students in learning; teachers enact instructional practices consistent with the development of the curriculum materials; and opportunities for assessment then align with what students learn through a curriculum, supported by teaching practices (Black et al., 2011; Wilson, 2018). These three elements should be aligned with the same vision and theory of learning.

Figure 1.1 helps us consider the relationship between these elements and helps to underscore the following argument: How we theorize learning should in turn influence how we design and enact curriculum, instruction, and assessment. Further, the ways in which that theory of learning is enacted must be mutually supported by instruction, curriculum, and assessment. Later in the book, we'll consider what happens when these vertices are out of alignment, or what can occur when

Figure 1.1. Instructional Triangle Centered on a Theory of Learning (adapted from Wilson [2018])

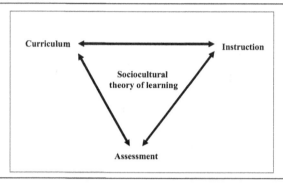

one vertex—for example, assessment—has an outsized influence on the other elements of the triangle (Black et al., 2011). For now, let's start by describing the ways in which theories of learning are shifting and their influence on the current vision for science curriculum and instruction. I will refer to these three interrelated conversations as science-as-practice, the new science standards, and critical perspectives on science education.

Science-as-Practice and Sociocultural Theory

In recent years, student learning in classrooms has been reconceptualized as participation in disciplinary practices (Ford & Forman, 2006). In science, this participation means the practices in which scientists engage as they ask questions, develop models, collect and analyze data, and develop explanations based on evidence. While science education reform has emphasized these processes of scientific inquiry for a long time (Rudolph, 2002), what's new is that we're seeking to redefine learning as engagement in these disciplinary practices or, more specifically, changes in participation in these practices over time. This is different from framing learning as changes in the knowledge in an individual student's mind.

The focus on disciplinary practices is connected to larger changes in how we think about student learning through the lens of sociocultural theory. While we'll dig more into this in Chapter 2, for now I will just emphasize a few elements of sociocultural theory that compel us to rethink our approach to assessment. Whereas traditional approaches to assessment focus on what an individual knows and can do, sociocultural perspectives encourage us to take a broader lens and consider how knowledge is distributed across individuals, and the ways that knowledge and meaning are situated in actual experiences (Gee, 2008b). Learning integrally involves students and their identities, in a process of being and becoming (Pryor & Crossouard, 2010). We view learning as a process of changing participation in disciplinary practice over time (Lave & Wenger, 1991; Wenger, 1998), as well as supporting the development of disciplinary knowledge (Board on Science Education, 2012; Ford & Forman, 2006). Students' lived experiences are viewed as foundational resources they bring to school, and as key points on which to build learning experiences (González & Moll, 2002).

Sociocultural theory encourages us to view learners as individuals in cultural and historical context (Board on Science Education, 2012; Ford & Forman, 2006) who are situated in larger activity systems with rules, routines, and divisions of labor (Engeström, 1999; Wertsch, 1998). Learners have individual, socially constructed identities that are constantly being formed and reformed, and changing from moment to moment (Gee, 2001; Luehmann, 2007). Curriculum, instruction, and assessment thus should be designed to engage learners' interests and identities to inspire them to investigate questions relevant to their lives.

The New Wave of Science Education Reform

These theoretical shifts deeply influenced the most recent policy initiatives in science education, best captured in the *Framework for K–12 Science Education* (Board on Science Education, 2012, p. 12), which then became the foundation for the Next Generation Science Standards (NGSS) (NGSS Lead States, 2013). The *Framework* coined a new vision for science learning that is called "three-dimensional" after its three core elements: science and engineering practices, disciplinary core ideas, and crosscutting concepts. Science and engineering practices are those disciplinary ways of knowing described in the previous paragraph, and which build upon and expand processes of science inquiry that were a major feature of the previous science education standards (National Research Council, 1996). The second dimension is comprised of disciplinary core ideas, or the big ideas in life, Earth and space, and physical sciences. Finally, crosscutting concepts—a new element of the NGSS—are the concepts that span and connect the various science disciplines. The unique feature of the new standards is that students' learning performances—what we expect them to know and do by participating in school—consist of all three elements.

This shift to three-dimensional learning is a big change from when I began teaching in the late 1990s, when it was commonplace to start the year with a "scientific inquiry" unit that focused on science practices like asking questions, drawing models, developing explanations, but in the absence of a particular scientific idea. I had all kinds of activities to support such inquiries, including students measuring how high plastic poppers would jump when they were flipped inside-out, or swirling a mystery liquid in a flask to see it mysteriously change color. In these lessons, the goal was to highlight how students participated in inquiry, but we didn't necessarily do anything to develop understanding of the scientific explanations or mechanisms underlying the phenomena we were investigating. In retrospect, I can see how these were missed opportunities to support students' science learning in authentic ways, and to look deeply into the phenomena we were exploring. We don't need to create content-free opportunities for students to engage in science practices; instead, we should always consider how students are learning about these practices in the context of a crosscutting concept and/or a disciplinary core idea.

As an example of how we are now seeking to intertwine the different dimensions, let's unpack a performance expectation for Earth's Systems in Middle School. MS-ESS-2-3 states that students will learn to analyze and interpret data on the distribution of fossils and rocks, continental shapes, and seafloor structures to provide evidence of past plate motions (NGSS Lead States, 2013). This performance expectation combines the three strands into a single statement to guide learning and teaching:

- Science practice: Analyze and interpret data
- Disciplinary core idea: Plate tectonics and large-scale interactions
- Crosscutting concept: Patterns

This performance expectation is intended to guide learning by foregrounding engagement in a disciplinary practice in order to uncover a disciplinary core idea: examining evidence in the form of locations of fossils, maps of geological formations on the seafloor, and examining similarities in the shapes of continents can support students in identifying patterns (e.g., fossils that can be found both on the African and South American continents; the location of the mid-Atlantic ridge or the Mariana trench). Curriculum materials have been designed to engage students directly with these kinds of data, including through interactive simulations. Teachers can support students in looking for patterns in the data through questions that lead them to look at similarities and differences in these data, and to examine how these patterns can be interpreted as evidence that suggest historical (and future) motions of plates. This contrasts with previous iterations of standards, which may have placed more emphasis on the concept of plate tectonics as a main learning goal.

Another key feature of the reform—again, building on sociocultural theory—is that students are expected to have the opportunity to engage in three-dimensional learning in the context of everyday phenomena or scenarios that are interesting and relevant to their lives and communities. Science lessons can then be framed as opportunities to make sense of and ask questions about these phenomena, and students are encouraged to start new curriculum units by learning about the phenomenon or question at hand, and then asking questions that arise based on their prior experiences, as well as their natural curiosity. Continuing with the example performance expectation above, curriculum materials have been designed to connect with students' own wonderings about the Earth and how it is constantly changing, using driving questions such as, "What will the Earth look like in 500 years?" from the Concord Consortium (www.concord.org), or "What causes Earth's surface to change?" from OpenSciEd, a nonprofit open-source curriculum (openscied.org).

We can support these three-dimensional science learning experiences by approaches to instruction that have been called *ambitious* (Lampert et al., 2013; Shepard, 2021; Windschitl & Thompson, 2011). This term refers to teaching that is rigorous, creates ample space for students' intellectual engagement, and connects learning experiences to daily life (Smith et al., 2001; Smylie & Wenzel, 2006). In science education, ambitious instruction involves planning learning experiences around big ideas and relevant phenomena to students' lives, drawing out their ideas, supporting ongoing changes in their thinking, and helping them to develop evidence-based explanations (Windschitl et al., 2018). They emphasize developing norms that support a classroom culture with high intellectual demand and attention to equity (Windschitl et al., 2018) in which students listen to each other and work together to make sense of the phenomenon at hand (Edelson et al., 2021). Teachers encourage collaboration and routines within the class where teachers and students routinely pause to appraise what's been learned so far, and to consider what to work on as the class moves ahead.

Science Education for Equity and Justice

Alongside these shifts in theory and policy have been larger movements emphasizing the need for radical and transformative changes in science education in the service of equity and justice. Science education sits at the crux of two intersecting systems of oppression: the scientific enterprise, which has been dominated by white, male, and Western perspectives, and which has disproportionately affected those living in developing countries (Latour, 2018); and the American school system, which has historically functioned in ways that marginalize students viewed as "other" from white, dominant culture (Kumashiro, 2000; Paris & Alim, 2017).

To counter these historical trends, the current era of reforms seeks to center the interests and identities of learners from a diversity of backgrounds, including students with disabilities, students of color, students living in poverty, and students from multilingual backgrounds (National Academies of Science, Engineering and Medicine [NASEM], 2018, 2022). This means that we seek to construct learning experiences in ways that create space for all learners to participate in three-dimensional science.

Equity and justice have emerged as explicit goals to better meet the needs of diverse learners in science education (Lee & Grapin, 2022; Philip & Azevedo, 2017). These goals include building bridges between students' interests and science and seeking to expand students' access and opportunity to learn science in and out of school. Further, these discourses include ways that what historically "counts" as science can be transformed and connected with larger social movements out of school. The National Academies of Science, Engineering and Medicine (2022) labeled the first two approaches as movements toward equity in science education, and the latter two movements toward justice in science education. These efforts to reform learning environments toward educational equity and justice compel us to address historical wrongdoings by reconstructing science learning environments to center the voices and identities of those students excluded in the past (Morales-Doyle, 2017).

Science education reformers are seizing upon opportunities to expansively reframe how student interests and identities can be placed at the center of learning environments (Board on Science Education, 2012). This means not only acknowledging but also deliberately creating learning opportunities around the ideas and experiences students bring to the classroom. This approach can help students know that they matter, that their communities matter, and that they have many resources upon which to draw in their science learning. For example, we should invite students to share stories about their experiences of familiar practices in science learning, such as growing vegetables in their gardens, home electronics repair, sewing, or kite making, and to make connections to disciplinary knowledge (Vossoughi et al., 2016; Wilson-Lopez et al., 2018).

This reframing values students' experiences as fundamental, not peripheral, to their science learning. Rather than considering how students' ideas are replaced by the science learning they access in school, we should instead consider how their identities, ideas, and experiences become interwoven with the scientific ways of knowing they learn in school, strengthening both (Tzou et al., 2019). Such reframing also compels science teachers to reorient their interactions with students toward the purposes of equity and justice (Burgess & Patterson Williams, 2022).

As an example of how we can attend to equity and justice in science learning, consider the Science and Integrated Language (SAIL) curriculum, a 5th-grade unit designed explicitly to support multilingual learners (Lee et al., 2019). Building on a framework for integrating language and science learning experiences (Lee et al., 2013), the curriculum is framed around a question of interest and relevance to learners' lives: *What happens to our garbage?* Students respond to a number of subquestions across a 9-week unit that all relate ideas about the structure and properties of matter to observable phenomena, including *What is that smell?* and *What causes changes in the properties of garbage?* (www.nyusail.org/curriculum). As they proceed through the unit, students make observations and predictions, engage in investigations, develop models, and construct explanations from evidence. The materials for the curriculum have "baked in" designs to support multilingual learners throughout, including sentence frames and starters, as well as using visual aids (Grapin et al., 2021). In addition, teachers preparing to use the curriculum had opportunities to learn about key science terms in students' home languages, and how to use classroom discourse strategies to support multilingual learners as they engaged in learning experiences (Lee et al., 2019).

FORMATIVE ASSESSMENT FOR AMBITIOUS AND EQUITABLE 3D SCIENCE LEARNING

The preceding sections have established how shifts in learning theory, science education standards, and the purposes of equity and justice should compel us to fundamentally re-appraise assessment in general, and particularly—getting to the purpose of this book—formative assessment. So what can we do as science educators, researchers, curriculum developers, and policymakers to reframe formative assessment to serve this new purpose? Let's explore the implications that each of these three trends has for the design and enactment of ambitious and equitable formative assessment in science classrooms.

Shifts in the way that we theorize learning should necessarily change how we consider formative assessment. If we consider learning as the knowledge one holds in their mind, then our assessments should simply look for changes in the amount of that knowledge accumulated over time. But if we consider learning to be changes in participation in disciplinary practice, we need to develop assessments that are sensitive to changes in participation over time, not just the knowledge one holds in one's mind. In addition, we expand our vision of learning to also include students' interests and identities so that learning is also a process of being and becoming (Nasir et al., 2022; Tzou et al., 2019). This means moving away from asking questions that get at knowledge alone and seeking to trace how students' models illustrate causal connections; to see how their explanations deepen and draw upon evidence; to witness how they reason and communicate about their ideas with others; and to view how their own ideas about science, and their perception of themselves as people who can contribute to science, also shift. It also challenges the way that we commonly assess individuals as an isolated event, and something individuals do. Instead, we shift to a vision of assessment as more authentic, responding to students' own questions, and embedded in accessible, everyday scenarios. Students should be allowed to work in groups, to share ideas with each other, and to revise those ideas as they participate in assessment. Shifts in how we theorize learning also compel us to broaden our view of assessment beyond an individual task or activity, and to consider the multiple ways students participate in learning over time in a variety of settings, both formal and informal.

Considering science learning as comprised of three dimensions—disciplinary core ideas, crosscutting concepts, and science and engineering practices—also pushes us to rethink the design of formative assessments; clearly, this vision for learning is complex and doesn't lend itself to assessment via simple short-answer or multiple-choice questions. A 2014 NRC assessment-focused supplement to the *Framework* argued that assessments should be constructed with multiple types of questions that together help us understand how students are engaging in scientific practices as they explain the big ideas, or disciplinary core ideas, in science (National Research Council, 2014). So a task might ask students to draw a model that demonstrates their understanding of the relationships involved in something they have experienced in their everyday lives, such as the need to wear a seat belt when driving (Kang et al., 2022), and then to write an explanation that illustrates their understanding of the relationships connected to a disciplinary core idea. Additional questions might encourage students to analyze data and apply the lenses of crosscutting concepts, such as looking at patterns or across different scales. Teachers conduct ongoing formative assessment that draws out and responds to students' developing ideas, supporting ongoing changes in students' thinking and engagement in science practices over time (Windschitl et al., 2018).

Finally, and most importantly, we must seize on these shifts in how we theorize and envision classroom science learning in ways that center equity and justice for the diverse learners in our classrooms. According to Burgess and Patterson Williams (2022), "equity work requires actively promoting all persons as equally entitled to the amenities of personhood, while acknowledging the contextual realities and barriers that foster inequities, and constantly working to name, address, and dismantle oppression" (p. 1074). When it comes to formative assessment, this means we must consciously attend to science assessment as parts of larger systems of curriculum and instruction (Furtak and Lee, in press; Kang and Furtak, 2021). We must design assessments around questions that interest learners and deliberately create space for all learners to be able to show what they know. It means we must attend to the ways we support learners and listen to and respond to them.

Given these trends, there are multiple implications for the design and enactment of formative assessment that is equitable, and that is supported by ambitious approaches to science instruction. First, we must consider how we design formative assessments as parts of larger systems of curriculum and instruction that center students' lived experiences, and which embed scientific questions in contexts familiar and interesting to students. Tasks should be designed in ways that provide scaffolding to help students show what they know and are able to do, allowing them to perform tasks in ways that sustain, rather than erase, their ways of doing and being. Multilingual students should be provided space to draw on *all* of their linguistic resources as they respond to the assessments. Furthermore, science teachers can consider their own identities and positionalities as teachers of science, and enact formative assessments in ways that make students feel safe, and that their ideas and experiences are not only valued but central to making sense of the scientific phenomena they are investigating in class.

Example: What Can We Do To Keep Our Community Healthy?

The remaining pages of this book will go into much greater depth around what formative assessment looks like when reframed around science as practice, with an emphasis on equitable participation in science lessons. As a preview, let's look at an example a formative assessment task written in 2020 to address students' experiences with COVID-19. This unit, part of the OpenSciEd open-source curriculum development effort, is designed for learners in grades K–2 (OpenSciEd, 2021). It addresses the driving question, "What can we do to keep our community healthy?"

14 | Framing

The unit is designed to engage students in multiple science practices such as asking questions and defining problems, developing and using models, and constructing explanations and designing solutions. In addition, for each lesson, the unit has specified what learners will figure out together about science, community, and COVID-19-related health inequities. Family and community members are engaged as an essential part of the learning experience through family tools.

Among the many formative assessments embedded in the unit is a paired set of tasks at lesson 2. At this point in the unit, teachers and students have surfaced their own questions; now, students draw an initial model about how COVID-19 affects the body, and then share that model at home. Figure 1.2 shows an example of the modeling task for

Figure 1.2. Sample Paired Formative Assessment (Top) and Family Tasks (Bottom). "Grades K–2 Lesson 2 Family Tool 2.1" and "Grades K–2 Lesson 2 Handout: Initial Drawings" by OpenSciEd, www.openscied.org

How does the coronavirus make a person sick?

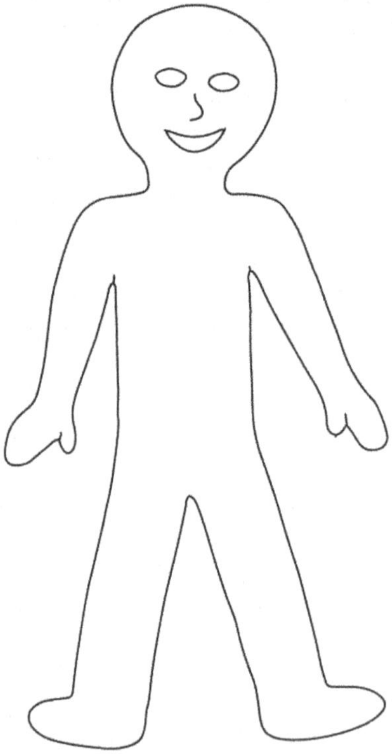

Licensed under Creative Commons License and without modification. View the Creative Commons Attribution 4.0 Unported License at http://creativecommons.org/licenses/by/4.0

students, as well as the family tool that guides students as they share their models and discuss them with their families.

INITIAL DRAWINGS

Directions: Use drawings to show what you already know or think you know about the coronavirus that causes COVID-19.

FAMILY ACTIVITY

Directions: First, have your child tell you about the model they created to explain how the coronavirus can make a person sick. Then talk about the questions that follow.

Part A: Model Sharing

Your child created a special kind of drawing called a model to show how the coronavirus can make a person sick. Models are used to represent a real thing (such as viruses that are actually too small to see with our eyes) and to explain how things work (such as how the virus interacts with a person). Ask your child to use their model to explain to you what they've learned about how the virus can make a person sick.

Part B: Answer These Questions as a Family

> **What part of the model was most helpful to you in explaining how the virus works? Why?**
>
> **How does this model connect to what your family already knows about the virus? Is there anything you want to change in your model?**
>
> **How are you feeling about the information in the model and/or the process of researching, modeling, and explaining?**
>
> **What other questions do you have that we could continue exploring?**

This paired set of tasks highlights many elements of the shifts in learning theory, science education reforms, and focus on justice and equity that I've introduced in this chapter. First, the task and unit center the interests and experiences of learners and invite them to engage in science practices as ways of representing and learning more. The task embeds a scientific question in students' lived experiences around the COVID-19 pandemic, and invites them to bring their experiences, as well as those of their families and communities, into the classroom. It engages them in drawing a model and then provides guidance for students to share these models and discuss them with their families. To make participation more accessible, both the task and the family tool are available in Spanish translation. Family members are explicitly invited to make suggestions to further refine the models based on their own experiences and ideas. Teacher guides for the lesson suggest that students be invited to add what they have learned to their models, and that students' models can be further refined through partner discussions and whole-class discussions.

HOW TO READ THIS BOOK

I've written this book at the intersection of science education and formative assessment research and practice, with the intention of creating a resource for multiple communities. In grounding my approach in learning theory, I hope to connect with researchers and graduate students looking for new framings for formative assessment in science. At the same time, I hope this theoretical grounding provides new and more comprehensive ways of planning for and enacting formative assessments that can guide preservice and practicing teachers, as well as science curriculum designers and district leaders.

The remainder of this book will unpack the benefits of these approaches, richly illustrated with examples, in three sections. The first part of the book will provide foundational assertions that will frame the rest of the book; in Chapter 2, I'll dig more deeply into sociocultural theory to develop a framework for formative assessment that will be applied in the remainder of the book. Chapter 3 will then describe how we can center equity and justice in the design of science formative assessments.

Part II of the book breaks the design and enactment of formative assessment into four sections, each addressed in its own chapter. Chapter 4 will present the reasoning for embedding formative assessment in accessible scenarios and phenomena relevant to students' lives, along with frameworks for identifying and selecting phenomena for assessment. Chapter 5 will then explain new ways in which tasks are being designed to center students' experiences, resources, and linguistic repertoires; the chapter also presents scaffolds to create space for students to show what they know. Chapter 6 unpacks ambitious approaches to classroom enactment of formative assessment tasks, providing frameworks for thinking about the classroom practices in which teachers and students engage as they enact these tasks. Chapter 7 then describes ways of thinking about and providing feedback from multiple perspectives, as well as approaches to self- and peer-assessment.

Finally, Part III expands outward from classrooms to look at larger influences on formative assessment. Chapter 8 explores various resources developed to support formative assessment design and practice. We then turn to perspectives beyond the classroom: Chapter 9 explores the importance and benefits of teachers co-designing formative assessments with their colleagues.

My intent is for the book to provide both a summary of where we are, as well as where we are headed with formative assessment at this moment in time. I warmly invite you to dive in and join me on the journey.

CHAPTER 2

Broadening Our View of Science Formative Assessment

Think of an outdoor space that you love. It could be anywhere—near your home or where you work, or even a place you have visited only once but that left an impression on your heart. For me, one such place is the Sonoran Desert outside of Tucson, Arizona (Figure 2.1). When I visit, I like to get out early in the morning; if it's late July or August, a monsoon may have dropped rain overnight. In the early morning light, water droplets glisten on the newly growing grass. I walk along the sandy, gravelly path, listening to a woodpecker chipping away at a black-barked mesquite tree. An agave, in its last season of life, has launched its tall, woody stalk into the sky, its blossoms reaching out to butterflies and hummingbirds. I pause to examine the mounded joints of a cholla cactus and discover its first flower buds poking out. An ocotillo's fingers fan out, its new green leaves concealing its poky spines. As I climb upwards in elevation, I come to the first saguaro cactus, the keystone species of this ecosystem. Songbirds have pecked holes in its tall sides, now healed over to make a cool, shady home.

One can contemplate the complexity of biotic and abiotic factors that contribute to this environment—the sporadic rains fed by the Gulf of California, the sandy soils, the intense sunlight. We can investigate the relationship between the saguaro cacti and the plants under which they grow until they are established enough to grow on their own. We can also examine the branching stumps coming from the cactuses to better appreciate the length of the lives the cacti have lived.

If we were to uproot the saguaro (or any other plant) from this environment, would we be able to fully comprehend it? Could we understand the complexities and interconnections in its habitat? Of course not.

I start the chapter with this example as a parallel to thinking about formative assessment in science. When we take a broader view of the saguaro cactus, we can appreciate all the interrelationships I've described above; and yet, when it comes to assessment, we tend to take

Figure 2.1. Saguaro, Cholla, and Ocotillo in the Sonoran Desert, Near Tucson, Arizona

a simpler lens. We tend to look at the individual learner, asking them questions alone, or giving them a written task to "see what they know and can do." What are we missing when we consider only what they individually know and can do during that moment of assessment in the classrooms? Is this a fair and accurate representation of who the student is and their life experiences? Of course, the answer to this question is no.

In this chapter, I'll argue for taking a much broader perspective on science formative assessment. My intention is that by doing so, science formative assessment will encompass a broader system of activity, and we will also gain a more nuanced and complex understanding of the learning environment, as well as the learners' role in that environment.

FORMATIVE ASSESSMENT IN A SYSTEM OF CLASSROOM ACTIVITY

Historically, when talking about formative assessment, the conversation has often focused on the tasks themselves, or the processes in which teachers and students engage when they are surfacing and responding to each other's ideas (Bennett, 2011). Focusing merely on the tasks and processes that surround them neglects many key interactions consequential to how formative assessment can support students on a daily basis as they learn: talking about learning goals, responding to interesting questions, sharing their thinking with their teacher and peers, taking and providing feedback that moves their thinking forward.

In this chapter, I'll broaden our lens beyond the individual learner completing a formative assessment task to take a broader aperture on what counts when we are looking at any instance of formative assessment in the classroom. As we do so, we must seek to better understand the student, their identities, their experiences, and the resources they bring to the classroom. We must understand the ways in which the teacher interacts with learners, and how learners interact with—and are held accountable to—each other's ideas. The teacher also brings their own lived histories and experiences and interpretations of the task, the content, and the students. We also must consider the school itself: the classroom and the culture teachers and students share in that space; the school and the policies it has in place; as well as the district, state, and national context. Figure 2.2 illustrates how these elements are brought into our view when we take a wider aperture on what we attend to in formative assessment in science.

Activity theory is one way of conceptualizing situative and sociocultural views of learning, and helps to shift our view from the tasks and interactions around them to encompass a wider system of interactions, the multiple voices in that system, the history of the activity and its purposes, the tensions that emerge in the enactment of formative assessment, and the possibility of expansive transformation (Engeström, 2001).

Figure 2.3 illustrates these elements of an activity system (Engeström, 1987), which we can then apply as a lens to help broaden what we

Figure 2.2. Broadening Our Lens on Formative Assessment

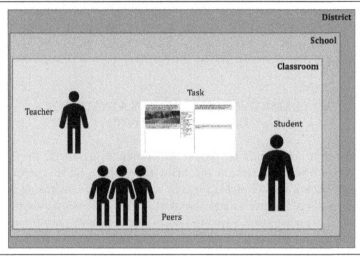

Figure 2.3. A model of an activity system; adapted from Engeström (1987, p. 63) and Gee (2008a, p. 90)

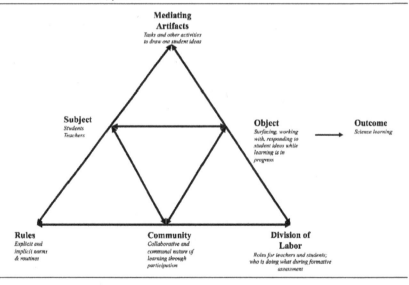

consider as we design and analyze learning environments dedicated to formative assessment. At the left of the triangle are the subjects of the activity—that is, students and teachers. At the right is the object or purpose of the activity, which is to draw out and work with students' ideas while learning is in progress, with the intended outcome of supporting students' science learning. At the top of the triangle are the mediating artifacts that support students and teachers in supporting student learning, most often in the form of tasks and other activities designed to draw out students' developing ideas and practices while learning is in progress. At the base of the triangle are the rules, community, and division of labor that support the other elements of the system. The rules are the implicit and explicit norms related to formative assessment, such as routines around sharing student thinking, and teachers and students responding to each other. The community refers to the potential collaborative and communal nature of learning through formative assessment when students and teachers participate in assessment that is discursive, not only paper-based (Duschl & Gitomer, 1997; Jordan & Putz, 2004). Finally, the division of labor refers to who is doing what in the ongoing activity, such as students listening to each other and asking questions of one another.

Following Kumashiro (2000), this vision of science formative assessment involves not just learning as an outcome, but also *unlearning* (Moss, 2008). That is, by the time learners have spent several years in school, they have come to understand how school works, the kinds of ideas (and whose ideas) are valued, and that assessment is for showing teachers that they know "the answers." Reframing formative assessment from a situated/sociocultural lens should compel us to support students (and teachers) in *unlearning* how they may have conducted assessment in the past. It encourages them to use assessment as a way of deeply connecting with students' ideas and interests, not just for evaluation. It pushes us to democratize classroom participation, and also to recenter our processes of assessment on the contributions and interests of marginalized learners.

DEFINING ELEMENTS OF A FORMATIVE ASSESSMENT ACTIVITY SYSTEM

The term "formative assessment" has been used in a variety of ways; for example, it is used to describe the tasks students might complete, as we might see in a set of instructional materials (e.g., "formative assessment at lesson 6"). But the term is also often used to describe a *process* that teachers and students might engage in, such as a class discussion about students' ideas, or students using a checklist to consider a model they have drawn to see what elements they have already included and what they might need to add in order to improve their work. In reality, as we broaden our view on science formative assessment, it will be useful to think about formative assessment *activity* that encompasses tasks, processes, and more (Bennett, 2011; Furtak et al., 2019; Moss, 2008).

To that end, we can now start our project of expanding the frame around formative assessment by asking a few simple questions—who, what, where, why, and how. Following Moss (2008) and Engeström (2001), we can articulate the questions as follows:

1. Who are the subjects of learning, and how are they defined and located?
2. What do they learn, and what are the contents and outcomes of their learning?
3. Why do they learn, and what makes them make the effort?
4. How do they learn, and what are the key actions or processes of their learning?

To these questions I add the additional queries of *Where* and *When* the students are learning. I summarize responses to these questions in Table 2.1, and will describe each in more detail in the sections below. In each section, I'll also use the situated/sociocultural framing to define common terms in formative assessment as I'll be using them in this book.

Who Are the Subjects of Learning?

As shown in the activity triangle in Figure 2.2, the object of formative assessment is to support students' three-dimensional science learning—so that we can consider the primary participants in formative assessment as students themselves, not only individually but in collaborative community with each other. We view these learners as humans with their own unique interests, motivations, and identities; when they come to school, they bring valuable life experiences that influence the ways in which they participate in learning with their peers. Students are able to formatively assess their own progress—that is, to engage in *self-assessment*—and can also work together to support each other's learning through *peer assessment* (Coffey, 2003; Sadler, 1989).

While the activity system shown in Figure 2.2 focuses on learning outcomes for students, it also involves teachers as key players. It follows that this book is not just about assessing student learning but also about how teachers learn to better support student learning, and each other's learning (Moss et al., 2008). As the facilitator/orchestrator of classroom learning environments, then, the teacher is considered a central participant in our formative assessment activity system. Teachers select and adapt assessment tasks, and then enact those tasks

Table 2.1. Guiding questions for broadening our lens on science formative assessment (adapted from Engeström, 2001; Moss, 2008)

Guiding questions	Science formative assessment involves...
Who are the subjects of learning? How are they defined and located?	Students
	Teachers
Where do they learn?	Both in and outside of school; formative assessments create space for students to share their ideas and experiences that aren't necessarily from school, and can be deliberately constructed to pull students' home experiences into their school learning
What do they learn? What are the contents and outcomes of their learning?	Phenomena related to their lives
	Disciplinary practices of scientists & engineers
	Phenomena that embed science learning in accessible contexts
	Disciplinary core ideas
	Crosscutting concepts
	Ways of collaborating, responding to others' ideas, holding each other accountable to the standards of the discipline
Why do they learn? What makes them make the effort?	Motivated to respond to questions that relate to their identities and interests; to participate in a classroom community of learners; to demonstrate developing expertise and grasp of practice that feels useful and relevant to their lives
How do they learn? What are the key actions or processes of their learning?	Tasks and activities that create space for students to share their ideas and experiences
	Cognitively demanding
	Multiple ways to show understanding
When do they learn?	On a day-to-day basis (informal formative assessment)
	At preplanned points in ongoing units of learning (formal formative assessment)
	Through formal and informal formative assessment experiences

with learners, framing the way the assessment is introduced, soliciting and facilitating students' contributions to small-group and whole-class conversations, and providing helpful follow-up questions and feedback to aid students in advancing their learning. Teachers also work with colleagues within the formative assessment activity system, collaborating to design and enact formative assessment tasks with students, and with the support of facilitators, such as instructional coaches, who may improve the ways an individual teacher enacts formative assessment.

Principals and other school leaders can also open up or constrain teachers' opportunities to learn new approaches to formative assessment, which in turn influences students' ability to participate in formative assessment. At a high school where I worked many years ago, the biology teachers did not have a common planning time because of the multiple varieties of biology taught at the school (grade-level biology; advanced courses, such as anatomy; biology for International Baccalaureate students; biology for students designated as English learners; etc.). So for teachers to work together to design formative assessment tasks, we needed to meet after school. However, the following year, after having some success in what we were able to accomplish together, we approached the principal, who agreed to leave one class period of the day with no biology taught so teachers could have their meetings within the bounds of the regular school day (Furtak, 2012).

We could also extend this circle farther out, to the district leaders and policymakers who afford or constrain environments in classrooms in ways that allow formative assessment to happen in support of student learning or—as we will see in subsequent chapters—may actually pull formative assessment into the orbit of a different purpose, more aligned with summative and large-scale assessment and demonstrating the "closing of gaps" (Penuel & Shepard, 2016; Shepard, 2009). As the book continues, we may think about the subjects involved in formative assessment in a series of concentric rings, and depending on our focus at a particular time, we may expand our view to include more participants beyond the individual teacher and their students.

What Do They Learn?

Students participating in science formative assessment are engaged in the disciplinary practices of scientists. As they complete formative assessments, they create disciplinary knowledge and multiple forms of representation. This knowledge and practice is built in ways that connect to compelling questions related to engaging and interesting phenomena in the world around them. Students also acquire "habits of mind" such as using evidence and seeking alternative interpretations that align with scientific ways of knowing. Students are empowered to ask their own questions of both the natural world and each other (and their teachers!).

Students also develop knowledge of the big ideas of science, or the disciplinary core ideas of life, physical, and Earth and space science. These ideas are bigger than memorizable bits of knowledge. They are the larger, orienting concepts within the disciplines, such as evolution in life sciences; kinetic molecular theory in chemistry; force and motion in physics; and geologic time in Earth and space science. These ideas are deeply connected with the compelling questions and embedded in everyday scenarios and examples, so that students learning about evolution may do so in the context of antibiotic resistance; kinetic molecular theory when learning about how to keep drinks cool in the summertime; force and motion when learning about snowboarders on a halfpipe; and geologic time when asking questions about landforms that surround their school.

We also look beyond these disciplinary core ideas to articulate how learning is not just the knowledge in one's head but also changes in participation in the practices of a discipline over time—for example, gradual improvements in students' ability to construct an evidence-based explanation, rather than "getting" a science concept in the moment. Second, and crucially, we are also interested in how students engage their everyday knowledge and resources as they learn, so that conversations about or references to everyday experiences are not "off target" but fundamentally related to connecting students' lived experiences to what they learn in school, and similarly, weaving together what they learn in school with their everyday and future lives and selves.

When we assess science practices, we don't just ask students what they know and don't get. We actively engage them in identifying scientific questions that might be asked, making models, analyzing and interpreting data, and constructing explanations. Assessments also engage students in these practices within a disciplinary context; for example, students might use a model to illustrate how changes in Earth's climate are related to energy flows in and out of Earth's systems. We also encourage students to develop identities as learners who contribute meaningfully to the classroom, to their own science learning, and to the learning of other students in their classroom by participating and collaborating with each other (Moss, 2008).

Crosscutting concepts can also provide opportunities for students to make sense of new phenomena or situations. Explicitly engaging students in considering patterns, systems and system models, scale, and cause-and-effect in settings that they have not before seen can be key ways to design a formative assessment. As Helen Quinn, a physicist and one of the authors of the *Framework*, put it, these concepts are the ways that scientists first engage with things they cannot initially explain (Furtak et al., 2021). Leading with questions linked to the crosscutting concepts provides new avenues into formative assessment that doesn't lead directly to conceptual understanding, but also provides opportunities for students to think through—to make sense of, to dynamically think through, and to figure out—the question being posed (Odden & Russ, 2019).

Teachers also learn as they conduct formative assessment in their science classes. They learn about students' experiences, ideas, and resources; they learn about how their class has participated overall in learning so far, and what they still have to learn. In addition, by listening carefully to student thinking, they have opportunities to interrogate and improve their own understandings of the science they are teaching, as well as strategies to help make this learning more accessible to their students.

How Do They Learn?

Formative assessment consists of a set of practices or routines organized by particular tasks, all aimed at providing useful feedback to learners to help them move forward in their understandings and engagement in science practices.

Formative Assessment Tasks

The word "task" is increasingly used in mathematics and science classrooms to describe a segment of a classroom activity dedicated to teaching or assessing a particular idea or disciplinary practice (Tekkumru-Kisa & Stein, 2015). A task can be defined as an event in which teachers and students jointly engage in work for an instructional purpose (Tekkumru-Kisa et al., 2020a). For the purposes of this book, I'll define a formative assessment *task* as an event conducted by teachers and students in a science classroom for the purpose of surfacing and working with students' ideas and grasp of science practices. We might often associate this idea of a task with an object or artifact that captures student ideas in a science classroom (Cowie et al., 2011), such as students' models, drawings, written explanations, or other representations that make their thinking visible. While a task might be a physical object handed out by a teacher, it could also be digital and conducted through some kind of online system. A task might be developed by a group of science teachers working together, or it might come as a part of a prepared set of curriculum materials.

These tasks support students in learning through features that explicitly encourage them to draw on their own ideas, backgrounds, and community and cultural resources (Kang et al., 2014). The tasks are open-ended and entail a high level of cognitive demand; that is, they invite students to engage in science practices as they demonstrate the knowledge they have developed (Tekkumru-Kisa & Stein, 2015). These tasks also provide students with the space and agency to share and display their ideas in a variety of modalities, such as drawing and writing (Fine & Furtak, 2020a). These tasks are supported by resources that help to mediate between students and teachers as they seek to understand each other's understandings and grasp of practices—things such as papers, whiteboards, sticky notes, markers, computers, tablets, and smartboards.

Routines and Interactions

Formative assessment tasks mediate participation in a set of interactions, such as statements, questions, and gestures through which students interact around ideas in a science classroom. These interactions are fundamental to thinking about formative assessment as existing in ongoing human to human interactions during science learning. At the foundation of these interactions are authentic questions in which teachers and students talk with each other about what they know; these questions go beyond simple "Did you get it?" questions but rather are seeking to understand "What do you think?" or "Where might you have seen this before?" Follow-up questions from teachers and students engage these ideas and push for more specificity and detail. "Why do you think that?" "Say more." This serves to deepen their ideas and explanations. Students also learn by participating in complex classroom environments that involve collaboration within groups as students work together to respond to instructional tasks and contributing to the construction of representations that capture their thinking. Students' participation in a variety of science practices changes over time, and their engagement in these practices helps them to develop and represent their understandings, and to apply crosscutting concepts to the ideas they are exploring.

We might also think about formative assessment interactions as being guided by a set of *routines* that support students and teachers in sharing their ideas with each other. For example, teachers and students might have a routine of pausing to appraise their progress in answering the central question driving a unit of investigation. In an OpenSciEd unit on Earth's Resources and Human Impact, for example, students are seeking to answer the question, "What causes Earth's surface to change?" (OpenSciEd, 2022b). While individual lessons address sub-questions like "Where were Africa and South America in the past?," a key formative assessment routine would be for teachers and students to zoom out from a particular investigation to see how they might apply their recent learning to the larger question driving the unit. In this routine, teachers encourage students to make sense of what they have been learning in school, and even to draw on examples from their everyday lives as they seek to answer the question. As new questions arise, the students and teacher capture those questions for the future; as they develop shared understandings of new words, those can be captured on a word wall.

All of these interactions are orchestrated by the support of strong teachers and leaders prepared to construct, facilitate, and engage learners in the kinds of classroom environments related to formative assessment described above. These teachers are committed to the principle that all students are able to learn and look to systemic sources of inequity as an explanation for students' learning challenges rather than blaming individual students. They collaborate in order to improve their own teaching practice, and they build on their own deep knowledge of science and science practices as they engage learners.

Feedback

Feedback is the crucial element of formative assessment that leverages student learning forward (Black & Wiliam, 1998; Wiliam, 2007). While some disagreement lingers as to the nature and form of feedback in education (Dunn & Mulvenon, 2009; Filsecker & Kerres, 2012), most agree that feedback consists of some form of response or information provided to students that can be used to positively influence their learning (Bell & Cowie, 2001; Ruiz-Primo & Furtak, 2006, 2007). Studies have deeply examined how feedback supports improvement in all types of human performance (Wisniewski et al., 2020). Thus, as we seek to understand how students are learning through formative assessment, we must consider how feedback plays a role.

Examples of feedback include a teacher providing a response in writing on student work, using that information to revisit a main idea the next class period, or shifting the planned sequencing of later learning experiences. In the case of peer or self-assessment, students might review their work with the support of a rubric or a checklist, which leads them to realize that key sections are missing from the explanation they have written. A teacher could ask several probing follow-up questions in response to a student comment to help that student think their idea through more deeply, or they may encourage students to make connections between science ideas and everyday ideas.

When we consider feedback from situated/sociocultural perspectives, we must consider not only how teachers are moving students toward understandings of the science ideas they are learning in school, but also the ways in which teachers draw on and encourage explicit connections between those ideas and students' ideas and experiences outside of school. We also consider how teachers not only support the development of students' science knowledge but also pay attention to and encourage students to become more sophisticated in their engagement with science practices over time, and how they create multiple spaces for students to learn from each other.

Where Do They Learn?

We most often think about formative assessment as taking place within the confines of a science classroom. In particular, students learn as they are engaged in the course of ongoing instruction, so formative assessment takes place in the context of a unit of learning where there are places—sometimes called "bends" or "joints"—where it's important to pause and take stock of what's been learned so far, and what students are still working on, before moving forward (Shavelson, Young, et al., 2008).

However, as we broaden the lens on what we attend to in formative assessment, we must also think about formative assessment as taking place beyond the four walls of a science classroom. It can occur when students make connections between the science they are learning and what they encounter in their daily lives. These interactions are multidirectional—a student may wonder why it's hard to walk up a hill near their home and connect that physical experience to ideas about gravity they have learned in school. They might notice a pattern in how snow melts faster on one side of the street than the other, wondering what causes that to happen.

Why Do They Learn?

Students engage in science formative assessment because they find it interesting and useful; they are motivated to participate because they want to explain compelling phenomena, to collaborate with their peers, and to be supported in sharing their ideas. They are able to recognize that through participation they receive support that helps to further their learning, and not at the expense of being evaluated or judged.

When Do They Learn?

Some of the instances I've described so far might be planned in advance, but others could arise spontaneously, or might not even be viewed formally as an instance of formative assessment at all. We might think about making a distinction between these types of formative assessment—sometimes, it is *planned* far in advance, and even embedded in a set of curriculum materials. In these instances, the teacher and students may pause during the course of instruction at a key point of learning to reflect on what's happened so far and leverage that learning forward (Penuel et al., 2019; Shavelson, Young, et al., 2008). This can happen either with planned tasks that the teacher will ask students to complete, or in preplanned conversations with students. We can call these *formal* formative assessments.

At the same time, formative assessment can also consist of informal ways of attending to what students know and are able to do. This ongoing attention to students' developing ideas is *informal* formative assessment and includes attending to student ideas during whole-class discussions and groupwork or asking students what they are thinking while they are working. To provide a little structure, we can use "back-pocket" questions—questions planned in advance and written on index cards that teachers can use to guide their interactions with small groups (Windschitl et al., 2018). In a way, this everyday noticing and attending to student ideas is just a part of what we might consider "good teaching," but it's worth tracking because these informal opportunities are crucial for supporting students' learning and helping them connect their ideas to larger concepts and practices in science.

We can thus envision our response to *when* students learn through formative assessment as existing on a continuum of formal to informal (Figure 2.4). I'll be using these key terms—tasks, practices, formal, and informal—throughout the book to describe formative assessment activity.

Figure 2.4. Continuum of Formal and Informal Formative Assessment (adapted from Shavelson et al. [2008, p. 23])

Formal Formative Assessment	Informal Formative Assessment
Preplanned, curriculum-embedded	On-the-fly, daily interactions
Planned tasks	Back-pocket questions
Facilitating whole-class discussions	Circulating to small groups

HOW ACTIVITY SYSTEMS WORK TO SUPPORT LEARNING THROUGH FORMATIVE ASSESSMENT

The collective responses to the previous questions build a conception of science formative assessment based on five principles: (1) learning occurs in a collective, artifact-mediated, and object-oriented activity system; (2) it is multivoiced, comprised of a community where participants bring multiple points of view, interests, and traditions; (3) it is embedded in cultural and historical context; (4) tensions are sources of change and development (not the same as problems or conflicts); and (5) there is a possibility of expansive transformation when "the object or motive of the activity are reconceptualized to embrace a radically wider horizon of possibilities than in the previous mode of activity" (Engeström, 2001, p. 137).

Formative Assessment as Mediated Activity

The first assertion that emerges from our conceptual framing of an activity system is that formative assessment is a mediated activity. That is, the activity of surfacing and attending to student thinking is mediated by a number of elements, including the teacher, the tasks, discourse, the materials available in a classroom, and other tools that support students in sharing their ideas. Given that formative assessment is a mediated action, it follows that examining any single element within the activity system would be misleading (Wertsch, 1998, p. 199).

Let's think about what this means in an instance of science formative assessment. One might be tempted to make a particular assertion about what a student knows and is able to do based on their response to a question. But we must acknowledge that any question asked frames or mediates the response that a student might give. In a study of 5th-grade students' responses to state test items, Noble and colleagues (2012) found that low-income students and those designated as English learners were more likely to answer questions incorrectly, even when they had elsewhere demonstrated the knowledge necessary to answer these items correctly. A sample item students answered in the study was, "If enough heat is taken away from a container of water, what will happen to the water?" (Noble et al., 2012, p. 791). This question is framed in an atypical setting of cooling something by "taking away heat," which is not consistent with the way that cooling is described in everyday language. Noble and colleagues found that many students misinterpreted this question, even though they understood the idea of freezing. One student reflected that they "never thought of it as freezing? . . . I just thought of it, I just thought of it getting colder and colder" (p. 792). A key takeaway from this study is that we must understand all the information we get from formative assessment in the context of how that information is mediated by the questions we ask, and other elements of the activity system.

Multiple Voices

Science formative assessment also features multiple voices. While a traditional learning environment might focus on the teacher's perspective and take on science, with students' ideas being compared to those ideas, a classroom focused on formative assessment is characterized by the many voices of students, with the teacher as the facilitator and mediator of those voices. We can also think about how students' communities and families are brought into these conversations, with their ideas and experiences represented by students in the formative assessment process (Tzou et al., 2019).

Given that these voices all bring different perspectives and experiences, we can better understand the unpredictability of formative assessment. While we can anticipate students' likely responses, if we are truly asking questions that draw on their ideas and experiences, it can be hard to tell what students will say, and where the discussion will lead. However, this openness to ideas and contributions is important as we expand the space for students to share their ideas and understandings. We should avoid limiting the types of responses they might give us, or funneling them toward particular answers.

I can conjure many instances of how formative assessment settings that I've either led as a teacher or observed as a researcher or teacher educator over the years featured multiple voices. They're usually opened up by a compelling question—not necessarily a long one, but one that really draws out student ideas—and then supported with an actively co-constructed space in which students are free to talk through their ideas (I'll provide many examples of these later). As a teacher, sometimes these conversations can feel like opening up Pandora's box, so to speak—it's like, "whoa, that's what they're thinking?" or perhaps, "wow, I'm not sure how to think about that." But rather than resisting and backing off, or putting the lid back on the box, we need to lean into these conversations and seize upon the ideas students are putting out there in ways that other activities—and definitely many assessments—would otherwise constrain. We're not just interested in whether the students can pipe back what the teacher has said—like repeating a set of notes played on a recorder—but rather a full chorus of responses. What's important is that formative assessment should aspire to be a truly dialogic space, where all participants are listening and responding to each other.

This process has been called "intentional engagement" of the naturally heterogeneous ideas in classrooms through posing questions (Rosebery et al., 2010). While the purpose of formative assessment might be identified as moving students toward a particular path by eliciting their ideas and providing feedback that moves them in a particular direction, the activity system lens encourages us to expand that vision by imagining "feedback" more broadly, as happening across a number of spaces and timeframes. From this perspective, the purpose of a formative assessment event could be conceived of as an opportunity at a preestablished time in a curricular sequence, or a less formal, everyday noticing, of the multiple ways in which students are grappling with ideas, turning them over in their heads, making connections, listening, and processing and reacting to the ideas of others. It is complex, it is messy, and it is deliberate.

Historicity

The preceding descriptions have all referred to participants in science formative assessment as having lived histories that they bring to any instance of classroom activity. Students bring multiple perspectives to science learning, informed by their own home cultures and communities. Anyone who has spent time around young children know they naturally ask questions about the world around them. They notice how hard it is to get the last drops of water out of a glass. They realize that if they add too much baking soda to a recipe, it rises much more. They wonder why stars in the sky appear to sparkle. They wonder why carbonated drinks lose their fizz when left open. These kinds of questions are the ones we should naturally engage through formative assessment—taking what students are learning in school and continuing to relate that science learning to other scenarios that may be similar to activities in their curriculum.

Unfortunately, students also sometimes learn that these natural wonderings don't have a place in school science, which historically has not been set up to draw out and engage natural curiosities. So students' participation in formative assessment is also influenced by their own learning histories in schools that are often oriented toward furnishing only correct ideas or showing compliance with the teacher's questions. Students can come to science lessons—particularly once they reach secondary school—knowing that their ideas and wonderings are not necessarily engaged in science lessons. This can be a big problem. Students know that in a situation called an "assessment," the game is on—they need to show teachers what they know. If they don't immediately get the answers correct, a penalty will need to be paid, such as a loss of points or a lower grade.

We thus need to fundamentally reframe science formative assessment to actively engage students' histories and experiences in ways that promote direct connections between students' ideas and the science they are learning in school. It's not separated; it's fundamentally intertwined. We also need to reframe learning environments to offer ways that students can participate without being at risk—or feeling at risk—of a loss of status or punishment if their ideas are categorized or heard as "wrong." Rather, we must help them feel safe to discuss their ideas, drawing on all their cultural and linguistic resources as they do so (Bang & Medin, 2010; Fine & Furtak, 2020a; Suárez, 2020).

Teachers, of course, also bring their own histories of learning science and engaging in assessment to any instance of formative assessment (Morrison, 2015; Windschitl, 2004). Many secondary science teachers primarily learned through lecture-style classes in which they were not able to actively engage in the scientific endeavor. As a result, their impressions of science may be influenced by the thick textbooks they read in their classes, or the labs they conducted that were aimed primarily at replicating results. Elementary teachers often have majors in other disciplines and may have taken only a few science classes. This can contribute to teachers forming "folk theories" about how science is done (Windschitl, 2004). Such theories include ideas that hypotheses are guesses, that there is a singular scientific method, that theory is optional and not a fundamental element of the scientific enterprise, and so on.

Deb Morrison (2015) drew a direct line between these experiences and teachers' formative assessment practices—when teachers are not sure how science is done, they are less likely to feel comfortable following the threads of students' ideas, or to use the analogy above, will want to put the lid back on Pandora's box. So just as we might anticipate that teachers with limited experience learning and doing science might need support as they learn to engage students in science and engineering practices, we can also recognize how their views of science could affect the ways they engage students in formative assessment.

Tensions

Inherent in this view of formative assessment are multiple tensions that emerge among different elements of the activity system. For example, we can consider the tension between the learner and their experiences, and the science that they are expected to learn in school. From the perspective of current science education reforms, we want to value both (National Academies of Science, Engineering and Medicine, 2018); however, school science has historically been given more value. Moving forward, teachers will have to grapple with how to truly listen to and honor students' ideas and experiences.

Studies of responsive teaching have wonderfully illustrated the complexity of student thinking and the ways in which teachers and students alike can listen and attend to each other's ideas and build on them as key resources when thinking about science ideas. For example, Suárez (2020) described the ways young learners express in language the sounds they hear when guitar strings are plucked ("ting, tang, tong"), and explored how this can be an entry point to understanding sound, wavelength, and the relationship between string tension and tone.

In addition, we can anticipate that as any element of the activity system shifts—for example, as new curriculum materials are introduced into the system—they may be in tension with other elements of the system. This is precisely the case we observe when new, *Framework*-aligned curricula are adopted in classrooms where routines, teacher experiences, and other elements of the system aligned with more traditional approaches to science teaching might be in place. Understanding the sources of these tensions can help us shift other elements of the system in ways that better support the outcome of students' three-dimensional science learning.

Possibility of Expansive Transformation

Within this system of multiple participants, their mediated actions, their histories, and the inherent tensions they comprise, we can envision emergent ways of conceptualizing formative assessment that can fundamentally transform learning environments toward a new vision of science learning. Indeed, the remaining chapters of this book will take deep dives into elements of this activity system, engaging the definitions developed in this chapter, and exploring from different angles how better-designed tasks, reimagined classroom participation, and new relationships with science goals cannot just reinforce but can become immutable, inseparable parts of the *Framework* vision.

As the book unfolds, it will continuously point to the possibility of expansive transformation that envisions formative assessment not just as an inextricable element of *Framework*-aligned learning but as a way of viewing the entire process of learning and teaching in science classrooms. Formative assessment is everywhere, and a necessary component of what teachers and students do together to constantly monitor progress and to push learning forward. In particular, it becomes an essential mode through which the multiple voices and experiences of a heterogeneous group of students are heard and respected in a classroom.

LOOKING AHEAD

Reaching the end of this chapter, you might be thinking, well, this sounds like a description of good teaching in general. And that's the point—formative assessment is in support of good teaching, rather than being entirely separate from learning. It is an activity deeply intertwined with teaching and learning, and yet serves the purpose of pausing, stepping back, and working with ideas to leverage learning forward more explicitly. And in order to do that, we need to deeply consider what students are learning, how they learn, and why they learn. Taken together, these descriptions paint a rich picture of science formative assessment activity systems. At its essence, this is the point of this book—to shift the scale from the teacher, the learner, and the task to a much broader picture that we must consider to truly understand and capture the potential of formative assessment to support student learning in general, and in particular in the context of science teaching reforms.

The remaining sections and chapters of the book will be organized from sociocultural perspectives and elements of the activity system I've described: participants, their histories, and why that matters for science formative assessment (Chapter 3); making assessment tasks relevant to learners, and designing those tasks in ways to make them more accessible to learners so they can share their ideas (Chapters 4 and 5); focusing on the interactions between teachers and learners, their routines and roles, and how feedback helps move learning forward (Chapters 6 and 7). Later chapters will explore additional influences outside the classroom activity system, including resources to support teachers as they design and enact formative assessments (Chapter 8) and professional learning (Chapter 9).

CHAPTER 3

Formative Assessment as a Vehicle for Equity and Justice in Science Learning

We know that children enter school full of curiosity and questions about their lives and the natural world, and that science can provide opportunities for them to investigate these questions (National Academies of Sciences, Engineering, and Medicine, 2022). Children also have a wealth of experiences and funds of knowledge to draw upon as they learn (González & Moll, 2002). They have multiple identities (Spencer et al., 2022), bring a variety of linguistic resources to science learning (Fine, 2021; Flores & García, 2022), engage in a wide range of ever-evolving cultural practices (Paris, 2012), and care deeply about pressing issues in their communities (Madkins & McKinney de Royston, 2019).

As we seek better approaches to the design and enactment of formative assessments to better serve *all* learners, we must step back and critically interrogate the degree to which formative assessment can broaden access and opportunities for *all* learners to engage in, and fully realize, the new goals for science learning. To that end, in this chapter we will explore how formative assessment in science education exists at the intersection of science as a discipline and the historical functions of assessment, both of which can have a constraining influence on whose ideas are valued in science learning. We will then discuss critical and decolonizing perspectives on science and assessment that compel us to reposition formative assessment as a vehicle for justice and equity in the current wave of science education reforms. The chapter concludes with rich examples of curricula that center justice and equity in formative assessment, and steps teachers can take to prepare themselves to broaden participation in science learning through formative assessment.

STRUCTURAL INFLUENCES ON SCIENCE FORMATIVE ASSESSMENT

In the previous chapter, I drew on conceptions of activity theory to broaden our framing for science formative assessment in this book. This activity system is situated in cultural and historical context. As we consider formative assessment and the ways it can broaden students' participation in science learning, we therefore need to begin by considering the larger context of this activity system, starting with the ways that science has traditionally been represented in schools and the interface between that science and the historical function of assessment.

"Settled" Science

Science, as it is constructed and represented in U.S. schools, is drawn from a variety of sources. State and national standards are the primary, and likely most important, way of articulating and communicating the science students are expected to learn. These standards documents—like any educational policy—are written by groups of educators, scientists, and policymakers who negotiate and argue as they seek to agree upon what's most important (Collins, 1998; NGSS Lead States, 2013). These standards represent the best of our knowledge about science and science learning; they are also impossibly long lists of what students need to learn in their formal schooling. Another key source is curriculum materials, often written by educational publishers, which seek to sell many copies across many regions. In seeking to cover the biggest ideas that students will learn, curriculum materials have in the past ended up seeking to cover too much content in shallow ways (Schmidt et al., 1997).

Educational resources such as standards and curriculum materials often reflect dominant perspectives on what science is, and how it is done, reflecting Euro-American ways of knowing (Aikenhead & Ogawa, 2007). Rather than being neutral, as it is sometimes conceived, science as we know it today has been constructed primarily by white, Western perspectives, with its beginnings in the Enlightenment and growing and developing into the modern day (Harding, 2008; Latour & Woolgar, 1979; Pickering, 1995). Science has also been used to justify extractive and consumptive actions on the Earth (Kimmerer, 2013), and positioning science as culturally neutral and objective has been used to justify harms (Marin & Bang, 2018).

Unfortunately, when we look at many of the science standards and curriculum materials, they can all come across as "settled science." Bang and colleagues (2012) have used this term in reference to how scientific consensus and dissensus are not well represented in the standards, as well as to refer to the outsized influence that colonizing perspectives have on how science is taught in schools. Science as taught in schools as a way of knowing and a body of knowledge is fundamentally different from perspectives of colonized societies who view humans as part of, not separate from, the world around them (NASEM, 2022).

Perceptions and values of dominant cultures tend to be most represented in curriculum materials and assessment. In the United States, this ultimately means white, middle-class values and perspectives. Paulo Freire (1968) has reflected that our methods of teaching result in repressing the cultural histories and values of minority communities in favor of promoting dominant paradigms. As a result, the process of schooling can easily become a process of pushing out students' ideas and experiences in favor of white, middle-class values.

My own identity as a white, middle-class woman who studied science as an undergraduate is similar to that of many secondary science teachers in the United States. National surveys with representative samples of science teachers in the United States have established that the science teacher workforce overwhelmingly identifies as white, and with content preparation in the science fields (Banilower et al., 2018). Although the student population in many regions of the United States consists increasingly of students of color, the majority of science teachers are still members of the dominant culture. We also know from decades of research that, despite huge efforts on the part of educational reformers, science continues to be taught in schools in ways that prioritize memorization and following science procedures. This is partly due to what has been called the "apprenticeship of observation" that is, science teachers experience science learning in particular ways throughout their own school experiences, and the sum of these experiences by far outweigh their own exposure to reform-oriented ways of teaching science in their teacher preparation. As a result, reform efforts can be slow to take hold, and science teaching continues to press the dominant paradigm.

Historical and Accountability Functions of Assessment

The activity theory perspective presented in Chapter 2 anticipates the ways in which influences outside a classroom will affect—and ultimately undermine—formative assessment in science classrooms. Classroom communities with teachers and students exist in cultural and historical contexts and are influenced by policy outside the classroom. This includes how assessment might be framed within the school, such as initiatives that certain percentages of students' final grades must be based on summative assessments, or that tests must feature certain kinds of writing organizers common across the curriculum. School district policies often mandate district-wide interim assessments that provide school and district leaders with information on how students are progressing toward meeting standards before higher-stakes tests. Even federal policies that dictate regular testing once a year, or in the case of science, every few years, will shape what teachers do with students on a day-to-day basis. Ultimately, what is possible to teach, and how that is assessed, is influenced by these multiple and interrelated influences from outside the classroom door. Before identifying the ways in which these external testing approaches might affect formative assessment, it's worth briefly stepping back for some historical context for educational assessment in the United States.

Legacies of the measurement of human abilities, as well as the way we teach science, are laden with artificial constructions of race (Donovan, 2014)—constructions that often uphold and maintain whiteness and European values as dominant (Gould, 1981). Educational assessment is often perceived to be neutral; we see numbers that indicate in some way something that is "true" about students' performance, particularly in a way that is supposed to be less value-laden or biased than what an individual person might conclude after talking to a student.

However, any assessment can also represent the perspectives, values, and cultures of its designers (Gipps, 1999). Even when assessments are carefully designed, any student's performance on them can never reflect everything the student knows, as assessment remains filtered through the questions being asked, the conditions under which the assessment is given, and the student's performance on any given day (American Educational Research Association, American Psychological Association, & National Council on Measurement in Education, 2014).

In the United States, the No Child Left Behind (NCLB) Act of 2001 intensified the consequences of assessments through mandated accountability testing in U.S. schools. While accountability testing had already been in place in the 1980s and 1990s, the NCLB Act created an environment in which external state tests were used to determine the quality and performance of schools, with all students expected to exhibit proficiency by 2014. States were required to track the performance of students from identified subgroups by gender, race/ethnicity, English language learners, special education, and socioeconomic status (Au, 2009).

NCLB led to annual testing that, rather than being used for program evaluation or to report to parents, was to be shared with the public and which carried consequences for school funding and school leadership. While states were left to determine their own mechanisms for this by developing their own processes for developing and administering tests, as well as reporting this information to the public, they were bound by federal law to report results for important subgroups as well as for total school and district populations. If they didn't comply, they risked losing federal funds. Testing was mandated for reading and mathematics grades 3–8 and once in high school. Testing in science was required only once at the elementary, middle, and high school levels. Proficiency in science was not part of accountability metrics, so resources and time flowed into mathematics and English Language Arts teaching, rather than into science, social studies, and other subjects. Elementary science—already a difficult subject to clear time for—disappeared.

These large-scale assessments are written far from the classrooms, with results analyzed outside the school and reported back on much longer timescales—on the order of months—rather than the shorter timescales needed for effective formative assessment (Wiliam, 2007). The design of the tests is also different by nature—large-scale assessments seek to establish the quality of learning across an entire school year, or even sets of school years or grade bands, and so cannot possibly be as closely tied to the curriculum as formative assessments; that is, they are *distal* to the curriculum (Pellegrino et al., 2001). Nevertheless, in recent years, teachers and schools have been under huge pressure to raise their scores on these tests. In some cases, formative assessment has been pulled into the orbit of the large-scale tests. Like large-scale, summative assessments, formative assessments also can also reflect dominant paradigms even while being perceived as objective.

CONSTRAINTS ON FORMATIVE ASSESSMENT

Together, the influences just discussed can manifest in approaches to the design and enactment of formative assessment in science classrooms in ways that can promote a unidirectional transmission of knowledge, with the knowledge perceived as coming from the teacher as a representative of the discipline of science, enforced through the mechanism of assessment. In these cases, science formative assessment can serve the purpose of checking to see if students have "the right answer" (Dini et al., 2020; Otero & Nathan, 2008).

Large-scale and interim assessments can further this constraining influence on formative assessment in science classrooms. As districts and schools have sought to systematically raise student test scores, approaches have emerged to support teachers in examining and taking action on the basis of student test responses (Penuel & Shepard, 2016). This trend involves disaggregating data into targeted subgroups of students and identifying low-performing students for "remediation." This kind of external pressure to raise scores can have a constraining effect on science learning environments. For example, middle school science teachers' goals to promote equitable engagement in science learning for their students were compromised when their school bundled initiatives to improve performance on mathematics and literacy accountability tests (Braaten et al., 2017). This resulted in students "learning about" rather than "figuring out" important science ideas. Teachers were less able to attend to student thinking as they promoted ways of knowing identified by school administrators. District leaders described this as "the price we have to pay" in order to raise test scores in other content areas (p. 441). Similarly, Garner and colleagues (2017) found that 6th-grade mathematics teachers asked to discuss student responses to large-scale tests ended up focusing on reteaching and remediation, which had the effect of reinforcing deficit-based views of students.

In progressive, reform-oriented educational settings—such as the practice-based science education reforms described in this book—teachers retain a large amount of control over how informal, classroom-based assessment is enacted with students, where student success is interpreted through the teacher's own criteria for what counts as quality performance or learning (Bernstein, 1996; Gipps, 1999). This type of assessment remains common in science classrooms (Dini et al., 2020), and in whole-class conversations can follow patterns where teachers ask questions, students respond, and the teacher indicates if students are correct. And this pattern can fit our definitions of formative assessment: A goal is set by an external audience or the teacher, the teacher elicits what students know, and then the teacher provides evaluative feedback in judgment of what students know and are able to do.

For students, teachers' expectations for what is "right" can be wielded through these day-to-day assessment interactions and can feel "like death by a thousand cuts—Slow. Humiliating. Painful. Dehumanizing" (Randall et al., 2021, p. 594). As an example, take the experience of Jahnay, a Black 7th-grade student, in her science classroom (Wright & Riley, 2021):

> One day in science class, the teacher discusses fevers and how aspirin should be used to support blood flow between the heart and the brain and to reduce the risk of blood clots in the arteries. Intrigued by the conversation, Jahnay raises her hand and shares that she often hears her grandmother talk about blood clots and will further inquire into how herbs assist in reducing them. The teacher responds by saying, "That's nice, but she should take aspirin; that's what actual scientists use." Feeling rejected and defeated by the response, Jahnay quickly replies, "I didn't ask you." The teacher takes offense to the comment and gives the student a "strike" for

talking back. From this incident, Jahnay learns a couple of things: (a) her teacher does not believe herbs can serve a medicinal purpose, (b) what "scientists" say is always right, and (c) sharing her interests in science will result in disciplinary reprimands if she does not agree with the teacher. Perhaps the most crippling component of this interaction is that Jahnay has learned that the knowledge she has constructed through family interactions is not considered trustworthy and valued in school science. (p. 497)

This story—which we can view as a moment of an informal formative assessment—illustrates how even through a short interaction a science teacher can close out learners' experiences. Wright and Riley (2021) envisioned a counter-story in which "the science teacher . . . viewed their role as a cultural broker for supporting Black girls' navigation of engagement in science" (p. 497). From this perspective, we could view knowledge as multidirectional rather than enforced by the teacher. Jahnay, for example, could support the science teacher—and the class—in making meaningful connections between the herbs her grandmother uses for her blood clots and the science knowledge and practices they are learning in school.

FORMATIVE ASSESSMENT AS A VEHICLE FOR EQUITY AND JUSTICE

The preceding argument helps us to understand how our perceptions of classroom and formative assessment as objective or neutral are inaccurate (Gipps, 1999), and should lead us to critically reconsider our own perspectives, positionalities, and purposes as we endeavor to design and enact better assessments in the context of *Framework*-era science education reforms. Critical, anti-racist, and anti-oppressive perspectives compel us to fundamentally reframe how we conceive of assessment (Kumashiro, 2000; Randall, 2021; Randall et al., 2021), and how formative assessment can promote equity and justice in science classrooms (Furtak & Lee, in press).

Equity in Science Formative Assessment

In Chapter 1, I described Philip and Azevedo's (2017) framework of discourses around equity in science education. NASEM's (2022) consensus report *Science and Engineering in Preschool Through Elementary Grades: The Brilliance of Children and the Strengths of Educators* builds on these discourses and defines equity as "ways—through changing policies and practices—to remove barriers to participation in science and engineering and increase achievement, representation, and identification . . .

Equity thus strives for comparable levels of attainment and/or participation" (p. 27).

This lens helps us to reimagine how assessment can be designed and enacted to support more equitable science learning (Furtak & Lee, in press). When it comes to formative assessment, this means that equity involves tasks designed around interesting scenarios relevant to learners' lives. For example, the unit described in Chapter 1 invites Courteney to create a dream car design for her mother. Similarly, students learning about osmosis might have a chance to consider how this process operates in the context of marinating carne asada (Brown, 2019). These approaches embed examples and scenarios in ways that resonate and connect with students, creating space for students to relate home experiences, such as gardening, to design projects at school (Wilson-Lopez et al., 2018).

Formative assessments can also have designs with baked-in structures that support learners in providing their responses, such as checklists that clarify what elements to include in a model (Kang et al., 2014), including key science terms in the languages students speak at home (Lee et al., 2016), instructions that invite students to translanguage, using all their linguistic resources in their responses (Fine & Furtak, 2020a).

Finally, centering equity in formative assessment means creating professional learning spaces that focus on supporting teachers in learning to help students participate in science (Kang, 2022). This acknowledges the key role teachers play in opening up opportunities to learn through formative assessment (Moss, 2008). Teachers can ask open-ended questions that create more space for students to share what they know, rather than narrowly constraining students to predetermined responses (Furtak, Kiemer, et al., 2016), and to invite students to bring examples from their daily lives (Kang et al., 2016).

Justice in Science Formative Assessment

The NASEM report defines justice as "addressing systemic oppressions that cause those barriers . . . seeking fair treatment of all people and supporting opportunities for self-determination and thriving" (p. 27). This approach to justice addresses structural elements of how we design assessment and whose ideas are centered in those processes of design (Randall, 2021). Justice means transforming how we think about student engagement in disciplinary practice in more expansive ways that value multiple ways of knowing beyond settler-colonial perspectives (Bang et al., 2012). Opening up science classrooms to interweave multiple ways of knowing can strengthen students' ultimate understandings of science and connect with their own ideas and the understandings they bring to school (NASEM, 2022; Tzou et al., 2019). These decolonizing views encourage us to name how mainstream, Western science has historically been positioned as the only way of knowing, promoting assimilation to white norms and ways of being (Likely & Wright, 2022).

Robin Wall Kimmerer, in her book *Braiding Sweetgrass* (2013), provides many examples of how Indigenous ways of knowing can strengthen our interactions with the natural world. Kimmerer presents a story of one of her graduate students who wanted to study how the Indigenous practice of selective weeding encouraged grasses to grow. The strategy ran counter to what the other science professors on the graduate student's committee knew, and they challenged the student's approach. However, the student proceeded with the study and discovered that selectively pulling sweetgrass from a field helped it to grow more lavishly as compared to leaving the field to grow without human intervention. Her findings astounded the committee and reinforced the value of Native American methods for maintaining grasslands.

Curriculum and assessments can be designed to build on similar principles, weaving together students' everyday experiences and community ways of knowing with the science they are learning in school, at the same time strengthening all of the elements (Tzou et al., 2019). We need to acknowledge and bring these sources of expertise into curriculum and our pedagogy (Belczewski, 2009). To authentically center this knowledge and these ways of knowing, justice-oriented perspectives compel us to design curriculum and assessments *with*, not *for*, communities (Bang, 2019).

Seeking justice can involve assessment experiences designed in partnership with learners, parents, and community members (Tzou et al., 2021). Educators are provided supports in recognizing and inviting students' experiences and knowledge into the classroom, and rather than supplanting this knowledge, creating ways to intertwine with science learning (Learning in Places Collaborative, 2021). Further, formative assessment for justice invites learners to show what they know in ways that sustain their own practices and creates space for students to take action in response to societal challenges, such as the effects of climate change or COVID-19 on their communities.

SELF-REFLECTION FOR AMBITIOUS AND EQUITABLE TEACHING

In science formative assessment, we often start with understanding the science we are teaching, as well as students' ideas and experiences so we can bring them into the science classroom. However, we also need to open space for teachers to understand their own understandings and identities, and how those intersect with their efforts in science teaching in general, and with formative assessment in particular.

We can easily slip into a mode in which we check to see whether students' ideas are the same as our ideas, or those that we want them to learn. These practices likely mirror our own experiences of assessment, which have been shown to be deeply influential on how we enact assessment ourselves (Looney et al., 2018). But where are these ideas really coming from? How are we creating space to listen and learn from our students, and the unique perspectives and experiences they bring, rather than prioritizing our own understandings?

This is where—as we seek to design and enact more equitable and just science formative assessments—we must consider own identities as science teachers. We might think of this process of self-reflection as spraying mist onto a window to see the glass we are looking through more clearly. How does the lens that we bring—colored by our own experiences as learners, and our identities as humans—influence what we see and hear as students are learning? And how are our own responses to students' ideas in turn influenced by that lens?

Reflection on our own identities and the science we are assessing should also extend to our questioning of the design of the formative assessments we are enacting with learners. This involves starting with self-reflection so that we are aware of how our own interests, histories, and identities intersect with those of our learners, and how this influences the way that they engage in processes of assessment in their classrooms (Patterson Williams et al., 2020; Randall, 2021).

These reflections can be framed as responses to questions that create space for teachers to consider their own identities as they interact with their work as teachers and assessors (Randall, 2021). Engaging in this process of self-reflection might be done individually before teaching a lesson (Learning in Places Collaborative, 2021), or with a group of colleagues seeking to design assessments to better center students' interests and identities (Kang, 2022). They might include such questions as:

- Who are we? What have our experiences been in the world?
- How do we understand science?
- How do we select assessments? Who designed these assessments? Whose ideas are valued?
- What kinds of strategies do we use to create space for students to share their ideas with us?
- How do we respond to students, especially when they say something we weren't expecting?

With guiding questions like these, teachers can work individually or together to reflect on their own lived experiences with science and science teaching, and on the ways their own values can play out as they interact with students. They can also reflect on how hierarchies of power can be enacted in classrooms, and their own role in recentering the classroom on students and helping to construct bridges between science and students' experiences.

These perspectives can help us open different approaches to formative assessment that prioritize students engaging in science practices in contexts relevant to their lives. They are critical of assimilative ways of teaching science, seeking to sustain students' cultural identities and ways of knowing and to build on teachers' processes of critical self-reflection.

CENTERING EQUITY AND JUSTICE IN FORMATIVE ASSESSMENT: EXAMPLES

While efforts to center equity and justice in classroom and formative assessment in STEM subjects are still emerging (Furtak & Lee, in press), some excellent models already exist in science education. The following sections provide examples of how formative assessments embedded in curriculum materials and with instructional supports can center justice and equity.

Lotions and Potions

Students' experiences in science—and science assessment—can be assimilative rather than embedded in everyday settings and sustaining cultural practices (Likely & Wright, 2022). In a unit that considers the intersections of Black girlhood, *Lotions and Potions: Science Through Hair Care*, middle school girls participated in science and engineering practices as they made hair care products and learned about skin and Black hair as science content (Likely, 2022).

The Lotions and Potions curriculum illustrates equity- and justice-centered approaches to science formative assessment in multiple ways. The curriculum focuses on equity by centering investigations and assessments on scenarios around skin and Black hair care, which are relevant to students' lives. Assessment tasks use multiple structures and scaffolds to support students in sharing what they already know, and what they are learning, in connection with these scenarios. Further, the curriculum and assessments promote justice by repositioning skin and Black hair care as foci for investigation through science and engineering

Figure 3.1. Overview of "Lotions and Potions: Science Through Hair Care" Curriculum, With Summary of Science and Engineering Practices (Bold) and Formative Assessment Activities for Each Lesson (adapted from Likely, 2020)

Lesson 1	Lesson 2	Lesson 3	Lesson 4	Lesson 5	Lesson 6
Around-the-room observations	Skin elasticity	How soap works	Hair lotion	Hair oil	Do-it-yourself (DIY) video
Obtaining, evaluating, and communicating information Observation statements	**Obtaining, evaluating, and communicating information** Observation statements **Developing and using a model** Hair pattern recording	**Using a model** Fill-in-the-blank Label the diagram Label the hair pattern	**Constructing explanations** Matching Whole-group conversation	**Engaging in argument from evidence** Pair-share activity	**Engaging in argument from evidence** DIY video

practices. Formative assessments of science practices were embedded throughout the unit, as shown in Figure 3.1.

Lesson 4, for example, was designed around the driving question, "What are the uses for the ingredients in the soap?" (Likely, 2020, p. 105). As part of this lesson, students were first asked to match ingredients with their uses in soap, and then to construct explanations and share with each other why lotion was an important component of soap. The formative assessment invited students to reflect on this question, and then students shared their ideas with the whole group:

> *Maci:* So you won't be ashy.
> *Rasheda:* Why else is lotion important?
> *Shauna:* It makes your skin moisturized.
> *Rasheda:* Why do you need your skin to be moisturized?
> *Shauna:* If it's dry, it could fall off.
> *Maci:* How your skin fall off?
> *Karesha:* Dirt could get in it, and you will get sick.
> *Rasheda:* What happens if your skin is too dry?
> *Maci:* If my skin is dry, it will crack.
> *Lanna:* And you can get sick.
>   (Likely, 2020, p. 109)

In this conversation, Likely (2020) found that students advanced several claims about lotion and engaged in a practice of collective argumentation in which a scientific argument was co-constructed by several students. Later in the lesson, students built on this and other explanations to create a video that would guide others in making lotions, with possible foci including things scientists do, skin and hair, soap/shampoo, hair and body lotion, or hair and body oil.

Learning in Places

The Learning in Places curriculum for Pre-K–3 learners is another example of how formative assessment can be embedded in storyline units of learning co-designed with communities (Learning in Places Collaborative, 2021). The curriculum is founded on transformative approaches to design that center ethical considerations in nature–human interactions. *Learning in Places* represents how equity and justice can be centered in formative assessment by locating assessment in students' neighborhoods and schools and inviting them to notice what is relevant to them. It invites stories about places that are important to their families into school and builds on the things students notice to help them think about histories of places, as well as futures. The curriculum—developed in partnership with teachers, learners, and community members—seeks to reframe how we consider knowledge in science classrooms by intertwining, and thus strengthening, multiple ways of knowing.

The curriculum materials include callouts that highlight not only science and engineering practices but also connections with families and communities. Teacher materials include explicit frameworks to support educators in enacting the materials (Tzou et al., 2021). Opportunities for formal and informal formative assessment are embedded throughout the curriculum, and are supported by tasks that invite students to bring in examples and ideas from their homes and families, as well as supports for teachers to recognize the science ideas in those examples (Bang, 2019).

The unit begins by inviting students to go on a neighborhood walk with a family or community member. These "family place walks" invite students and their families first to write or draw who or what they share their neighborhoods with, and then to go for a walk and write or draw who or what they observe in their neighborhood. The curriculum provides supports for children and families that highlight science practices that they engage in during these walks, such as making observations and asking questions. In turn, *Learning in Places* provides supports for teachers because students bring their writings and drawings from their neighborhood walks into the classroom. Teachers are provided explicit supports to consider the places in which they are teaching in historical context, and to de-settle their own understandings of Indigenous peoples and places (Learning in Places Collaborative, 2021).

Assessment opportunities are embedded throughout these lessons. For example, at the beginning of the unit, teachers engage the class in whole-class or pair discussions about the kinds of places and peoples that have histories, as well as the places and peoples that have futures. The goal of the formative assessment is to help students understand that all people and places have histories, as well as futures. Students share their ideas on sticky notes, and later these sticky notes are sorted onto a whole-class graphic organizer.

Later in the unit, teachers bring students on a walk around the schoolyard in order to engage with similar sets of questions about what they notice. Informal assessment opportunities include "back-pocket" questions that guide teachers to help notice relationships in their observations ("You found flowers! Who else besides humans do you think would like to find flowers and why?") and purposes ("How did this place come to be this way? Why do you think it's important for us to learn about this place and who we might share it with?") (Learning in Places Collaborative, 2021; LE1.3: Sharing Places, p. 4).

Students are encouraged at multiple points to bring their families' stories and perspectives into their school learning. In LE1.4 Learning Across Places, students are invited to identify a place that is important to their families, and then to draw it. They are invited to reflect on how their family came to be in this place, how they feel in this place, how the place has changed since their family arrived, and who and what else they share the place with (pp. 2–3).

At the end of the learning sequence, teachers are invited to look across the different tools students have completed in school and at home, and to identify patterns they see in student and family thinking, relationships students see, what students and families do in these spaces, and how power and historicity are represented. The goal is to support learners—as well as teachers—in going back and forth between their homes and school, and to make meaningful connections that enrich both sets of knowledge and practices.

Learning in Places integrates teacher self-reflection tools as prework for teachers as they are preparing to enact units. Teachers are invited to self-assess with the same graphic organizer that will be used to guide their teaching of the unit and to organize students' ideas, and then to reflect on questions such as, "What do I know from prior experience and research I have conducted? What questions or wonderings do I have? How can I support students' sensemaking within and across

Figure 3.2. Guide for family neighborhood walk. Adapted from *Learning in Places Collaborative (2021). LE 1.A Sharing Places: Neighborhood Walk. http://learninginplaces.org*

PART 1: BEFORE OUR WALK

We share our neighborhood with many others, including animals, plants, water, and other humans. We can learn a lot from others about our neighborhood by making observations and asking questions.

Before you go outside for a walk, create a picture of **who** and **what** you remember is outside around your neighborhood. You can include words, symbols, and drawings.

What kinds of things do you think you can learn from walking in your neighborhood?

---

scales of time?" (Learning in Places Collaborative, 2021; LE1.1: Socio-Ecological Histories of Places Launch, p. 2).

EQUITY AND JUSTICE: CONNECTIVE THREADS FOR FORMATIVE ASSESSMENT DESIGN AND ENACTMENT

We've dedicated some time to developing clear understandings of constraints on formative assessment in science, as well as the potential for formative assessment to expand participation in science learning for all learners. The remainder of this book will pull on these themes of equity and justice as connective threads to inform how we design and plan for formative assessment; how we enact those tasks with students; the tools we develop to support formative assessment in classrooms, and professional learning approaches; and the ways that larger educational systems can constrain, or enable, transformative formative assessment in science classrooms.

Part II

TASKS AND PRACTICES

CHAPTER 4

Questions Worth Answering: The Role of Phenomena in Formative Assessment

A few summers ago, my children and I took a hike near Rocky Mountain National Park; at the time, they were in preschool and 2nd grade. Within minutes of leaving the car, I found myself barraged by questions. Why is it harder to walk uphill than downhill? Why are so many roots covering the path? Why aren't we seeing any animals? Why is it so hot today? Why am I more thirsty when I'm exercising? Are we there yet? I was amused, and a little exhausted, by their queries; we didn't discuss all of their questions, but they represented children's innate curiosity about the natural world. All children in all cultures, as part of their normal developmental processes, find themselves curious about their surroundings.

These questions from children don't just come out in the grandeur of a National Park—if we listen carefully, we will hear them every day. A few weeks ago, my son (now age 9) stared into the glass from which he had just been drinking, and asked, "How come I can never get all the water out of my cup, even when I think I've drunk it all? There's always a little water left in the bottom." Of course, science ideas popped into my head when I heard this question—surface tension? the properties and shape of the glass? There are simply so many directions we can go with kids when we listen to their questions.

If we marvel that our kids ask these questions at home, but not as much at school, some have argued it's because of the way we traditionally teach science—as a catalog of facts that tells kids their questions aren't as important as what's in the textbook, or what's on the next test. Recent research on learning has compelled us not to just move these real-world applications to the front and center of students' experiences of learning but to have them *define* students' science learning in school (NASEM, 2018). Students' questions and natural curiosity should drive them to learn science; and for assessment to support these shifts in instruction, we must also design assessments around these interesting scenarios and real-world questions. Why would we take the rich learning experiences students have in these phenomenon-driven units and distill them down to simple recall of facts? As the world exists in all its complexity, we want students to take what they've learned through investigating interesting questions in science learning and show it on assessments that engage that learning in new scenarios and contexts around them. Just like when they're out for a walk with a family member or quenching their thirst at home.

In this chapter, I'll provide a few ways of thinking about phenomena to inform the way we select and use them to frame formative assessments.

CONSIDERATIONS FOR PHENOMENA

Let's start by making connections to the larger role that phenomena play in science curricula. The *Framework for K–12 Science Education* (Board on Science Education, 2012) and follow-up publications (NASEM, 2019) have emphasized that curriculum and instruction should start with students' natural interests as a way into the science practices, disciplinary core ideas, and crosscutting concepts they learn about every day. Rather than having curriculum units framed around a science idea (e.g., "Force and Motion"), we instead would start by asking a question that students can relate to and which they find engaging, such as, "How can we design an exciting roller coaster?" Or, instead of learning about the "structure and properties of matter," students might ponder the question, "What happens to our garbage?" (Lee et al., 2016).

When we have designed instructional units centered on these kinds of contextualized and interesting questions, it's important for assessments to follow suit (Randall, 2021). Assessments that revert to concepts alone, or science practices in the absence of a larger disciplinary context, will not align with these kinds of units. Instead, assessments should be framed in everyday contexts that are interesting to students so they are compelled to answer them, and so they align with phenomenon-based units of instruction. Phenomena aren't just written scenarios but also may be represented in pictures, diagrams, and data as contexts for students to interpret. They may also involve a degree of uncertainty to compel students to engage in sensemaking about the scenario at hand (Furtak et al., 2021).

When we're identifying and selecting phenomena to contextualize an assessment, I find it useful to think about phenomena in four ways: they should be engaging, observable, place-based, and sustaining the knowledge and practices of minoritized learners. While these criteria clearly overlap, each provides a dimension through which we might consider how, and why, a phenomenon can be an entry point for students—and for which students (see Figure 4.1).

Interesting and Engaging

When we think about science assessments, "interesting" might not be the first word that comes to mind. Often, assessments are taken simply because they are required. But what if we were to radically rethink assessments as needing to also be interesting and engaging for students? If the questions asked are ones that students already wonder about, might they not be more motivated to show us what they know and are able to do? Scholars have studied the link between interest, motivation, and learning for years; what they have found is that when students' natural interest is engaged, they are more motivated to participate in learning (NASEM, 2018). By asking questions that students want to figure out an answer for, we stimulate their natural curiosity and sensemaking as they try to understand the world around them (Odden & Russ, 2019).

Observable

Phenomena can also start with a scenario that is observable. An observable phenomenon might be caused by something happening at the molecular level; think, for example, of asking students why a seat belt's metal tongue gets so hot on a summer day that it could burn you, but the webbed belt itself doesn't get as hot. Why is that? The deeper explanation involves thermal energy and the underlying properties of the materials themselves, but the seat belt is something they can touch, feel, experience. As an example, consider how an assessment for energy transfer and transformation might be given in the context of asking students to design a better coffee cup to insulate a hot beverage, rather than going immediately to the intramolecular processes at play. While the latter ideas can certainly be addressed in the assessment, framing the assessment question around the observable phenomenon reinforces the connections between scientific processes and students' everyday lives. At the same time, when the question being asked can't be directly observed, students might benefit from data or images they can observe that illustrate the phenomenon in the same way, such as showing figures or videos of changing temperatures of ocean water at different times of year.

Contextualized in a Real Place and Time

While many assessments might construct a fictional scenario, or one that could in theory happen any time, and at any place, we can go a step further by embedding assessment questions in a specific place and time. This kind of design enables us to draw upon specific, real-world data that students can analyze, model, and explain as part of the assessment.

As an example, we can turn to a task intended to draw out student thinking about falling objects and gravity. Envision that a teacher passes out a type of formative assessment task called a Predict-Observe-Explain assessment (White & Gunstone, 1992). This assessment was designed based on research that suggests students will predict larger and heavier objects will fall to the ground faster than smaller and lighter objects.

The teacher holds up two balls—one rubber, one steel—and explains she will drop them at the same time. First, she asks students to predict which ball will reach the ground first and to write down their prediction and reasoning. After a few minutes, the teacher sets the balls on a shelf and releases them. The two balls hit the floor simultaneously; the teacher then asks students to connect their prediction with their observation.

This scenario—dropping two balls of differing mass but similar size simultaneously—may be happening in real time in front of the students, but it is still decontextualized from students' daily lives and sets them up to be incorrect, framing their ideas as needing to be replaced (Posner et al., 1982). However, air resistance is something students have experienced before, such as when they stick their arm out the window of a moving vehicle, or even when they walk against the wind. When we more intentionally place our assessments, as well as students' learning opportunities, in communication with students' daily experiences, we position them differently, as bringing assets and resources that are fundamentally related to their science learning. We create opportunities to interweave their ideas and experiences with science, and to engage the practices of scientists as they develop models and explanations connected to these everyday contexts.

The NGSS Sample Task "A Tale of Four Cities," for example, examines variations in weather in four cities in the Western United States (Achieve, Inc., 2014). The task provides data from the four cities, basing the phenomenon at the center of the task in those specific places. The task also creates space for teachers to provide additional data from their own communities. Similarly, Penuel and colleagues (2019) developed a task that presented average heart rate data for visitors to the Tibetan Plateau, and those living at high elevations (Achieve, Inc., 2018).

Sustaining the Knowledge and Practices of Diverse Learners

The final criterion follows from Chapter 3 and seeks to create access and opportunities for students to draw on their own histories and experiences in learning, particularly for students whose communities have been historically marginalized in science. Doing so raises the questions about the three preceding criteria—the phenomenon is interesting and engaging to *whom*? Observable and based in the space and time of *whose* community?

Thus, as we are designing assessments, we must seek to make the science students are learning relevant to the cultures and experiences of the racially and linguistically diverse students in our classrooms. The idea is that by allowing students to share what's interesting and relevant in *their* lives, teachers and curriculum and assessment developers can then identify links to the science they are learning and use the culturally relevant phenomena as an entry point.

We can push this even a step farther: assessment scenarios can do more than just be relevant to students and their communities. Designing formative assessment tasks that are relevant and responsive to students' interests is clearly an important step (Taylor, 2022); at the same time, scholars encourage us to look beyond using culturally relevant scenarios to teach only canonical knowledge (Paris, 2012). Instead, we can push ourselves to explore how assessment scenarios can sustain the interests and practices of students and their communities (Paris, 2012; Randall et al., 2021), such as by asking students to share what they know through videos, as in the Lotions and Potions example in Chapter 3 (Likely, 2022). Further, when we consider justice-oriented and anti-racist approaches to assessment, we should consider how the phenomena and scenarios in which we embed assessments can decenter dominant perspectives and be embedded in contexts and historically marginalized communities (Randall, 2021).

As an example, we can look to the set of resources developed by the Stanford Project *Science in the City*, a partnership among teachers, teacher educators, and educational researchers. A series of lessons explore how the practice of redlining—the historical practice of banning people of color from securing mortgages in particular areas—is related to climate change (https://scienceinthecity.stanford.edu/resources/redlining-urban-heat-a-lesson-in-climate-change). A formative assessment embedded in the series of lessons invites students to animate and record an explanation of how redlining and climate change are connected in Powtoon, an online tool that allows students to make and record animated videos. Students are prompted to use specific terms, including greenhouse effect, city planning, urban heat island, ozone, and CO_2.

Figure 4.1. Four Considerations for Formative Assessment Phenomena

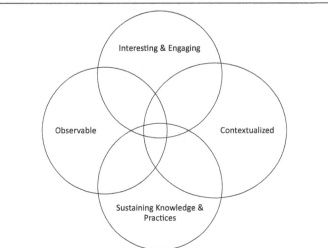

Taken together, we can envision how a particular phenomenon might meet one or more of these criteria. We might assume that better phenomena would meet several of these characteristics, while acknowledging that few phenomena would be able to meet them all. A phenomenon might be interesting and observable (e.g., how a comet nearing the sun would begin to melt and display a long tail), but may not be relevant to students' everyday lives. A good way to think about these criteria might be to determine how a phenomenon could be made even better to frame an assessment—for example, the comet tail phenomenon could be framed in the case of a specific comet the students may have seen or heard about, such as the NEOWISE comet in summer 2020.

What's important is when deciding whether to use a particular phenomenon, we are clear about the underlying reasons for any trade-offs being made when we prioritize one consideration over another. For example, in a unit on force and motion, we might want to ask students about the movement of an object without accounting for friction; this might lead us to work with a phenomenon such as a ball rolling along a frictionless surface, which is decontextualized. Similarly, we might not always be able to center the knowledge and practices of *all* communities of students on every single task; we should thus consider how we are ensuring that all students have opportunities to locate themselves and their experiences in a phenomenon framing a task at some point in a unit.

TYPES OF PHENOMENA FOR FORMATIVE ASSESSMENT

As mentioned at the beginning of the chapter, our purpose is to consider how phenomena should be involved in the design of formative assessments embedded in three-dimensional curriculum units. The term "formative assessment" alone in many ways obscures the reality that it can be placed at different points in units and serve different functions. For example, assessment opportunities may link back to students' developing abilities to respond to the driving question for a unit. However, teachers are likely also interested in students' ability to transfer or apply their learning to related, but different, scenarios in assessments. This may involve students seeing a phenomenon that draws upon the same scientific principles but that poses questions in a different context.

Ultimately, this comes down to the size of the phenomenon. Selecting a phenomenon for a formative assessment task should involve selecting a question that can be addressed within the time allotted for the assessment. We should also consider that the task should provide students with the right amount of information to engage in the task, with no extraneous details to cause confusion or distraction.

Jason Buell and colleagues (2019b) presented a framework for thinking about phenomena for assessment in relation to units of instruction, and I'll summarize and build on elements of that framework here. The relationship of any kind of assessment to instruction can be described using the language of same, close, proximal, and distal (Pellegrino et al., 2001; Ruiz-Primo & Li, 2004). These ways of thinking about the relationship of an assessment task to classroom learning experiences can also be used to examine the relationship between the phenomenon driving a whole curriculum unit and those that might be used specifically for formative assessment (Buell et al., 2019b).

Same Phenomenon

As the unit begins, teachers conduct formative assessment to find out students' prior experiences with the phenomenon, and the ideas and experiences they leverage to develop an initial model or response to the question. Then, each time the class returns to this question can serve as another chance to gather more information and to better understand students' learning as it develops through the unit. We can think of this as the *same* phenomenon (Buell et al., 2019b). As an example, in the unit described in Chapter 1, students could return to the driving question, "How are modern cars designed to keep you and your family safe during a collision?" several times through a unit to appraise progress and to see how new learning has helped students advance toward answering the question (Kang et al., 2022).

When this is done at the beginning of the unit, such as by making an initial model, asking students about the same phenomenon serves as a form of preassessment that centers students' experiences and resources at the start of a learning sequence. Later in the unit, students may return to the central question to revise their models based on evidence collected as part of the learning sequence, or to refine or better develop their explanations. In this way, using the *same* phenomenon is not just a simple way to do formative assessment. It's also interwoven into the way we think about unit sequences in three-dimensional instruction.

As students return again and again to the anchoring phenomenon, they provide evidence in the course of ongoing learning about the ways they are developing their grasp of scientific practices, their understandings of disciplinary core ideas, and their application of crosscutting concepts. They create posters, draw models, and talk to their peers and their teachers about their ideas and understandings. They ask questions of each other to refine their understandings. They revise their ideas and evaluate their models and explanations given new evidence gathered in investigations.

Close Phenomenon

The next type of phenomenon for a formative assessment can be close to, but not the same as, the phenomenon framing the unit (Buell et al., 2019b). These phenomena might have many similar features or dimensions to what is seen in the framing phenomenon for the unit, but with some elements or contexts changed; however, the underlying concepts are essentially the same, and create space for students to show what they know in a closely related scenario. These phenomena are still embedded in the unit—that is, they are activities built into the unit, about which students learn and investigate—but they are not the same as the anchoring phenomenon driving the unit.

As an example of a close formative assessment phenomenon, we can consider the Oil Tanker Unit for high school chemistry in Ambitious Science Teaching (Windschitl et al., 2018). In this unit, students seek to understand why an oil tanker train car crushes inward after being steam-cleaned and then sealed and left overnight. A formative assessment that is the same as the driving question of the unit can happen as a preassessment or an embedded assessment later in the unit, when students return to the question, "Why did the tanker crush? How did the tanker crush?"

However, students cannot directly investigate the phenomenon of the oil tanker, so a close phenomenon can serve both as an opportunity for students to better understand the underlying phenomenon, as well as a chance to formatively assess students' main takeaways from the activity. In this unit, students conduct an investigation in which they boil water in soda cans, filling them with small amounts of water and heating them before dipping them into cold water, causing them to crush inward (similar to what is observed in the video). A close formative assessment might ask them questions about key relationships (volume, pressure, temperature) that also apply to a complete model of the crushing oil tanker phenomenon, but they are framed in the context of the soda can (Windschitl et al., 2018). See Table 4.1 for an overview.

Proximal Phenomenon

A phenomenon might be considered proximal if "the assessment task was designed considering the knowledge and skills relevant to the unit, but **content was different to the one studied in the unit [emphasis added]**" (Ruiz-Primo & Li, 2004, p. 75). The main focus of a proximal assessment is *transfer*, or the process through which students are able to apply their practices and understandings from one context to another. As a result, these tasks will be more challenging for students than same or close assessments. At the same time, though—and a key distinction in the context of the NGSS—is that proximal phenomena should still assess the same set of standards that students have learned during instruction (Penuel et al., 2019). Schwarz and colleagues (2009) identified this ability to address new contexts with the science practice of modeling as the most sophisticated level of that practice, such as

Table 4.1. Same and Close Formative Assessment Phenomena for Oil Tanker Unit (adapted from Ambitious Science Teaching, n.d.)

Type of Phenomenon for Formative Assessment	Question
Same	Why did the tanker crush? How did the tanker crush?
	Draw an initial model and discuss in small groups and as a whole class; create a whole-class consensus model.
Close	Think back to your experiment with the soda cans. State your results as a rule. How did changing the manipulated variable affect the amount of crushing? When _____ the can crushed more because _____.

when students spontaneously make models for phenomena that are not necessarily the same as those driving their unit.

As an example, we can explore the high school unit, "Why Don't Antibiotics Work Like They Used To?" (Next Generation Storylines & iHub, 2019; Penuel et al., 2019). While the unit itself provides opportunities for students to develop understandings of evolution through the process of natural selection as they examine data, model, and explain, as well as apply multiple crosscutting concepts, the proximal transfer tasks present new scenarios for students to apply these practices and understandings at the end of units of instruction. While the driving question for the unit focused on antibiotics, the transfer tasks used phenomena about Galapagos ground finches, swallows, and humans on the Tibetan plateau as contexts.

While we might ultimately hope that students can transfer what they have learned to a phenomenon proximal to that driving the unit on a summative assessment, we should provide them with opportunities to show what they know in other phenomena through the unit.

Distal Phenomena

A distal phenomenon is farther away from what is being investigated in a unit of instruction, and as a result less likely to be of relevance for formative assessment. These kinds of phenomena are based on state or national standards and are more likely to be encountered on an interim or large-scale assessment.

HOW DIFFERENT PHENOMENA SUPPORT FORMATIVE ASSESSMENT ACROSS AN INSTRUCTIONAL UNIT

All units that build on an anchoring phenomenon are rich with opportunities for multiple kinds of formative assessments that are the same, close, and proximal. As an example, we can look at the OpenSciEd thermal energy unit for 6th grade that has as its anchoring phenomenon, "How can containers keep stuff from warming up or cooling down?" (OpenSciEd, 2020b). See Table 4.2 for a summary. Each subsequent lesson in the series of units engages students in investigations with cups, lids, containers, and contents such as liquids as students explore elements of the system and its relationship to the conservation of thermal energy inside a regular and insulated cup. Throughout the unit, students return again and again to this phenomenon, making and revising models and explanations based on evidence collected during investigations. In

Table 4.2. Same, Close, and Proximal Formative Assessment Phenomena for Thermal Energy Unit (adapted from OpenSciEd, 2020b)

Type of Phenomenon for Formative Assessment	Question
Same	How can containers keep stuff from warming up or cooling down?
Close	Cold lemonade on a hot day! Sarah and Michael were visiting their friend, Regina. They were in Regina's backyard enjoying cups of ice-cold lemonade. They noticed droplets on the outside of the pitcher of lemonade. The three friends made the following claims: A. **Sarah** said, "Those droplets must be lemonade leaking from inside the pitcher." B. **Regina** said, "The droplets on the outside of the pitcher are water. They came from the air outside the pitcher." **Michael** said, "I agree that the droplets on the outside of the pitcher are water, but the water comes from the melting ice cubes inside the pitcher." Based on what you have figured out from our investigation, pick the claim that you most agree with. Use words and pictures to explain why you agree with it, and support your thinking with evidence from our investigation. Use reasoning to explain why each piece of evidence supports the claim. [Text reprinted from 6.2 Lesson 5 Assessment Cold Lemonade on a hot day!]
Proximal (Transfer)	In emergencies, shelter or a place to sleep is very important. People often spend nights outside on the ground. The government is trying to identify a solution that will keep people warm when they need to sleep directly on the ground. They are considering three types of blankets and evaluating how well each works to keep people warm. Below are their criteria and constraints. Criteria: 1. Will keep people warm and alive sleeping outside for 6 hours at night, with no more than a 10°F (5.5°C) temperature change in the air on the inside of the blanket where the person is. 2. Can also be used to keep people warm during the day. 3. Needs to be lightweight.

(continued)

Table 4.2. Same, Close, and Proximal Formative Assessment Phenomena for Thermal Energy Unit (adapted from OpenSciEd, 2020b) (Continued)

Type of Phenomenon for Formative Assessment	Question
	Constraints:
	4. Keep costs low and affordable.
	5. Environmentally friendly and can be reused.
	(Data provided on three types of blankets, average nightly temperatures, human body temperatures, and results of initial tests)
	1. Why is the government so concerned about people getting too cold if they sleep directly on the ground?
	2. Use the information and data from the tests to make a recommendation for which blanket the government should choose. In your response, include scientific reasoning to support your recommendation.
	Choice: _____
	Reasoning: Explain using scientific principles and connect the test results to the criteria and constraints.
	(Text with data omitted reprinted from 6.2 Lesson 18 Assessment Disaster Blanket Design Assessment)

Note: Task prompts summarized with modifications described above from "Thermal Energy Unit" by OpenSciEd, www.openscied.org. Licensed under Creative Commons License. View the Creative Commons Attribution 4.0 Unported License at http://creativecommons.org/licenses/by/4.0

addition, a more formal embedded assessment partway through the unit (Assessment 6) also uses the same phenomenon but focuses on one element of the system: the design of the cup's lid.

We can also see several opportunities within the unit for assessing transfer through the use of various phenomena. While the anchoring phenomenon of the unit addresses the comparison between the ability of different kinds of cups (insulated and not insulated) to keep a beverage at temperature, the proximal phenomena—which are included as both formative and summative assessments—use different phenomena with similar opportunities to model and explain thermal energy as students are learning in their experiences in the curriculum unit. Students are asked about the formation of water droplets on the outside of a pitcher of lemonade on a cold day (Assessment at Lesson 5), as well as to explain energy transfer and transformation when placing ice on bodily injuries (Assessment at Lesson 14). Then, at the end of the unit, students respond to another transfer task, framing questions in the context of different designs for disaster blankets (Assessment at Lesson 18). All three of these phenomena are related to the phenomenon that anchors the unit but also provide opportunities to model, argue, and explain in a different context.

RESOURCES FOR IDENTIFYING PHENOMENA FOR FORMATIVE ASSESSMENT

Student interest surveys are an emerging way to identify phenomena for use in assessments (e.g., Edelson et al., 2021; Penuel et al., 2018). These surveys provide candidate scenarios and phenomena that students can read, rate, and comment on, thereby helping those designing the assessment tasks to be sure to build upon scenarios and examples that are both relevant and interesting to students. Students can rate the tasks on a scale ranging from "Not at all interesting—I don't have any questions about this" to "Very Interesting—I have a lot of questions and I want to know more!" While these surveys have historically been used for students to share their interest in phenomena for summative assessments, teachers might also use them to identify candidate scenarios for formative assessments.

PUTTING IT ALL TOGETHER: FRAMING FORMATIVE ASSESSMENT TASKS WITH PHENOMENA

In this chapter, we have looked at two ways of thinking about phenomena for formative assessment: first, a set of four criteria for thinking about how phenomena engage students and connect with their lives, and second, a way to consider the relationship between a phenomenon for formative assessment and its connection to the larger unit in which it is embedded. Appendix A contains a Phenomenon Planner based on these ideas that you can use to identify phenomena for different points, and for different purposes, in a unit.

Ultimately, as we shift our approaches to curriculum and instruction in science, formative assessment must follow; that means that if our curriculum and instruction are centered on compelling scenarios and questions that drive inquiry in science classrooms, our formative assessments should do the same.

CHAPTER 5

Formative Assessment Tasks: Artifacts and Material Representations of Student Thinking

When I think back to my experience in teacher education in the late 1990s, it can be encapsulated in a task. As part of my student teaching experience, I—like so many of us—was asked to design a unit, complete with embedded and summative assessments. Although I studied biology as an undergraduate, I found myself also teaching two sections of 9th-grade Earth science, so I decided to challenge myself to construct an inquiry-based unit on the relationships between the Earth, moon, and sun. These were the early days of the National Science Education Standards, which primarily separated content and inquiry. The unit covered Earth and Space Science standards about the location of these celestial bodies in space, working examples of eclipses, as well as the reasons for the seasons.

As part of the unit, I wrote what was my first—but definitely not my last—ambitious assessment. On the assessment at the end of the unit, I asked students to respond to the question that starts this chapter, which was intended to draw on students' knowledge of the Earth's orbit around the sun (that it is slightly closer to the sun when it is summer in the Southern Hemisphere), as well as relationship between the tilt of Earth's axis and the angle of incidence of solar radiation. It was built on the misconception that Earth being closer to the sun is what causes it to be warmer, as compared to the angle of incidence of solar radiation on the surface of Earth:

> *Why might you have a hard time explaining to a person living in Australia that the distance from Earth to the sun is not related to increased temperatures in summer?*

I was excited to give the task to my 9th-graders, who—to my surprise and disappointment—almost uniformly left it blank or said they were confused by the question. My bubble had burst. On reflection, I now understand that I was trying to write an ill-defined task that drew deeply upon students' understandings, mental representations, and what I perceived as common misunderstandings of these relationships.

All in one question.

Clearly, the task fell short of what I hoped it would do. I missed the mark in connecting with students' own experiences, instead trying to frame the question from the perspective of a faraway location. Looking back, I think I am still trying to write a better version of that question.

This chapter will focus on formative assessment tasks, particularly those that start with the kinds of phenomena discussed in Chapter 4 and that use multiple components to create space for students to share their developing engagement in three-dimensional learning. We'll also look at the different features of formative assessment tasks that make them more accessible to multilingual learners.

WHAT DO WE MEAN BY "TASKS"?

To start this chapter, I want to be very clear: the ideas at the foundation of this book are intended to push against the idea that the phrase "formative assessment" is interchangeable with a task, or a "thing" that we might download from the internet, a set of questions that we assign to our kids, or a guide for self-reflection that we distribute and then ask kids to complete. Throughout the book, I am intentionally aiming to think much more broadly than that.

Let's start by identifying the ways in which tasks can serve as the centerpiece of a classroom activity system focused on finding out what students know while learning is in progress. I draw on the following definition of a task:

> any instructional or assessment-related unit of disciplinary work that is assigned to students to intellectually engage them in science or mathematics . . . a segment of a classroom activity devoted to the development and assessment of a disciplinary idea and/or a practice. (Tekkumru-Kisa et al., 2020b, p. 607)

Building on this definition, we can consider a formative assessment task as

- designed to mediate participation in disciplinary work,
- defining what the work is that students will do, and
- serving as a tool to surface students' developing understandings and practices.

A formative assessment task can also create opportunities for students to share and work on those understandings and practices with their peers and teacher. Research tells us that tasks are an important way to support the adoption of new and ambitious forms of teaching in science (Tekkumru-Kisa et al., 2020a).

In this chapter, we'll start by examining the role that formative assessment tasks play in a classroom activity system. Then we'll unpack the conversation about formative assessment tasks in the context of the *Framework* before we identify several elements of task design found to support students in sharing their developing ideas and engagement in practice. Then we'll examine a few examples that illustrate these points.

THE ROLE OF FORMATIVE ASSESSMENT TASKS

The purpose of considering a whole classroom activity system is to help us understand—from a wider viewpoint—all of the elements that go into surfacing and working with student ideas and practices when formative assessment is happening. A key response to the question *How do students learn?* is through tasks—tasks that build on prior knowledge, both from their home experiences and from school; tasks that are cognitively demanding; tasks that engage them in practices, such as using evidence and modeling; and tasks that allow them agency to show what they know, to ask their own questions, and to develop their own representations.

Looping back to the activity system presented in Chapter 2, we can see how and why tasks are so important when we think about a larger assessment activity system. To make this more concrete, I'll work with the Oil Tanker modeling task from Ambitious Science Teaching discussed in Chapter 4 (Windschitl et al., 2018). The task asked students a question that was the same as the phenomenon driving the unit: *Why did the tanker crush? How did the tanker crush?* Students were asked to draw an initial model and discuss in small groups and as a class, and then to create a whole-class consensus model.

In the Oil tanker example, the task is comprised of a set of **tools** that mediate classroom activity as **students** (subject/s) work toward the **purpose (object)** of sharing and gradually refining their ideas and disciplinary practices (Cowie et al., 2011). This includes the video the teacher showed her students of an oil tanker crushing inward after being steam cleaned, sealed, and then left overnight; the question itself, shown on a projector to the class; and a handout with places for students to draw their initial models, showing the oil tanker before, during, and after it crushed (Ambitious Science Teaching, n.d.; Windschitl et al., 2018). Students used large pieces of poster paper to draw their initial models in small groups.

This task then helped to guide the **division of labor** among student and teacher participants in a variety of ways—for example, students working together to create group models of a phenomenon; students reviewing and responding to each other's developing explanations; and later, the teacher facilitating students sharing their ideas with the whole class.

The task can also define who participates as members of the classroom **community**, creating the expectation that students work together, not alone, and that they are held accountable to their peers' ideas, as well as to the standards of the discipline (Engle & Conant, 2002). In the Oil Tanker example, the task is set by the teacher with the explicit expectation that students will participate in a larger community of learners that will develop a consensus model. We can also think of how the community can be defined beyond the classroom and school—for example, by engaging the knowledge and resources of students' families and community members (such as in the "Learning in Places" curriculum presented in Chapter 3).

Finally, the tasks can set the **norms and expectations** (**rules**) for how students will engage. For example, the task might contain scaffolds that specify the kinds of notation students might use as they make a model, or a checklist to identify the elements of an explanation they need to include (Windschitl et al., 2018). The task might also specify that after creating their model, students are expected to participate in a "gallery walk" of others' models, using different colors of sticky notes to denote various forms of comments, contributions, or questions about the models (Ambitious Science Teaching, n.d.). In the case of the Oil Tanker task, norms and expectations for making the model were shown in a handout that asked students to "Talk together and agree on some things to include before anyone starts drawing" and "In each phase—before, during, and after—draw and label with words what you can see and what you think might be happening that is unobservable" (Windschitl et al., 2018, p. 123). The task also suggested that students could use dots for air particles and arrows to show direction of movement.

Even this brief analysis of the role that tasks can play within an activity system focused on formative assessment helps to highlight their fundamental role in realizing the object of reforms in science classrooms. In fact, Tekkumru-Kisa and colleagues (e.g., 2015, 2020b) have argued that tasks are fundamentally related to students' opportunity to engage in the kinds of ambitious science learning environments currently advocated in the NGSS.

The "thingness" of tasks is something I want to hold onto in this chapter—by material representation, I mean something that's planned, recorded, and/or written down. Students may or may not get their own version on paper or on a personal device (think of a teacher displaying a graph, or a short video, on a screen for students to see). The students might access the task through a link on their own devices. They might have a question they're answering as they make a model as a small group on a whiteboard. But this is all organized by something we'll call a task.

Tasks are more formal and preplanned than informal formative assessment, when teachers attend to what students are saying and doing throughout instruction, ask follow-up questions, give feedback, and modify their instruction on a day-to-day basis. Although tasks may take many forms, as mentioned above, they are embedded in an ongoing course of learning yet different in purpose than a regular learning activity. The purpose is to pause—to take stock of what's been learned so far and where learning is ultimately headed—and then to use that information to inform subsequent steps in the learning process.

Ultimately, since the structure of the task is integrally related to students' opportunity to learn, it's important to better understand how the design of the task itself is relevant to what students can share. In the next sections of this chapter, I'll unpack different ways of thinking about the design of tasks that are most likely to create space for students to share their thinking.

INTEGRATING THE THREE DIMENSIONS IN FORMATIVE ASSESSMENT TASKS

As described in Chapter 1, part of the new vision for science learning is to go beyond tasks that might assess just a disciplinary core idea or a science practice independently. Instead, we are seeking to design tasks that are at least two-, and possibly three-dimensional, inviting students to show us what they know and can do in a richly contextualized task. So let's take a little time to talk about each of the three dimensions, and how to represent them in formative assessment tasks.

Disciplinary Core Ideas

I'll start with disciplinary core ideas, as this is the dimension of the NGSS that we might be most familiar with as we design and adapt tasks. Resources spanning decades have provided many examples of what formative assessments focused on concepts can look like. These assessments often featured questions specifically designed to elicit students' common misunderstandings, often called "misconceptions."

In the current wave of reforms, we want to push beyond framing student ideas as "mis" or "incorrect" and to think about how the ideas and experiences students bring to science classes are essential to connect with the learning they're doing in school, rather than needing to be replaced.

We also want to focus on how disciplinary core ideas are represented in science classrooms—most of the new standards are deliberately written at a larger grain size, as opposed to catalogs of atomized knowledge. Some concepts that might have been a big focus in the past, such as memorizing the names of cellular organelles, reproducing the stages of mitosis, or creating a physical model that makes an analogy between parts of the cell and a factory or some other system, are no longer included (I'll admit—these are all things I experienced as a student, and which I taught and assessed for in my high school biology class!). Instead, when we look closely at the middle school standards for biology, we see that it focuses on the function of a cell, and how parts of cells contribute to the function:

> MS-LS1-2. Develop and use a model to describe the function of a cell as a whole and ways parts of cells contribute to the function. (NGSS Lead States, 2013, p. 67)

This performance expectation might leave much to interpretation; fortunately, in each NGSS Performance Expectation, we also see additional information (in brackets or parentheses) that are called *Clarification Statements*, which provide additional information and examples, and *Assessment Boundaries*, which specify the limits of an assessment based on the performance expectation. For MS-LS1-2, we see these in the following text:

> [Clarification Statement: Emphasis is on the cell functioning as a whole system and the primary role of identified parts of the cell, specifically the nucleus, chloroplasts, mitochondria, cell membrane, and cell wall.] [Assessment Boundary: Assessment of organelle structure/function relationships is limited to the cell wall and cell membrane. Assessment of

the function of the other organelles is limited to their relationships to the whole cell. Assessment does not include the biochemical function of cells or cell parts.] (NGSS Lead States, 2013, p. 67)

These boundary statements are key as we interpret how to formatively assess students' developing understanding of disciplinary core ideas; that is, we want to be sure that we step back from the granular and focus on the big-picture, core ideas within a discipline. What's important is that we go beyond asking questions only about disciplinary core ideas but push ahead to combine questions about concepts with science and engineering practices, as I'll explain in the following sections.

Science and Engineering Practices

The science and engineering practices create natural opportunities for formative assessment, particularly when we think about tracing the development of students' understandings and grasp of practices over time. By nature, the practices ask students to *do* something, not just to remember something, and as a result, this learning performance creates space to listen to and to view their abilities and understandings, and to provide support as they move ahead. So when designing or adapting formative assessment tasks, we can use the practice that is included in a standard as a place to start.

As an example, let's consider an elementary unit focused on the science practice of modeling (Schwarz et al., 2009). The unit is anchored by the simple question, "What causes a shadow?," a question that many children spontaneously ask and wonder about based on experiences from everyday life. Students begin by drawing initial models of light shining on an object, such as a box or their own bodies, at the beginning of the unit as an opportunity to pre-assess and elicit student thinking and experiences as students develop questions about the phenomenon. Students then construct models, which become material representations of students' ideas that teachers may see and interact with (Cowie et al., 2011). As the unit progresses, students conduct empirical investigations that test the relationships in the model; when they complete the investigations, they return to evaluate and revise their models multiple times. Each of these stages of the task can be considered an opportunity for formative assessment. The task itself is embodied by the students' models, and the making of models over time allows us to track and support not just the development of students' conceptual understanding, but also their ability to model.

In the middle school life sciences example above, science and engineering practices help us see how students are asked not just to understand the structure of a cell, but to develop and use a model to show their understanding. The OpenSciEd unit on Cells and Systems (OpenSciEd, 2022a) is oriented around the question, "How do living things heal?" Students start the unit by engaging with community and family members to understand their stories of healing, and then create initial models of how healing might happen on a person's body. About halfway through the unit, students return to the question of healing, this time in a task related to a wound on a person's leg (a proximal phenomenon to the one driving the unit). A modified version of this task is shown in Figure 5.1.

This task shows how students are invited to create and use a model based on what they have learned, integrating a science practice with a disciplinary core idea.

They can build more examples for the other science practices as well: We can engage students in identifying a scientific question, analyzing and interpreting data, and constructing explanations. Table 5.1 provides a list of the kinds of questions that could be embedded in tasks, adapted from STEM Teaching Tools Practice Brief 30 (Van Horne et al., 2016).

Crosscutting Concepts

Crosscutting concepts might not be the first of the dimensions to come to mind, but they can provide ample opportunities for students to make sense of new phenomena or situations in formative assessment (Furtak et al., 2021). Explicitly inviting students to consider patterns, systems and system models, scale, and cause and effect in settings they have not before seen can be an effective way to design a task. As Helen Quinn, a physicist and one of the authors of the *Framework*, put it, these concepts are the ways that scientists engage with things they cannot initially explain. Leading with questions linked to the crosscutting concepts provides new avenues into formative assessment that don't lead directly to conceptual understanding, but also provide opportunities for students to consider—to make sense of, to dynamically think through, and to figure out—the question being posed (Odden & Russ, 2019).

As an example, let's consider the phenomenon of cuts healing, discussed above. Leading with crosscutting concepts invites us to ask a range of questions that invite students to make sense of what's happening in the pictures; a teacher might show the pictures and then set up the task to invite student sensemaking with several questions: *How is the leg changing over time (patterns)? What structures can you see? What*

Figure 5.1. Formative Assessment Task for Unit on Healing, Aligned to MS-LS-1-2. Modified from *OpenSciEd Unit 6.6 Lesson 8*, "Time-Lapse Video of Skin Healing Observations" by OpenSciEd, www.openscied.org

Marie fell on a hike and scratched her leg. She took a picture at the doctor's office, and then more pictures over three weeks to track how her leg was healing.

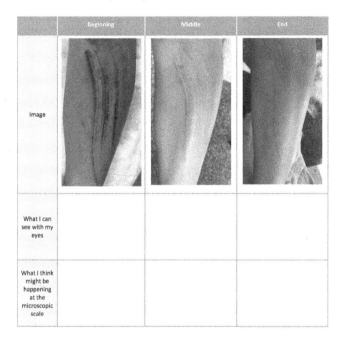

Develop a model of what you think is happening as Marie's skin heals at a microscopic level.

- Using what we have figured out about different parts of the body at different scales, the different systems in the body, and the structure and function of these parts, develop a model to predict how cells help make new skin form on the leg.
- Use words, pictures, symbols, or zoom-ins.
- Be sure to include how the cells fill the gap caused by the injury.

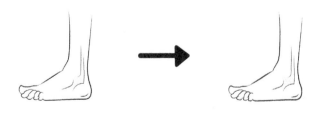

Injured Foot   Healed Foot

Licensed under Creative Commons License and with modification of text and images. View the Creative Commons Attribution 4.0 Unported License at http://creativecommons.org/licenses/by/4.0

Table 5.1. Questions That Help Teachers Attend to Student Engagement In Science Practices

Science Practice	Sample Questions
Asking Questions	• What kind of question could we ask to help us investigate that phenomenon? • What other questions could we ask?
Developing and Using Models	• How does the model show your thinking? • Which of these models better explains the evidence we've seen? • What are the limitations of the model?
Planning and Carrying Out Investigations	• How might we investigate that question? • What might we measure to understand what's going on? • What kind and how much data might we need to collect?
Analyzing and Interpreting Data	• How could you organize or represent the data you've collected? • What causal relationship do you find between the different sets of data you've collected?
Using Mathematics and Computational Thinking	• How might we use mathematics to help us understand this relationship? • How can we predict how this relationship will continue in the future?
Constructing Explanations	• How do you explain what's happening? • What is the cause of what you're observing? How do you know? • How does your model help you to explain the phenomenon?
Engaging in Argument from Evidence	• How well does the evidence support your claim? • What are possible alternative explanations to the claim you have made? • What other evidence might we need to support your explanation?

Note: Some questions adapted from STEM Teaching Tools #30: Integrating science practices into assessment tasks (Van Horne et al., 2016).

function do those structures have? How are the structures and functions related (structure and function)? How might this be different if you observed it under a microscope (scale)? These kinds of questions based on crosscutting concepts provide entry points for students with a range of prior knowledge and experiences.

The task for this phenomenon, adapted from OpenSciEd (2022) and shown in Figure 5.1, explicitly builds on the crosscutting concept in

MS-LS-2-1: Structure and Function. Complex and microscopic structures and systems can be visualized, modeled, and used to describe how their function depends on the relationships among its parts; therefore, the complex natural and designed structures/systems can be analyzed to determine how they function (NGSS Lead States, 2013, p. 223). The task includes this in the bullet that prompts students to draw on what they know about structure and function. It also integrates another crosscutting concept—scale, proportion, and quantity, which notes that processes that can be observed at one scale, such as cell regeneration and growth, cannot be observed at another scale but will manifest in the observable phenomenon of cuts healing.

Since crosscutting concepts replicate the ways that scientists proceed when confronted with new phenomena or problems, they provide space to reframe assessments as opportunities to apply *crosscutting concepts to make sense of novel phenomena* (Furtak et al., 2021). In particular, they provide students with opportunities to leverage their experiences from their daily lives, promoting more equitable participation in science learning. Table 5.2 provides more sample questions based on the crosscutting concepts, based on STEM Teaching Tools Practice Brief 41 (Penuel & Van Horne, 2018).

ELEMENTS OF MULTICOMPONENT FORMATIVE ASSESSMENT TASK DESIGN: SUPPORTING LEARNERS TO SHOW WHAT THEY KNOW

Now that we've broken down the three dimensions of NGSS standards and highlighted how each can contribute to the design of a formative assessment task, let's think about how to explicitly create tasks that go beyond assessing one dimension at a time. We move far beyond simple factual recall, or simple engagement in procedures (which we might call one-dimensional tasks, which have lower cognitive demand—see Tekkumru-Kisa et al., 2020a). Instead, we seek to develop tasks that will engage students in two-dimensional (e.g., science and engineering practices + disciplinary core ideas, or disciplinary core ideas + crosscutting concepts) or three-dimensional tasks in the service of doing science—that is, responding to an engaging and puzzling scenario or phenomenon (see Chapter 4), and then responding to a series of questions that support students in engaging in science practices, their application of crosscutting concepts, and their understanding of disciplinary core ideas. These more challenging tasks have been described as having higher *cognitive demand* in that they can be ambiguous without a clear pathway to an answer; they require students to demonstrate a grasp of scientific

Table 5.2. Crosscutting Concepts as Opportunities to Ask Students Questions That Engage Them in Sensemaking

Crosscutting Concept	Sample Questions
Cause and Effect	• What is the relationship between _____ and _____? • How can a small change in _____ have a big effect on _____?
Structure and Function	• How does the structure of this object relate to its function? • If the structure changed, how would that affect its function?
Systems and System Models	• What are the boundaries of this system? • What is inside the system and what is outside the system?
Scale, Proportion, and Quantity	• How does the amount of _____ relate to the amount of _____? • How might you measure _____? • What is the difference in the patterns you observe at different scales?
Stability and Change	• What is the rate of change? • In what ways is the system staying the same? In what ways is it changing? • How might this system be disturbed by a sudden change in _____?
Energy and Matter	• Where does the energy in this system come from? • How is energy transferred or transformed? • What is the relationship between matter and energy?
Patterns	• What patterns do you observe? • How is _____ changing over time? • How do changes in _____ relate to changes in _____?

Note: Some questions adapted from STEM Teaching Tools #41: Crosscutting Concepts Prompts (http://stemteachingtools.org/assets/landscapes/STEM-Teaching-Tool-41-Cross-Cutting-Concepts-Promptsv2.pdf) (Penuel & Van Horne, 2018)

practice, and to apply crosscutting concepts and draw on disciplinary core ideas (Tekkumru-Kisa et al., 2020a).

We also want to design tasks that meet the goal of engaging all learners with these tasks. More specifically, we want to use our formative assessment task design as an opportunity to interrogate whose interests and identities are centered in that task, and how the task can explicitly create space for students to see a place for themselves and their experiences in the task, and for students with a wide range of linguistic backgrounds to be able to show what they know. Rather than thinking about this after the task is designed, it can and should be done as the task is being created, as considering how the language used in the task supports all learners in understanding it is essential to realizing the goal of broadening access to and participation in science for all learners (Lee et al., 2019).

To do so, I'll build on a framework I developed with Caitlin Fine, which integrates recommendations on science formative assessment task design with research on supporting emergent bi- and multilingual learners (Fine & Furtak, 2020a), as well as approaches that explicitly center justice and equity (e.g., Randall, 2021). I'll also draw on a foundational analysis by Kang and colleagues (2014) that summarizes how different features of formative assessment tasks support students in showing what they know.

Culture and Language

A culturally sustaining approach to formative assessment task design encourages us to start the entire design process with students' knowledge, experiences, and practices so that we create tasks that authentically connect with them. In addition, we seek to allow students to use all of their linguistic resources as they respond to an assessment question that is relevant to their daily lives.

A key starting point for a quality formative assessment task is that it is framed in the context of a phenomenon or scenario for students that helps them locate the science they are learning in school in everyday examples and scenarios that matter to them. Refer to the previous chapter for more resources for thinking about which kinds of phenomena are best suited to the purpose and function of the assessment.

Teachers can create space for students to share their responses in languages other than English. Teachers I have spoken with who regularly work with students from multilingual backgrounds noted that with Google Translate they can still understand what students have shared even when they don't speak the same language, and that by allowing students to write a response in another language they are assessing the students' knowledge of science, not their knowledge of English. Teachers can make this explicit for students by letting them know it's okay for them to use all their linguistic resources.

In schools where the majority of multilingual students speak the same language—such as Spanish—tasks can be translated into that language, or instructions can be provided in multiple languages. For example, the formative assessment shown in Figure 5.2 features a commonly sighted animal in the Denver area, and students were encouraged to respond to the task using all their linguistic resources (this student

Figure 5.2. Student Responding in Spanish to an English-Language Biology Formative Assessment Task

There is a population of foxes living together in foothills of Denver Colorado where there is a large variety of habitats from trees and open grass fields. The fox populations consist of these three types of color variations. Imagine that there is a major fire in the area where these foxes lived. Now there are fewer trees in the area

Fox 1   Fox 2   Fox 3

1. Predict which of these fox populations would be more successful in surviving in order to reproduce under these new conditions.

   los zorros se reproducen muy rapido esto yega a estar en todos lados gracias a su reproduccion

2. Explain your reasoning?

   yo pienso que estos animales se reproducen muy rapido y asi pueden yegar a habitar los pueblos de esa manera

3. What could we do to find out if your prediction is correct?

   podriamos avenguar mas sobre estos animales para saber sobre su reproduccion y asi yo podriamos saber mejor.

---

responded in Spanish). Figure 5.3 provides an example of how teachers can embed this kind of support into the directions on a formative assessment task.

At the same time, when writing formative assessment tasks, we should be mindful of the ways that language complexity can influence how students engage with and respond to the questions we are asking (Taylor, 2022). We want to write short sentences and avoid technical words unrelated to the task at hand. In addition, we should be

Figure 5.3. Excerpt of Task Illustrating How Task Directions Can Invite Student Translanguaging, and How Instructions Can Be Included in English and Spanish; see Appendix B for the Complete Task (adapted from Fine & Furtak, 2020)

Directions: Read the story below and use it to draw and explain a model about energy. You may use all your linguistic resources to do so, and write your response in any language.

Instrucciones: Lea la historia a continuación y úsela para dibujar y explicar un modelo sobre la energía. Puede utilizar todos sus recursos lingüísticos para hacerlo y escribir su respuesta en cualquier idioma.

Imagine you are heating a cup of water in the microwave to make a warm drink. You het the water for just about a minute, so it doesn't start steaming or boiling.

1. What kind of warm drink are you making?

2. Draw a model that shows what is happening to the molecules in the liquid before and after it is heated.

- Model Checklist
- Show what's visible and invisible
- Label your drawing
- Make a key
- Explain ideas that we've been talking about:
    - Molecules
    - Thermal energy
    - Kinetic energy

Before | After

Figure 5.3. Excerpt of Task Illustrating How Task Directions Can Invite Student Translanguaging, and How Instructions Can Be Included in English and Spanish; see Appendix B for the Complete Task (adapted from Fine & Furtak, 2020) (Continued)

3. In the space below, explain what is happening when the liquid in the mug is heated. In your explanation, you need to include:
- ❏ How the molecules are moving before and after the cup is put in the microwave
- ❏ How the motion of the molecules is related to the temperature before and after heating
- ❏ How the motion of the molecules relates to kinetic and thermal energy

Adapted from "Heated Cup of Water" at the NGSS Task Annotation Project, original task available at https://www.achieve.org/files/sites/default/files/18-126%20Heated%20Cup%20of%20Water_Annotations.pdf

mindful of words that might have multiple meanings within the subject area (such as using "graph" as a verb in the sentence, "graph these data using a bar chart," rather than saying "create a bar chart to represent the data," p. 42). We should avoid idiomatic phrases that have particular meanings in American English but are likely to be unfamiliar to students from other cultures, such as saying a person is "under the weather," instead of saying they are sick, or to "pull someone's leg" instead of "making a joke." Finally, we should reduce sentence complexity by omitting dependent clauses, which do not express a complete thought, and breaking longer sentences into shorter ones. As an example, we could change the directions to a task from "The task which is shown below asks you to draw a model and write an explanation" to "The task is shown below. Draw a model and write an explanation."

Alignment and Rigor

As we seek to create tasks that connect with and sustain students' knowledge and cultural practices, we also want to maintain that the tasks are creating opportunities for students to show what they know at grade-appropriate levels. I have encountered resistance when working with teachers and administrators around designing tasks that are more accessible for bi- or multilingual learners due to the assumption that the tasks might be "watered down"; however, I always emphasize that we need to do so in ways that maintain, rather than decrease, the rigor of tasks for students. The sections above on the three dimensions have illustrated the ways in which we can unpack standards to identify their different dimensions; as we design formative assessment tasks, we want to continually monitor the ways in which those tasks align with the standards for the grade level at which students are learning.

Tasks should encourage students to use academic language in their responses. Formative assessments should not only contextualize scientific questions in relevant scenarios but also provide specific guides for students to use academic language (Brown, 2019). A regular classroom question such as "Describe how water moves in the process of osmosis" can be rephrased to ask, "Explain how osmosis describes why marinade works when making carne asada (be sure to use words like *semipermeable membrane, random kinetic motion,* and *concentration gradient*)" (Brown, 2019, p. 109). This reframing embeds the question in something the teacher knows the students may have encountered at home, and at the same time requires learners to practice academic language as they write their explanation.

This kind of support can also extend to words beyond the science terms embedded in a standard. Mandy Watson, an experienced secondary science teacher and administrator at an international school, keeps the vocabulary at a high level in all her assessments. However, when there's a word she doesn't expect students to know, she'll provide a definition. For example, in her environmental science class, Mandy will do this with words like *evaluate* or *deduce*, such as in the following examples:

> Evaluate the solid waste disposal method of composting as a method to introduce into our school community to deal with leftover food waste. *When asked to evaluate, it is important to include a final sentence of conclusion after weighing up the benefits and limitations.*

> Deduce the relationship between the acceleration of the object and the force acting on it (*deduce* means to reach a conclusion based on the evidence).

Mandy emphasizes that adding this additional information helps make the task more accessible for multilingual learners in her classes.

To constantly monitor the rigor of a given standard, I find it helpful to refer to the "Evidence Statements" developed for each of the NGSS performance expectations. The easiest way to access these is via the NGSS website (www.nextgenscience.org); for each performance expectation's web page, the link to the Evidence Statements can be found on the righthand side. Table 5.3 provides an example of the Evidence Statements for MS-LS-1-2, the performance expectation we worked with earlier in the chapter. The evidence statements help us to see the kinds of student performances we should expect as students are learning about the standard and can help us keep in mind the level of rigor we are aiming for in our assessment task design.

Task Components

The question I wrote as a student teacher—*Why might you have a hard time explaining to a person living in Australia that the distance from Earth to the sun is not related to increased temperatures in summer?*—helped to illustrate that trying to ask students everything in one question is not just difficult to design but also difficult for students to answer. Instead, we can support students in showing what they know when we design tasks comprised of multiple parts or components in order to fully assess all the elements of the learning goal (NRC, 2014). These multiple components might consist of background information, questions, pictures, diagrams, data, and multiple outcome spaces such as places where

Table 5.3. Evidence Statements for MS-LS-1-2 (adapted from NGSS Lead States, 2013; see nextgenscience.org for the complete evidence statements)

MS-LS1-2: Students who demonstrate understanding can develop and use a model to describe the function of a cell as a whole and ways parts of cells contribute to the function.		
Science and Engineering Practices: Developing and using models	*Disciplinary Core Ideas:* Structure and function	*Crosscutting Concepts:* Structure and function
Observable features of student performance by the end of the course include:		
Components of the model	To make sense of a phenomenon, students develop a model in which they identify the parts of cells relevant for a given phenomenon (e.g., components, such as the nucleus, cell wall, the function of a cell as a whole)	
Relationships	In the model, students describe the relationships between the components, including:	
	1. The particular functions of parts of cells in terms of their contributions to overall cellular functions (e.g., mitochondria's involvement in cellular respiration)	
	2. The structure of the cell membrane or cell wall and its relationship to the function of the organelles and the whole cell	
Connections	Students use the model to describe a causal account for the phenomenon, including how different parts of a cell contribute to how the cell functions as a whole, both separately and together with other structures. Students include how components, separately and together, contribute to:	
	3. Maintaining a cell's internal processes, for which it needs energy	
	4. Maintaining the structure of the cell and controlling what enters and leaves the cell	
	Functioning together as parts of a system that determines cellular function	

students can draw models, write explanations, or create tables or other representations.

Using multiple components in tasks can also support multilingual learners as they share their ideas on formative assessments. Different kinds of questions break the tasks into smaller pieces and allow students multiple points of entry to use drawings or graphical representations, not just words, so they can show their ideas in ways not only dependent on language. These representations can also support students in sharing their ideas, as the representations can mediate their communication about their ideas during formative assessment tasks (Cowie et al., 2011). For example, a student explaining their ideas in Spanish can support their communication with speakers of other languages by allowing them to represent their ideas in graphical format, as shown on the left panel of Figure 5.4. In addition, using other representations such as sorting cards and gestures can support students in speaking across languages with each other.

Scaffolds

As we design tasks for students that are rigorous and include multiple components, we must also consider how we are supporting them in responding to the questions on those tasks. We can think of these as *scaffolds*, just like the ones we might use when building a structure. Scaffolds have three key features: they support structures while they are being

Figure 5.4. Two Examples of Students Using Visual Representations to Mediate Conversations About Science in Multiple Languages; Left, a Student Speaking Spanish and Using a Representation of a Halfpipe; Right, Students Speaking German While Sequencing Notecards Written in English

constructed, allow for easier access during that process, and then are later taken away. We can think similarly about scaffolds in formative assessment tasks: they support students as they are learning to be able more easily to show us what they know, and we can gradually remove or fade out those scaffolds as students progress in their learning (McNeill et al., 2006). Examples of scaffolds I've already included in this chapter are lists of words to include in a student response, such as in Brown's *carne asada* task. The healing task in Figure 5.1 includes a checklist that clarifies the elements they should include in their model.

Kang and colleagues also found that including what they call *sentence frames* can support students in learning to articulate scientific explanations. These frames help focus students on particular aspects of a phenomenon, or to make deeper connections as part of their explanations. For example, students might be focused onto an element of a phenomenon with a sentence frame such as, after observing an inflating balloon, "What I saw was . . ." Inside [the balloon] the particles were_____ . . . . I know this because_____" (Kang et al., 2014, p. 687). A deeper connection might be supported by the following frame: "Evidence for _____ comes from the [activity or reading] because_____" (p. 687).

As we embed assessments in a unit of learning, or even across the course of a school year, we can envision how these kinds of scaffolds could fade out. Checklists that help students understand what to include in their models, for example, could be provided early in a unit, or early in a school year. As learning progresses, and expectations increase as students have more opportunities to create and use models, teachers could reduce the amount of information included in these checklists as a way of assessing students' knowledge of what should be included. The same approach might be used for sentence frames, which might not be necessary as students better understand how to make causal explanations.

Clear Objectives and Scoring Criteria

All learners benefit when learning objectives are made clear on assessments, and when the criteria by which they will be scored are shared. This helps to make often unstated expectations about how to present work—which may vary across cultures—explicit for students. A 12-year veteran science teacher with whom I met, who has worked in schools in international settings in multiple countries on three continents, uses checklists, rubrics, and plentiful examples on assessments to help students understand what is expected of them, and the quality of work they can produce.

Formative assessment researchers have long established that showing students rubrics to support their self-assessment can improve their understandings of expectations. In turn, those self-assessments can improve the quality of their responses or participation (Andrade, 1999; Sadler, 1989). While a detailed rubric might not be necessary on an embedded formative assessment task, we can still make our assessment criteria explicit to learners in multiple ways. Students can also collaborate with their teachers to co-create criteria for their work (Coffey, 2003); this can be a great way to encourage learners to draw on their previous experiences. For example, middle school students have had many opportunities to represent data in elementary school; in an early year formative assessment that involves creating graphs, teachers could ask students to work together and as a class to develop a list of criteria for what makes a good graph, such as clearly labeled axes and a title.

When we want to give students quick and targeted feedback on a formative assessment, sharing rubrics with students can help them know what to include. For example, student arguments and explanations can be assessed using a simple rubric, as shown in Table 5.4 (Zembal-Saul et al., 2012). This rubric was developed to guide students and teachers in evaluating the quality of podcasts that 3rd-grade students created in which they made claims about what was required to light a light bulb.

Teachers can also provide students with their own self-evaluation tools, such as checklists for what can be included in elements of their responses, or even for their own participation in class discussions or arguments (Taylor, 2022). This can help support students as they engage in cooperative learning, such as listening to and responding to each other's ideas. Using these as checklists can help reinforce students in participating and make explicit what might otherwise be unspoken norms in science classrooms. Table 5.5 provides an example of a self-evaluation checklist for participating in group discussions that is provided as part of the OpenSciEd Teacher Handbook (OpenSciEd, 2020a).

You can find a full checklist of the task design elements from this section in Appendix C.

PUTTING IT ALL TOGETHER: REDESIGNING A MULTICOMPONENT FORMATIVE ASSESSMENT TASK

Now that we've taken some time to review what we know, I want to revisit the task I was working on for my high school Earth science students 20 years ago. That idea that tasks should have multiple components extends beyond everything I was trying to do as a student teacher,

Table 5.4. Sample Rubric for Evaluating Quality of Student Arguments and Explanations (adapted from Zembal-Saul, McNeill, & Hershberger, 2012, p. 131)

	Claim	Evidence	Pieces of evidence include:
	A statement or conclusion that answers the original question/problem	*Scientific data that supports the claim. The data need to be appropriate and sufficient to support the claim*	*Check all that apply:*
0	Does not make a claim, or makes an inaccurate claim like "all you need is a light bulb."	Does not provide evidence, or provides only inappropriate evidence or vague evidence, like "the data show me it is true" or "Our investigation is the evidence."	☐ Bottom of the bulb on the positive end of the battery and wire on the side of the bulb leading to the negative end of the battery
1	Makes an accurate but vague claim like "We got the bulb to light by connecting the wire to the battery."	Provides 1 of 4 pieces of evidence using drawings and photos. All four ways should include a complete circle with one wire, one bulb, and one battery; may also include inappropriate evidence.	☐ Side of the bulb on the positive end of the battery and wire on the bottom of the bulb leading to the negative end of the battery
2	Makes an accurate and complete claim like "A complete circuit is required to light a bulb.	Provides 2 of 4 pieces of evidence using drawings and photos. All four ways should include a complete circle with one wire, one bulb, and one battery; may also include inappropriate evidence.	☐ Bottom of the bulb on the negative end of the battery and wire on the side of the bulb leading to the positive end of the battery
3	Makes an accurate and complete claim like "A complete circuit is required to light a bulb."	Provides 3 of 4 pieces of evidence using drawings and photos. All four ways should include a complete circle with one wire, one bulb, and one battery; may also include inappropriate evidence.	☐ Side of the bulb on the negative end of the battery and wire on the bottom of the bulb leading to the positive end of the battery
4	Makes an accurate and complete claim like "A complete circuit is required to light a bulb."	Provides all 4 pieces of evidence using drawings and photos. All four ways should include a complete circle with one wire, one bulb, and one battery.	

Table 5.5. Self-Evaluation Checklist for Participating in Group Discussion. "Self-Evaluation: Engaging in Classroom Discourse" by OpenSciEd, www.openscied.org

Setting	Criteria	Absent: I do not do this	Developing: I occasionally do this (sometimes)	Proficient: I often do this	Mastery: I consistently do this
In large/whole-group settings (Scientist Circle discussions, gallery walks, etc . . .)	Shares one's own thinking by contributing new ideas, questions, and additional clarification				
	Listens actively to others, rephrasing, repeating, and/or reusing the ideas others have shared and asking others to repeat their statements or to clarify an idea when they are difficult to hear or understand				
	Respectfully provides and receives critiques about explanations, procedures, models, and questions by citing relevant evidence and posing and responding to questions				
	Invites others to share their thinking and contribute their ideas				

(continued)

Setting	Criteria	Absent: I do not do this	Developing: I occasionally do this (sometimes)	Proficient: I often do this	Mastery: I consistently do this
In small-group settings (partner talk, small-group discussions, lab work)	Shares one's own thinking by contributing new ideas, questions, and additional clarification				
	Listens actively to others, rephrasing, repeating, and/or reusing the ideas others have shared and asking others to repeat their statements or to clarify ideas when they are difficult to hear or understand				
	Respectfully provides and receives critiques about explanations, procedures, models, and questions by citing relevant evidence and posting and responding to questions				
	Invites others to share their thinking and contribute their ideas				

Licensed under Creative Commons License and without modification. View the Creative Commons Attribution 4.0 Unported License at http://creativecommons.org/licenses/by/4.0

when I was trying to do too much with one single question. Instead, a multicomponent task breaks down the complex learning goal or learning target represented in a task, and then uses multiple components as scaffolds that engage students in different elements of that learning goal.

As an example, we might consider the following NGSS performance expectation that would have encompassed that assessment I was trying to write back at the turn of the millennium:

> HS-ESS2-4: Use a model to describe how variations in the flow of energy into and out of Earth's systems result in changes in climate. (*Clarification Statement*: Examples of the causes of climate change differ by timescale, over 1–10 years: large volcanic eruptions, ocean circulation; 10s–100s of years: changes in human activity, ocean circulation, solar output; 10s–100s of thousands of years: changes to Earth's orbit and the orientation of its axis; and 10s–100s of millions of years: long-term changes in atmospheric composition.) (*Assessment Boundary*: Assessment of the results of changes in climate is limited to changes in surface temperatures, precipitation patterns, glacial ice volumes, sea levels, and biosphere distribution.) (NGSS Lead States, 2013, p. 285)

We can pull out the different dimensions and components combined together in this performance expectation—"Use a model" (modeling, science and engineering practice); "Cause and Effect" (crosscutting concept), and the Earth and the Solar System, Earth Materials and Systems, and Weather and Climate (disciplinary core ideas). An assessment linked to the Performance Expectation then might provide space for students to use a model of the Earth-sun system representing the tilt of the Earth on its axis, and the relative position of the Earth to the sun at four different times of year.

Now, looking back at the original task that started the chapter, I have several insights that could lead me to design the task a different way. First, I can see how my own perspective on what might be "interesting"—locating the phenomenon for the task in Australia—didn't take my students' interests and experiences into account. Second, I can see how the specific combination of disciplinary core idea, crosscutting concept, and science and engineering practices could lead to providing a wide range of information to students to support their engagement in the task. Third, I can see how using multiple sets of questions could build students up to responding to the question.

These insights led me to design a new version of the task that gets at the same central question of how the climate could be so different at various places on the planet. Kang and colleagues (2014) presented a similar task co-designed with a teacher working at a school

Formative Assessment Tasks

with high populations of students from families that had emigrated to the United States. The question framing the task asked, "Why don't countries near the equator, like Samoa, seem to have seasons like we do here, in Seattle?" (p. 23). Students were then given a template model of the position of the Earth and sun at different seasons and were asked to choose a country near the equator to work with, such as Kenya or Cambodia. Students were then asked to fill in the model of the Earth and sun, and to make a claim and support it with evidence to respond to the question.

This task inspired me to re-create the "Australia" task for the High School Performance Expectation above, using multiple components similar to the task in the Kang article, and integrating the science practice of analyzing and interpreting data (Figure 5.5). We

Figure 5.5. Redesigned Task for Energy Flows and Seasonal Patterns in Weather

Rafa called his grandmother in **Santiago**, Chile on FaceTime last week, and saw that it was warm and sunny there, but it was snowing here in **Denver**. But then his friend Chi told him that in **Lagos**, Nigeria, the weather is more or less the same all year.

Why is the weather so different in these three places?

1. Draw four Earths that show *what causes* each of these three locations to experience:
   a. Winter   b. Spring   c. Summer   d. Fall

2. Label each Earth with the season

3. Label the location of the three cities at each Earth

4. Write a claim that answers the question *Why is the weather so different in these three places?*

5. Use evidence from what you've learned in class to support your claim.

6. What are some possible limitations of the model and explanation you've provided?

can start the task by basing it on a phenomenon that is relatable to students in the class. While the sample task provided here uses example locations, these could be updated using Google Maps based on teachers' knowledge of students' connections to various countries in the world.

The task uses five different questions to provide space for students to draw a representation that shows the position of the Earth and sun at different times of year, with a prompt to include the intensity and distribution of sunlight falling on Earth. Students then are prompted to make a claim based on the model, and to use evidence in class, supplemented by pictures or other representations, to support their claim. The complete task is included in Appendix D.

While this task helps place the phenomenon in the context of a student's experience, it could be even further adapted to start from an observable event that students might see outside their doors. A student from Colorado, for instance, might notice a common winter phenomenon where there is more snow and ice on one side of the street than the other. This question gets at the same essential principle as the Australia task—the angle of the sun's rays in summer compared to winter—through a more accessible phenomenon that students in Colorado would have experienced in their daily lives.

Melissa Braaten, an author of the Ambitious Science Teaching suite of resources and my colleague as an associate professor at the University of Colorado, uses a similar question in professional development workshops. She helped me to develop a similar task that illustrates how multiple components can support students in sharing and advancing in their learning.

The task could be redeveloped to include multiple components and scaffolds. For example, the initial question could accompany a picture of the observable phenomenon. The task could provide space for students to draw an initial, individual model, with a checklist and other criteria provided to help students know what to include in their model. Students could then be prompted to provide an explanation. Finally, a teacher might include some small-group conversation in which students shared their initial models, and then students could draw a revised model in the final space of the task (Figure 5.6). The complete task is included in Appendix E.

Braaten emphasizes that a task like this can be enacted through a layered approach, in which students are supported to complete an initial model, and then to layer on new lines of explanation as they proceed through a unit of learning. They might return to the task multiple times at the beginning, mid-, and late in the unit, such as after they

Formative Assessment Tasks

Figure 5.6. Multi-Component Version of Snowmelt Formative Assessment Task, With Space for Initial and Revised Models

It makes a big difference which side of the street you're on after a snowstorm in Colorado. As the picture below shows, one side of the street can be completely melted out, while the other side of the street is still covered in snow. How might this happen?

Draw a model that shows how the snow might melt faster on one side of the street than the other. Label your drawing and symbols. Use a key to show what colors and symbols mean.

Model checklist
Include ideas about the Sun and solar energy that we've been working on together:
- How does sunny versus shady matter?
- How does angle of sunlight matter?
- How does the amount of direct sunlight matter?
- Is there a pattern of East, West, North, or South sidewalks? Why or why not?
- Other ideas from our class's explanation checklist.

---

figure out how the angle of sunlight matters, and then begin to wonder about directions that the street is facing and vice versa.

These layers could be built in over the course of the unit; for example, the teacher might ask students to work together in a small group. Through conversation with their peers, they could see where an additional layer is needed and, and in turn, it could help their peers revise as well as helping their own model/explanation when they revise after seeing their classmate's model and explanation.

This example walks us through how using multiple components not only made this task more accessible but also took it from what was essentially a knowledge-only question into a three-dimensional space. Linking the question to an observable phenomenon related to students' experiences helped create the need to know.

BEYOND PAPER AND PENCIL: TECHNOLOGY-ASSISTED FORMATIVE ASSESSMENT TASKS

I recognize that the examples I've provided so far skew heavily toward analog technologies—that is, paper and pencil, whiteboards, or other physical tasks. While many of the tasks we might envision as formative assessments might take paper form, we must consider not only how schools have increasingly migrated student work online during and following the COVID-19 pandemic, but also how engaging technologies to help students show what they know reflects what kids do every day when they use computers, smartphones, smartwatches, tablets, and other devices to make and participate in their world.

I would be remiss to conclude the chapter without mentioning that for many years teachers have experimented with digital technologies to support formative assessment. I'll be careful to do this not just from the teachers' and schools' perspectives but from those of students as well. Christopher Wright and Bryan Gravel have investigated how culturally sustaining perspectives encourage us to center not just students' knowledge and interests but also the practices in which they are already engaging. In today's smartphone-enabled world, this includes video-recording apps such as TikTok and music-playing apps like Spotify. Wright and Gravel asked how assessments could create space for students to show what they know using these technologies they already use, such as creating videos that illustrate their understandings, or analyzing Spotify playlists to infer elements that programmers use to create algorithms that suggest the next songs that might be played (Gravel et al., 2022). Earlier in the chapter, I provided an example of how 3rd-grade students could use spoken-word podcasts to record their verbal explanations rather than writing them on paper (Zembal-Saul et al., 2012).

In a recent review chapter, I worked with Sara Heredia and Deb Morrison (Furtak et al., 2019) to identify major themes in how technology was supporting formative assessment tasks in science teaching. We found that the most common approach was student personal response systems, such as clickers, that have been used more widely in higher education (see Ruiz-Primo et al., 2011, for a summary) and which have been adapted to K–12 settings through web-based platforms such as Kahoot (kahoot.com). These kinds of technologies most often involve teachers using or uploading a selected-response question that they display to students, and then students using the personal response technologies—which could also be cell phones, tablets, or personal laptops—to vote. Tasks administered this way are not a sufficient intervention to improve student learning but should rather be considered in a larger activity setting where they support particular kinds of interactions, including cycles of posing the question/task to students, allowing students to think about the question on their own or in groups, students sharing their responses, the teacher displaying those responses, and then the whole class discussing the result (Beatty & Gerace, 2009).

The pandemic school shutdowns and sudden switches to digital learning also compelled many teachers who hadn't yet used digital approaches to conduct formative assessment with apps or other technologies. In 2020–2021, I worked with several secondary science teachers as part of a long-term partnership to create an asynchronous, interactive online space in the Flipgrid software so that teachers—who at the time were teaching hybrid and remotely—could share ideas they were developing to support student learning in digital and online settings. Flipgrid (info.flipgrid.com) provides a "simple, free, and accessible video discussion experience." Flipgrid integrates with a user's video camera and allows short videos to be quickly and easily recorded and saved to topic-specific Flipgrid "pages," that can then be viewed by other viewers on the site.

Several teachers shared examples of how they had adapted versions of tasks they already used into Google Docs and then provided students with feedback using the comment function, while others branched out into collaborative technologies such as Veed.io, Gizmos, and Peardeck. Common features of these kinds of technologies is a shared medium—such as a diagram, image, or video—and possibilities for students to share responses with both their teacher and each other, and to receive feedback on their responses.

For example, a high school physics teacher used Veed.io to share videos with his students of an egg breaking in one scenario but not the other, and prompted students to use specific terms they had learned about in their explanations. Students were able to view the videos and then to write in their own responses, all collected via the app. Another science teacher liked sharing pictures and questions through Peardeck, as it also collected students' written (qualitative) responses, which she said helped her get a quick sense of where her students were in their learning.

There are even online technologies that allow students to go beyond votes or written responses to move objects around and share their diagrams and models. One teacher used Desmos to adapt a Process-Oriented Guided Inquiry Learning (POGIL) activity in a way that students were able to sort cards showing molecular representations sorted into mixtures or pure substances; another example was adapting Google Slides so that students could use particle representations as they balanced equations (Figure 5.7).

New technologies are emerging that allow students to draw models and other representations more flexibly in online spaces. The Illuminate

Figure 5.7. Student-Drawn Models Created Using Illuminate

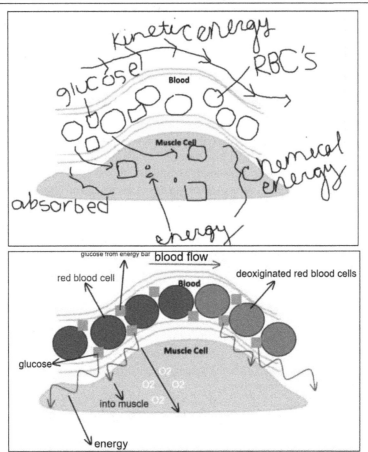

platform, for example, includes tools that allowed high school biology students to create the models shown in Figure 5.7 above. Students were able to use color, arrows, text, and other annotation resources to draw their models, which teachers could then view to provide feedback.

An important principle to keep in mind, though, is that as formative assessment tasks shift to these digital technologies, they must still be considered in the context of an overall activity system, and the same guidelines for the quality of the task apply. A multiple-choice question shared with students in Kahoot is still a closed-ended, single-component task. We can raise the level of the task by asking an open-ended question, as we see in the physics egg example. We can also provide students with scaffolds for them to share their learning (such as the list of terms to include) and encourage them to share their ideas in an open outcome space.

LOOKING AHEAD: THE IMPORTANCE OF PRACTICES AND FEEDBACK

In this chapter I've put together how we can unpack three-dimensional standards to create multicomponent tasks that are more accessible to learners, and that center the ideas and experiences of students historically marginalized in schools. In order to achieve broader participation in science learning, we will need to have many more tasks such as those described in this chapter to support student learning across grade levels and science disciplines.

That said, the tasks are just one piece of a larger classroom assessment activity system. The next two chapters will present in greater detail two more essential features of formative assessment: classroom practices and activity structures that support students in sharing their ideas, and the feedback that teachers and learners create on the basis of these tasks in order to move learning forward.

CHAPTER 6

Norms, Routines, and Community: Classroom Enactment of Formative Assessment

When we hear the phrase "formative assessment" we might immediately think of the tasks in Chapter 5 that are the focus of classroom activity. However, we've now established that these formative assessment tasks are just one element of a larger formative assessment activity system. When we take a broader lens on formative assessment, we need to consider how the tasks are enacted with learners—that is, teachers' questions, actions, and feedback as they create space for students to share their science ideas and engage in science practices. These include questions that teachers ask of students, and the ways that students respond to each other. These practices are embedded in the social and historical context not only of schooling but also in the cultural practices and experiences of teachers and students.

Considering enactment is essential because we know from research that teachers enact formative assessment tasks in a variety of ways—just as we would anticipate they would enact anything else, such as investigations or curriculum materials (Furtak et al., 2008; Furtak, Kiemer, et al., 2016; Kang et al., 2014). Clearly, some support and guidance from the teacher is essential for formative assessment to realize its purpose—but how can we think about enacting tasks in ways that support students in sharing their thinking?

WHAT DO WE MEAN BY "ENACTMENT"?

In this book, the idea of "enactment" comes from our overall sociocultural framing—namely, the social and historically situated structures that help to organize the classroom activity of teachers and students as they engage in formative assessment activity. Enactment encompasses the **division of labor** among student and teacher participants in a variety of ways, which I'll call *participation structures*, such as students working together in small groups, or talking together or with their teacher in a whole-class discussion. Enactment also involves how teachers and students interact within the classroom **community**, such as the ways they ask questions of and respond to each other as they encourage each other's thinking. Finally, enactment encompasses the **norms and routines** (**aka rules**) for how students engage with each other, such as creating initial and revised models, engaging in particular ways of sharing, and arguing ideas as they develop explanations with each other.

Being explicit about how we plan to enact formative assessment tasks with students helps us consider how we are making our teaching more equitable. How do participation structures create space for all students to contribute their ideas? How are we building a classroom community that centers students, their interests, and their experiences? How do norms and routines help to make explicit ways of participating as we further develop our thinking and engagement in science practices?

In this chapter, we will focus on three key elements, represented in Figure 6.1, that can help us envision how we'll use formative assessment tasks with students: participation structures, norms and routines, and classroom community. We can think of these three dimensions of classroom enactment as surrounding or encompassing a task, while also being organized by that task.

PARTICIPATION STRUCTURES

Something I have always loved about formative assessment is that while it's an activity that seeks to find out where students are in their learning, it also invites us to break the traditional script of individual testing and assessment, where we have students complete a task silently and individually, and then hand it in to be evaluated by the teacher. Formative assessment invites us to embed assessment opportunities in the rich set of classroom activities that we use every day. A formative assessment task then becomes an opportunity to change things up, to talk with students, to invite them to work with each other, and to respond to their ideas in ways that are intended to support students as they develop in their learning.

Lemke (1990) called these kinds of settings "episodes" of classroom activity; this helps us think about a lesson like parts of a TV show. There's a beginning, a middle, and an end. Depending on the purpose of the scene, how students and teachers are working together might shift; the teacher could bring things together at the beginning of a lesson and remind students of what they're working on before sending

Figure 6.1. Major Elements of Formative Assessment Practices

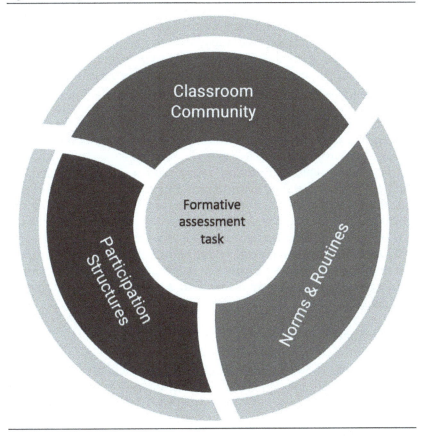

students into small groups to reflect on their learning so far, and perhaps to revise models or explanations they developed earlier in a unit of learning.

These are common ways that teachers might think about planning a lesson: It has a combination of scenes or episodes that might include framing the task, individual and pair-work or groupwork, and whole-class discussion. A formative assessment task is well-suited to span a number of these participation structures. The task might be introduced, and students could have some individual thinking time to articulate, draw, model, or otherwise represent their ideas. Then students can turn to their neighbors and share their ideas, and perhaps refine their own models and explanations in response to sharing with their peers. Later, the teacher might bring the class together for students to share their thinking with the class, and they might make a model together.

Individual Students

Perhaps the most common image we have of students in an assessment context is students responding individually to a task. While we are certainly interested in what individual students know and are able to do, we also want to know how they are *participating* in learning experiences in the classroom, and how that participation shifts over time. This means we want to attend to how they listen to and discuss ideas with their classmates, how they make connections with their everyday experiences, and how their engagement in science practices becomes more sophisticated from lesson to lesson.

That said, there is certainly a time and a place for individual students to consider their own ideas and experiences, and to represent those some way in a formative assessment task. Thus, it is still worthwhile—even when we want students to participate with others as part of their learning through formative assessment—to provide some individual time for students to reflect and to capture their own ideas before interacting with their peers or the teacher. Later on in a unit of learning, students can benefit from taking a step back to reflect on their own progress as well.

Student-Student

Ultimately, as we shift toward classroom activities that empower student participation, we want to create more spaces in which students are interacting with and held accountable to each other, rather than having all interactions facilitated by the teacher (Engle & Conant, 2002). Some of these participation structures are ones we might use regularly in classroom activities that are well-suited for formative assessment settings, such as pair- or groupwork. Or, increasingly commonly, students might learn to facilitate their own conversations, which teachers might listen to and thus learn more about how students are thinking and interacting with each other.

Pair- and Groupwork

Students can work together in pairs or in small groups, depending on the purpose of the formative assessment activity. For example, students might join together in pairs after a brief time to think on their own to get them talking with each other about their responses before turning to a whole-class discussion (i.e., a think-pair-share). While simple, these paired conversations can "prime the pump," so to speak, in a lower-risk environment before sharing ideas with their teacher or the whole class.

Even in settings where students are unaccustomed to talking about their ideas in formative assessment, a simple think-pair-share participation structure can quickly lead to a room buzzing with students sharing with each other. These conversations might be supported with scaffolds such as rubrics or checklists to support the students in reflecting on their own or their partner's work, or to be sure that each student has a chance to participate equally (see Chapter 5 for examples of self-reflective rubrics and checklists).

Students could also work in larger groups of up to five students to have more in-depth conversations about their ideas, to share their models and explanations, to analyze data, or to talk about their prior experiences and questions as they relate to the phenomenon being presented in the formative assessment tasks. These groups might be of differing size depending on how many minds might be necessary to think through a challenging, and possibly loosely structured, task (Cohen, 1994).

Scientist Circles

An emerging approach that can serve as a formative assessment is to gather students together as a whole class to discuss and share their ideas, and to argue their perspectives on and interpretations of data and evidence as part of formative assessment. These settings, sometimes called "science seminars" or "scientist circles," involve students sharing their ideas and responding to each other with little or minimal structure by the teacher (Affolter et al., 2022; OpenSciEd, 2020a).

Scientist circles literally decenter the teacher as the holder of expertise in the classroom by having students gather in a circle, facing each other. The teacher might join the circle as a participant, or hover on the outside of the circle to provide support and facilitation. The circles can become a sensemaking space for students over time, where they share and listen to each other's ideas, ask questions, and think together about what they have figured out and what they still have to learn.

Teacher-Student

Finally, we can consider participation structures that involve the teacher interacting with the whole class, small groups, or one on one with students. I'll emphasize that in the context of formative assessment enactment, these interactions should serve the specific function of sharing and responding to student ideas. If the teacher does most or all of the talking, they aren't able to really listen to students expand upon and develop ideas. Instead, these kinds of conversations should create ample space for students to talk about their ideas, using the task to guide them in inviting student talk about key questions to support their learning. Duschl and Gitomer (1997) called these "assessment conversations," as they are dialogues among teachers and students intended to allow participants to listen to and respond to each other's thinking.

Teachers might circulate around the classroom while students are working individually or in small groups, moving among tables to ask questions to see how students are progressing, and providing in-the-moment support. Windschitl and colleagues (2018) encouraged teachers to use what they call "back-pocket questions"—questions written on index cards that teachers might keep in their back pockets, as mentioned in Chapter 2—to organize these kinds of interactions and guide students through a task.

Shifting Participation Structures Within and Across Lessons

Teachers can enact formative assessment tasks using a variety of these participation structures based on the placement and purpose of the assessment (see Table 6.1). If teachers want to find out what individual students know, they could have students work individually first, and then discuss their ideas in pairs before participating in a whole-class discussion; if they want students to listen to and develop each other's

Table 6.1. Participation Structures for Formative Assessment Activity

Participants	Structures	Description
Individual Student	Seatwork	Students provide their own responses to a task; students reflect on their own progress in learning
Student–Student	Pair-work/elbow partners	Students work together on a task
	Groups	Larger groups of students collaborate, depending on nature of task
	Scientist circles	Students interact directly with each other in a whole-class setting without facilitation by the teacher
Teacher–Student	Whole-class discussion/assessment conversation	Teacher facilitates a whole-class discussion in which teacher supports and helps students develop their ideas
	Circulating to students/groups	Teacher works with individual or small groups of students to draw out and support their thinking

ideas, they might work in small groups and eventually shift to a scientists' circle to share evidence for their ideas.

To illustrate how a task can be enacted across different participation structures in one class session, let's consider a formative assessment task co-designed by a group of high school biology teachers (Deverel-Rico & Furtak, 2022). This task was designed by teachers working in a university–school district partnership to have multiple components that invite students to draw initial and revised models, and to explain the phenomenon of football players' performance being affected when they play games at altitude. Figure 6.2 shows a student-drawn initial model in response to the framing phenomenon; the complete task is included in Appendix F.

The task had several phases, including initial models and explanations, revised models, and space for students to describe their conversations with partners about their models. Teachers created guidance for themselves to help them enact the task across different participation structures, supported by the student handouts (Figure 6.3).

The instructions the teachers wrote for themselves help to illustrate how the task was designed to be launched and enacted across different participation structures, as well as the interplay between the task and those structures. We see that the teachers planned to introduce the task and then show a video to stimulate student interest and thinking, and then invite students to talk in small groups about the phenomenon. Then the students and teacher would come back together for a whole-class discussion of the ideas that came up in their small-group conversations before the teacher would pass out the task and invite students to complete their model and initial explanation. The whole class would then discuss their models before students again return to their small groups to complete a revised model.

NORMS AND ROUTINES

When we invite students to share their thinking with us and their classmates, they are taking many risks: the risk of being perceived as wrong, the risk of being misunderstood, the risk of exposing a closely held aspect of their own backgrounds or identities. Therefore, when we enact formative assessment, we must start by creating a classroom culture that values all students' contributions, where students feel safe to share what they know—and what they are still learning. We can do this by establishing clear norms for participation in formative assessment. In addition, we can further support students by establishing set routines that are recurring processes and approaches that we use when formatively assessing their learning.

Figure 6.2. Student-Drawn Model in Response to High Elevation Formative Assessment Task for Cellular Respiration

Part 1

Scenario: The Oakland Raiders are at the Mile High Stadium this weekend. They have had a good season overall, but at this game they aren't playing as well as they usually do. Team members experience increased heart rate, breathing rate and **overall fatigue** (tiredness, low energy). The Broncos win by a large margin.

Cellular Respiration Equation

$$C_6H_{12}O_6 + O_2 \rightarrow 6CO_2 + 6H_2O + \text{Energy}$$
glucose

Part 1

Including matter and energy from the cellular respiration equation, draw a model (picture, chart, diagram etc.) to show how the Oakland Raiders running back gets and uses energy to play the game against the Denver Broncos. Show things that you can see, and things that you cannot see. *Use arrows and labels to show the flow of energy and cycling of matter.*

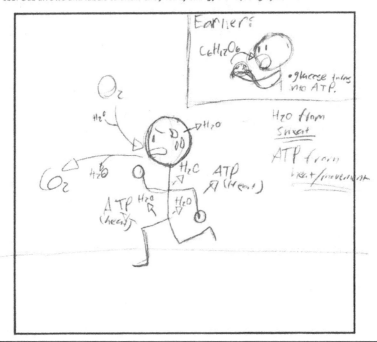

Setting Norms for Sharing and Responding to Each Other's Thinking

We can start by creating new ground rules for formative assessment that flip the script of typical classroom interactions and making that known to students. Teachers can do this at the outset of a lesson, helping to frame what's ahead. Even a brief statement when launching a formative

Figure 6.3. Guidance Written by Teachers for Enactment of High Elevation Cellular Respiration Task

Show video

Elevation 5280: Altitude Sickness Broncos Stadium video

Read: *"Since 1975, the Denver Broncos sport the best home record in the NFL. Since 2007, the Colorado Rockies have the 14th-best home record in the MLB—yet rank dead last in their away-game record during that same span. Since 2003 (the longest data set I could find), the Denver Nuggets have the fourth-best home record in the NBA yet rank 13th in their away-game record. Coincidence? I wouldn't count on it."*

Prompt for discussion: Why might visiting teams struggle more when it comes to playing at the Broncos' stadium or another Denver sport stadium?

Students talk with their table groups about the prompt

Come back together as a full class and discuss

[Students will likely come up with elevation, air is thin—may not know what that means exactly—students may bring in altitude sickness; they might talk about the oxygen masks on the sideline]

Questions to prompt in full-class discussion:

What does it mean that the air is thin?

Why does it matter that the air is thin? How could that impact visiting teams' athletic performance?

Why might they have oxygen masks on the sideline?

Part 1

Hand out part 1

Students independently do questions 1–3 and model

Come together as a full class and discuss questions 1–3 and model

Share out ideas—volunteers from each table

Where does the energy come from?

Discuss oxygen as a limiting factor

Look for the breakdown of sugar and the breaking of bonds of sugar

Prompt students to consider oxygen, glucose, carbon dioxide, water, and energy.

Part 2

Hand out part 2

Students work with a partner to revise their model; encourage students to include inputs and outputs, oxygen, glucose, carbon dioxide, water, and energy. If time allows, students work with a partner to trace energy back to the sun.

assessment task can help make expectations clear for what is to follow (Kang et al., 2016). Ann, a 7th-grade science teacher, launched a task for a unit on energy by saying the following to her class:

> Okay, now we are going to revisit our whole-class model of the roller coaster . . . We are trying to understand, as a class, which roller coaster design gives the car enough energy to make it through the loop twice—once forward, once backward. We will do this by using "red light," "green light," and "yellow light" stickers. Generally, we know that scientists can't just say "yes" or "no" to a question. They have to back up their claims with evidence. The red, green, and yellow stickers will help us do that as scientists. . . . The idea is that you tell me both the activity and the evidence you got from the activity to support a model or to show how a model is faulty. We want to have one per class, so that we can start to use evidence across classes to build a stronger case for one or two models. The goal here is to come to a class understanding what works and what doesn't, before we move onto final explanations. Remember that we are scientists and we use evidence (p. 1327).

In this statement, edited for inclusion here, Ann reminds students of the task they had completed earlier, and then asked students to use a "stop-lighting" process of a green light (evidence supports the model), red light (evidence does not support the model), or yellow light (not sure). She clarifies that the idea is to see what they understand and don't understand at this point, as they move toward a final, evidence-based explanation.

It's helpful to give students a set of norms as a starting point; these might include suggestions such as those listed in Table 6.2.

Table 6.2. Norms for Participating in Formative Assessment (adapted from OpenSciEd, 2022)

	Norm
Equity	Monitor the time we spend talking
	Encourage others to participate
	Respect the perspectives, ideas, and experiences of others
Community	Share our thinking to help others to learn
	Listen closely and ask questions of each other so we can understand each other's thinking
Moving forward in our learning	Use and build on each other's ideas
	Be open to changing our minds
	Recognize that we are all here to learn

Coffey (2003) provides examples of how teachers can set norms like these with students so that everyone in the class has a chance to participate in and contribute to a group understanding of how to share and respond to ideas in formative assessment. For example, a 6th-grade teacher I once worked with, Ms. Schafer (pseudonym), set the stage for formative assessment with her students by asking them to identify how she listened to their ideas, and then using that as a foundation for what she wanted students to do as they listened to and responded to each other (Furtak, Glasser, et al., 2016). Ms. Schafer kicked off a formative assessment by asking her class:

> Let's have a conversation. I'd like you to close your books, and I'll put away my books. I want to talk about how I've been listening to your ideas. Can you tell me what you've seen about how I listen to any idea you've said? How do I listen to your ideas?

Her students shared astute reflections of Ms. Schafer's teaching style, noting that she repeats students' ideas so everyone can hear them, she listens intently, she respects what students are saying, and she calls on everybody. One student noted, "You don't tell people their answers are wrong." This last point is key—her students had already figured out that Ms. Schafer was there to support their learning, not to tell them they were right or wrong; this helped create the conditions to make them feel safe to share their ideas. Teachers' actions speak louder than words. These statements can be made at the beginning of an activity but are reinforced by daily teaching practices that support the explicit goal of working with student ideas. If the teacher's practices imply that some ideas have more value than others, students will nevertheless feel evaluated, and the formative function of the activity may not be achieved.

If a whole-class conversation like this feels challenging, teachers can start by providing students with a set of sample norms, as shown in Table 6.2, and then having students talk in small groups to discuss and adapt the norms and suggest additional ones for the whole class to consider.

As we strive to democratize students' learning in science classrooms, we seek to have conversations involve more students talking with each other, and less active intervention from and mediation by the teacher. We can support students through scaffolds like sentence starters, not just on written tasks but also displayed on a projector, poster, or whiteboard, to aid students as they share their ideas with the class. These sentence starters could include statements such as, "I agree with Zander because _____," or "I think that _____ causes _____ because of [evidence]."

We can also set norms for how we listen to each other, holding students accountable to listening to and understanding their peers' ideas, not just to their teacher. Inviting students to ask each other to rephrase or repeat helps to set the expectation that they listen to and respond to each other, as shown by this example from the Inquiry Project (TERC, 2011):

Lucas: Maybe where the ships are is a basin, so all the water got drained out into the river?

Teacher: Oh. [pause] Can anybody repeat what he just said? If you can't repeat what he just said, are we practicing our norms?

Tyla: Can you please repeat what you just said, Lucas?

Tavon: Lucas, can you repeat what you said please?

Lucas: Maybe that the ships right now are in a basin, so all the water got drained out into another river.

Teacher: What do you . . . maybe you should say a little more about a basin.

Lucas: Like a basin is like—once there was water in there, right? Maybe, and there could be rivers connected to that basin, and the rivers are flowing the opposite direction from the basin, so maybe the water is getting drained out.

We can also explicitly encourage students to translanguage to provide more access and opportunity for multilingual learners. This lets students know they don't have to share in formal English but may draw on their other languages, make gestures, and use informal ways of describing their observations, ideas, and understandings (Fine, 2022; Menken, 2006; Suárez, 2020). Inviting familiar language into the classroom can help make conversations about ideas more accessible to students, particularly those who are emergent multilingual learners. For example, allowing students to describe the sound of a guitar's different strings with onomatopoeias (e.g., "ting, tang, tong") shows that students notice changes in tone without privileging scientific terms and descriptions (Suárez, 2020).

Routines for Formative Assessment Activity

We can support students in engaging in these norms through larger patterns of classroom activity or sets of routines that teachers and students engage in regularly to aid their learning (NASEM, 2022). Routines have taken hold in the current wave of science education reform to describe the kinds of interactions in which students and teachers might engage, such as sharing questions or initial ideas about models (Thompson et al., 2013), or with students engaging in evidence-based arguments with each other (Lowell et al., 2022).

When it comes to science formative assessment, we can identify several kinds of routines that help to surface and attend to student ideas. These routines can be used regularly within and across units, so that students come to understand sequences of activities and how they support their learning (OpenSciEd, n.d.).

Sharing initial ideas about the anchoring phenomenon at the outset of a unit. The beginning of a unit is a perfect time to draw out student ideas as they dive into a new sequence of learning. It sets the expectation for a unit as seeking to answer a question students find compelling and interesting and invites students to locate that phenomenon in the context of their own experiences. The routine can start by sharing the driving question or phenomenon in some way, such as by showing a video, sharing some kind of data or story with students, or inviting students to share their experiences from their homes and families. Students can then write, draw, make models, or even just talk with each other as they try to make sense of the phenomenon, using their prior knowledge to figure out what might be going on.

This routine can carry across multiple kinds of participation structures, with students first making sense of the phenomenon on their own, and then moving into increasingly larger groupings, first with another student or in a small group, and then in a whole-class conversation where a wider variety of ideas are shared (Windschitl et al., 2018). Students can then think together and discuss other places they may have seen this phenomenon or related examples in their everyday lives before posing questions that might guide their further study (OpenSciEd, 2020a). In this way, the anchoring phenomenon routine provides students and teachers with a sense of how students leverage their prior ideas and experiences into a new unit of learning, so that their subsequent activities might build on them and be pulled throughout the unit.

Taking stock of learning and putting pieces together. We often talk about formative assessment as a process that is ideally embedded within units of learning, allowing students and teachers to step back to reflect on what they've done so far as well as on what they might do going forward. It creates space for students and teachers together to think about their learning up to a particular point, what they are doing now, and what they might study next (Black & Wiliam, 1998).

In the case of Ms. Schafer's class, this involved whole-class discussions that encouraged students to apply the main findings of investigations they had completed to the main question framing their unit, *Why do things sink and float?* (Ayala et al., 2008). Over the course of the unit, students learned that the purpose of investigations was not just to develop an explanation of the findings but to use those findings to help them develop a more sophisticated understanding of the driving question. The routine also helped students to identify what questions they still had, and what they still needed to figure out.

Students might revisit their science notebooks to see what they've done so far, or even look back at the questions they posed at the beginning of a unit to think about what they have learned that moves them closer to answering those questions. A key element of this step is using these reflections on prior learning to identify, individually or as a class, what they might do next; this reflection and metacognition helps students reflect deeply on their learning (NASEM, 2018; White & Frederiksen, 1998).

This routine might include students working together to share and respond to each other's ideas and to come to a consensus model and explanation of what they've learned so far. Students might start by working individually with checklists that include elements of their models or explanations that they need to integrate; they might then share their own work with a partner or small group before participating in a whole-class discussion where they share their evidence for their models and explanations and negotiate with other students to come to a consensus.

TALK MOVES: ESSENTIAL ELEMENTS OF FORMATIVE ASSESSMENT CLASSROOM PRACTICES

A common thread throughout the previous sections is that in different participation structures and across routines it is crucial that teachers and students learn together in discourse-rich environments. These conversations are perhaps the most important element of the enactment of formative assessment tasks, as they are the ways in which ideas are shared, responded to, challenged, and revised in formative assessment settings. As we seek to fundamentally shift power dynamics in science classrooms from teachers telling students what they should know to centering classroom talk on student interests and ideas, certain statements and questions can help teachers and students listen to and respond to each other.

These are sometimes called "talk moves" that support ongoing student conversation and sensemaking. While teachers can use talk moves to encourage students to expand on their ideas, to respond to each other, and to deepen or provide evidence for their thinking, we can also consider how talk moves can be modeled and ultimately used by students as they interact with each other in small groups and whole-class conversations. In my own experience, even just trying out a few of these talk moves shifts the balance toward student ideas and reasoning. Each question is *authentic*, or a genuine request for something the teacher doesn't already know, as opposed to a question that has a set answer (Cazden, 2001).

In my own teaching, I've found it useful to have specific talk moves in mind to help support ongoing conversations about student thinking and to encourage students to talk with each other. Rather than asking questions that have simple answers, talk moves get students talking so we can all listen, learn, and respond. Asking someone what they think, what their experiences have been, what they already know, and to talk through their model or explanation are invitations for students to provide extended responses. Then, to keep students talking, we can follow up by asking them to share more information, to "say more," or to provide additional examples. We can similarly draw more students into the conversation by asking them what they think about another student's response, to add on to their idea, or to ask them who agrees or disagrees, and why. I've provided an overview of these talk moves in Table 6.3.

PUTTING IT ALL TOGETHER: A FORMATIVE ASSESSMENT CONVERSATION TO SUPPORT THE DEVELOPMENT OF STUDENT THINKING

Now that we've unpacked three elements of how classroom enactment can support formative assessment activity—participation structures, norms and routines, and talk moves—let's return to the example of the Broncos task from earlier in the chapter to better understand how teachers can organize classroom practices around a formative assessment task. In her dissertation research, Clarissa Deverel-Rico has examined how a high school biology teacher, Mr. Riley (pseudonym), enacted a three-dimensional formative assessment task across multiple participation structures in an anchoring phenomenon routine using talk moves to create space for students to connect their everyday experiences with the phenomenon (Deverel-Rico & Furtak, 2022; Furtak & Deverel-Rico, 2021). You can find the complete task in Appendix F.

Let's first take a look at the way that Mr. Riley used different elements of the Broncos task to enact the task across different participation structures, as shown in Figure 6.4. Appendix G contains a similar version of this figure that you can use to plan your own formative assessment enactment.

Students first watched the video as the teacher launched the task in the first 3 minutes of class, and then students talked in small groups and participated in a whole-class discussion before they made initial models

Table 6.3. Formative Assessment "Talk Moves" to Support Student Thinking and Sensemaking

Talk move	Function
Encouraging students to share their ideas and experiences	
"What do you think?"	Asking students to share their own ideas and understandings (instead of asking them to provide specific responses)
"Can you tell me what's happening in your model?"	Asking students to explain in their own words what they have drawn in their own model and/or visual representation
"Why/How do you think this is happening?"	Encouraging students to provide explanations that get at underlying mechanisms
"What experiences have you had with _____?"	Encouraging students to share their own experiences in class
Follow-ups to push students to explain, elaborate, and expand on their thinking	
"Say more"	Asking students to share more about their idea/explanation/model to expand their thinking
"What makes you think that?"	Pressing students to provide evidence-based reasoning
"So, you are saying . . ."	Clarifying or revoicing an idea previously shared so a student can verify and/or clarify the teacher's interpretation
"Can you give me an example?"	Asking students for examples (from both inside and outside of class)
Making connections between ideas	
"How have you changed your thinking?"	Encouraging student reflection and metacognition
"How does what you're saying connect to other ideas?"	Helping students make connections between the current conversation and previous ideas from class
"Who else agrees or disagrees?"	Encouraging students to agree or disagree with ideas that have been shared
"Who wants to add on . . . ?"	Inviting other students to contribute to the ongoing conversation

Note: Adapted from Michaels et al., 2010; NASEM, 2019; vanZee & Minstrell, 1997; Windschitl et al., 2018. https://inquiryproject.terc.edu/shared/pd/Goals_and_Moves.pdf

Norms, Routines, and Community 121

Figure 6.4. Levels of Grouping, Routines, and Talk Moves From High School Biology Formative Assessment (figure by Clarissa Deverel-Rico)

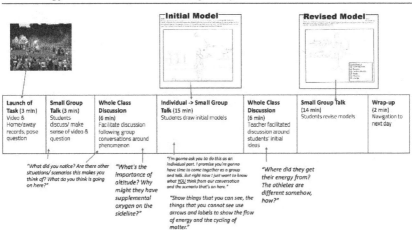

in small groups. After another whole-class discussion in which the students shared their ideas, students then returned to revise their models.

The lesson began with Mr. Riley showing the video and reading the task aloud to students before guiding the students to talk in small groups:

> What I'll ask you to do—take 2 minutes at your table and talk about this prompt. Why might the visiting team struggle more when it comes to playing at Broncos Stadium or another Denver sports stadium? So talk at your table for a couple of minutes. We're gonna come back together, okay?

Students talked animatedly in their small groups for several minutes as Mr. Riley walked around to listen to students as they shared their ideas about the phenomenon with each other.

He then invited students to come back together as a whole class:

> *Mr. Riley:* So, we're going to talk in a big group about why that might be going on . . . okay, so you can wrap up conversations. 3, 2, 1, all right, cool. *I heard some great, great ideas at the tables I got around to.* Just kind of wanted to come back together as a big group before I ask you to produce something with these ideas. Ah, so *what kind of ideas do people have*? Yeah, what do you got?
> *Student:* So, since we're at such high, like high altitude, a lot of these people aren't used to it—okay—and be like altitude sickness.

Mr. Riley: Okay. Great. Yeah, I think every table I went to mentioned this word *altitude*, and then altitude sickness. We kind of saw that in the video. So, what, *what's the importance of altitude then for it?*

Student: Well near or at sea level, a lot of the water heats up and mixes with that air and stuff, so it makes it like heavier. And now that we're up here it's so much lighter, so much drier it like affects our lungs more so the people who travel from, say, New York to here, they have, they're used to like a bunch of water being in their lungs when they come up here. It's like more dry.

Mr. Riley: Okay, *so water may be a component* that we certainly do have a dry climate here.

Mr. Riley kicked off the conversation by referring to ideas he overheard in the small groups, placing value on the ideas that students shared and encouraging them to share these with the whole class. He then asked an open-ended question about what ideas students had—not what the answer was, but their ideas. A student shared an extended response with ideas about altitude, moisture, air, lightness, and heaviness, and Mr. Riley picked up on the word "altitude" and asked the student to share more of their thinking. Then, after the student talked more about altitude, Mr. Riley repeated what the student had said, signaling that they identified what might be an important component of the model they will be making.

Mr. Riley then followed up on another word the student shared, when they talked about how being at sea level makes the air "heavier" as compared to altitude, where the air is "so much lighter":

Mr. Riley: I'm interested in one word you used, and that was that, I think you said the air was lighter.

Student: Yeah.

Mr. Riley: So we're talking about, like, thinking back to last year in chemistry. What would be the term maybe that we would be using for, um, oh, I heard it—density. Yeah, okay, so how would we change that statement from lighter to using the word density then?

Student: The air is less dense.

Mr. Riley: The air is less dense here. Okay. All right, all right. So I think we're on to something there.

Student: Um, people in Colorado, the air is less dense with oxygen, and you need oxygen to have your muscles work correctly, so when people who are used to a lot of oxygen in the air, or at least more of it in a bigger area, then when they come here then their bodies struggle to get enough oxygen in the air into their lungs because their capacity would fill up . . .

Mr. Riley: Okay, great. So moving from density and thinking about one of the main components of air, and that's oxygen. Okay, so I heard that our muscles need oxygen. Okay, *so why do our muscles, why do our muscles need oxygen?* Yeah. [calls on student].

Student: Because they need it to do cellular respiration.

Mr. Riley: Ah, okay. So cellular respiration requires oxygen. Okay, so that can be a big part of it. Okay, *any other things that people want to add to that conversation?* What? What was your example that you talked about [student name] *You had some friends who play soccer.*

Student: Well like, I guess that in Argentina is like a great team, like one of the best in the world. Every time they like, go to Peru, they, they're struggling because of the high elevation, because they get tired faster, it's harder to breathe for them.

Mr. Riley: Okay, great. So maybe we could see that happening in another country, even besides National Football League we see that happen in soccer games as well.

Mr. Riley then turned students to making models in small groups, where they were guided by the task to show energy transfers and transformations, and to label their models. He also asked students to respond to the questions on the next page of the task, which were intended to focus students on key indicators of the equation for cellular respiration. After an extended amount of time in small groups, Mr. Riley brought students back together and used the questions from the task to help students reflect on elements of their models, and to highlight key indicators of respiration that would be affected when athletes performed at altitude.

Throughout the lesson, Mr. Riley supported his students through making norms for participating in the lesson explicit, as well as engaging in routines to support them in sharing their thinking. At the beginning of the lesson, Mr. Riley let the students know he was interested in *their* ideas, not necessarily only looking for what might be the "right" answer for the task: *"Right now I just want to know what YOU think from our conversation and the scenario that's on here."* Then, at several points in the lesson, Mr. Riley set the norm that students were encouraged to share their thinking, and to relate everyday examples to the question posed on the task, as illustrated when Mr. Riley encourages students to share the idea about the Argentinian soccer team.

Mr. Riley also used the routine of launching a task with a phenomenon, and then asking students what they noticed and wondered about the phenomenon, before asking them to create initial and then revised models following conversations with other students and with him. As students made their models, Mr. Riley reinforced norms for how to make models by using the guide on the task to encourage students to show what they could and could not see.

After the unit was completed, Mr. Riley reflected on the lesson and how different classroom practices supported students in sharing and moving ahead with their thinking:

> So, that little video clip—that was a pretty effective tool of kind of hooking them in a little bit. And then started—they had a little bit of time to converse with the people at their table about it. And the phenomenon of the Raiders are coming to town. And the running back couldn't—was running out of energy and they had to propose reasons why that was happening, and make connections to the cellular respiration aspect of it. They had to draw models, which I thought was really great. And then, we also gave them time to come back and revise those models once they had talked to their group. Which, I thought was a really cool part of it. After they got some input and we had discussions, to be able to go back and revise those models.

In this chapter, we've seen multiple examples of how formative assessment tasks can organize the sharing and responding to student thinking through various kinds of practices that include grouping, talk strategies, norms, and routines. We can envision how different combinations and sequences of these elements of classroom practices can be put together around separate tasks in ways that help students to develop in their thinking and respond to each other. Key across these examples is how students can make connections between their own thinking and the phenomenon that frames their task, and then get support from their teacher and peers across multiple forms of classroom participation, embedded in routines, and with talk moves to help them develop their thinking.

CHAPTER 7

Feedback

We've put in the work. We've designed, adapted, or selected formative assessment tasks that are multidimensional, and which embed multiple kinds of questions for students in the context of a phenomenon that's interesting to them and relevant to their lives. We've given the task to students in a classroom environment where they know their ideas are valued, and that provides them ample time and space to share those ideas with each other, and with other students in class.

So . . . now what?

When those ideas are shared, what do we do?

This is where feedback—the way we respond to students to support their learning—comes in. Feedback is a broad term that describes the information that goes in multiple directions between participants in formative assessment about the status of ongoing learning and understanding. Teachers and learners are engaged in ongoing, endless cycles of feedback. Hattie and Timperley (2007) defined feedback as consisting of responses to three fundamental questions: Where am I going? How am I going? Where to next? These three questions provide information that can feed outward toward learning goals, feed back to the learner as to how they are doing, and feed forward to inform subsequent learning.

Feedback has received a lot of attention in the last few decades because of its established potential to positively influence learning (Black & Wiliam, 1998; Hattie & Timperley, 2007; Kluger & DeNisi, 1996; Wisniewski et al., 2020). I use the word "potential" because feedback can also have a negative influence on learning. How we listen to and respond to student ideas—particularly in the multivoiced learning environments we seek in current science education reforms—is hugely consequential to students' opportunities to learn science. As we seek more equitable learning environments, we must consider how our feedback—the ways that we respond to student ideas and support students in moving ahead in their learning—is broadening students' access to ambitious science learning.

So while this chapter will address elements of the formative assessment activity system that we've already investigated—tasks, practices, and so on—it will highlight the crucial role that feedback plays in how students experience formative assessment, and the ways in which it can support—or inhibit—their learning.

FEEDBACK TO SUPPORT SCIENCE LEARNING

Let's start by stepping back to talk more broadly about the larger milieu in which feedback happens, and why that matters for formative assessment. I will view feedback as part of a larger system of interactions between the teacher and students, mediated by particular artifacts, following particular roles and divisions of labor, with the object of supporting learning. In keeping with the instructional triangle that I presented in Chapter 2, we should also consider feedback as an element of classroom instruction that is integrally related to assessment and curriculum.

We can start with the object of supporting disciplinary learning. In a classroom focused on engaging students in learning science as practice, students and teachers work together to understand each other's ideas, to design and conduct investigations, to create iteratively better models that represent relationships, and to communicate their interpretations of evidence with each other. Students' abilities, ideas, and experiences are all resources that we want to build on as we support their subsequent learning. This participation metaphor for learning, and taking learning as changes in participation in disciplinary practice, has implications for how we conduct assessment. From this perspective, the object of formative assessment is to support students in increasing their participation in disciplinary practices in ways that acknowledge their cultural and historical backgrounds and encourage them to bring these into the classroom. The teacher is repositioned as a fellow learner; they seek to learn what the learners know and are open to understanding learners' understanding. In this way, they are seeking knowledge with learners (Gutiérrez, 2008), and assessment is done with, not *to*, the learners.

Feedback is a vital part of formative assessment and should be aligned with and support this vision of learning and purpose of formative assessment. Feedback is the answer to the third question we use to frame formative assessment—that is, how can we get from where we are now to what we want to learn? Feedback provides information about aspects of the current state of learning. Assessment activities assign roles and responsibilities for the actors in the activity system, and also some kind of "telos" or trajectory of progress in learning. To that end, feedback should be the continuous process through which the actors in the activity system—students and teachers in the case of formative assessment—perceive and take action upon the current status of learning in order to move forward toward learning goals aligned with the vision of learning I provided above.

A MODEL OF FEEDBACK

As we get more specific about what constitutes feedback in formative assessment, we can think about the multiple directions feedback can take between the participants in a learning environment. Feedback, like other forms of learning through participation, is a mediated activity, often through artifacts such as checklists, rubrics, representations of students' thinking, or even some kind of technology. Feedback can also be mediated by written artifacts, such as teachers' comments to student work. In this section, my focus is on the learner's reflection on their own learning process, rather than just the artifact itself; the importance is on feedback that is contextual and consequential for subsequent learning (Hickey, 2015). Figure 7.1 represents the many different directions feedback can move between teachers and learners.

Learners

We can start with the ways that we support learners in the formative assessment process, so they are able to provide themselves with feedback that supports their learning. This process can be supported by resources such as rubrics or checklists, as described in Chapter 5 (Andrade,

Figure 7.1. A Model of Multidirectional Feedback

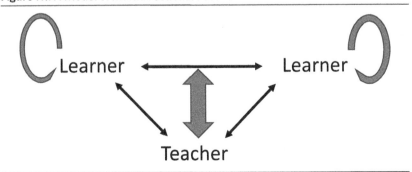

1999). These resources mediate feedback for students as they represent goals and criteria for the quality of work, such as how to annotate a model with arrows to show relationships or to zoom in to show processes not visible to the naked eye. Elements of what goes into a causal explanation, or how to create a visual representation of data can also be supported by these kinds of checklists. By comparing their work to the checklist or rubric, students can see areas where they can change it and make improvements.

These same kinds of resources can support students as they look at each other's work, such as when they have worked individually to create models and then compare and discuss them with each other. A simple approach through which students can annotate and provide each other feedback on their models and explanations is using colored sticky notes (Windschitl et al., 2018). This approach reflects the reality that models and scientific explanations are meant to change as new evidence and ideas become available. Students can learn to use sticky notes with different colors that correspond to types of comments, such as suggestions that students add or remove as they revise elements of their models, or questions that help the maker of the model think more deeply. These sticky notes can be added to models as students do a gallery walk of others' models, drawing on their own ideas and experiences to annotate and make suggestions for their classmates' models.

Mr. Riley, the teacher whose lesson we explored in Chapter 6, had his students make models and provide each other with feedback via sticky notes for a unit on energy cycling within ecosystems. Students were making models trying to capture how energy was transferred and transformed in the closed system of an ecosphere with shrimp and other organisms living in it. Mr. Riley reflected:

> Kids . . . were pretty blown away with the fact that it could survive on its own for years and years with zero inputs. And that kind of drove our question is how—how does that happen in terms of energy and carbon? So, they did models, they drew models themselves. And then, they got to get together with their groups and talk about their models. And then, produce one final model. Once they finalized their group model, we did a gallery walk. So, they hung up the posters out in the hallway, and they all had sticky notes and they had to write one positive, and one [area of] growth for the posters.
>
> And then after the gallery walk, students got to come back, look at the feedback, think about it constructively and then make some final changes to their posters based on that feedback. So, I thought that one was a good

cycle of kind of using models, getting feedback a couple of different ways from their group. And then, from an outside audience that was anonymous.

In this way, the students' ideas as represented in their models can mutually inform each other's work, mediated by sticky-note comments that students can then use to revise and improve their models.

Teachers

As the facilitator of classroom learning environments, it makes sense that a great deal of feedback in the classroom involves the teacher. We can consider the ways that teachers provide feedback directly to individual students or to groups of students in classroom conversations, and also the ways in which their feedback can be provided in writing.

Feedback in Classroom Conversations

Teachers give students feedback daily and moment to moment through their responses to their ideas and questions. This is an essential element of how the larger discourse communities within science classrooms are constructed (Duschl & Gitomer, 1997; Pryor & Crossouard, 2008). When teachers and students engage in talk about ideas, this talk exists in social, cultural, and historical contexts (Gutiérrez & Rogoff, 2003). Individual students bring multiple and differing linguistic, cultural, and historical repertoires to classrooms that reflect their background experiences and interests. As we engage students in formative assessment conversations—those that are aimed at students sharing, listening to, and responding to each other's ideas (Gitomer & Duschl, 1998)—feedback should be provided in ways that encourage students to share and build on their ideas, to provide evidence for their understandings, and to apply other standards of the discipline. From this perspective, feedback goes beyond telling students they are right or wrong, or even giving neutral responses. Instead, our feedback is responsive to the ideas they are sharing, as we ask them to tell us more about their thinking ("That's an interesting idea—can you tell us more?"), and to back up their ideas with examples from inside and outside of school ("How do you know that? What examples have you seen of this? What did our investigation help us understand about that?"). Our feedback can also refer students to our developing understandings of how scientific knowledge is developed—for example, by refining models ("Can you add a zoom-in there to help us see what's happening at the molecular level?" "What do the arrows show?") or developing evidence-based explanations ("I hear you making a claim—how can you support that with evidence from our investigation?").

Feedback matters because the ways we respond to students in formative assessment communicates what we count as legitimate (Pryor & Crossouard, 2008). We telegraph to students whether their ideas have value or not through the ways we respond to them. Taking that idea one step further, in science classrooms that privilege white, formal English-speaking ways of knowing, then the ideas, cultural understandings, and linguistic resources of students from nondominant backgrounds can be further marginalized and excluded through the feedback provided to students (Randall et al., 2021).

Clearly, the ways teachers attend to and listen to student ideas—and *who* is sharing those ideas—matters (van Es et al., 2017). It doesn't take students long to figure out that their teacher is going to evaluate what they know, and that evaluation has serious consequences for their progress in school. To that end, there is substantial risk for students to feel their ideas are not valued. If students reveal what they think, and that is found inadequate, incorrect, or inappropriate, then their grades, their progress, and their status in school are all at risk.

We want to encourage students to share their ideas. We want to respond to those ideas. We want to invite students to share their everyday experiences, understandings, and practices, and to empower them to answer questions relevant to their daily lives (Pryor & Crossouard, 2008). This approach to formative assessment is in dialogue with student thinking, seeking to interweave, not replace, students' ideas and perspectives with school-based teaching (Brown, 2019; Robertson et al., 2016; Tzou et al., 2019). In this framing, feedback is not to indicate whether students have the "right" answer but rather to encourage them to make sense of the phenomena and scenarios in the assessments as a core function of the assessment process (Deverel-Rico & Furtak, 2022; Odden & Russ, 2019).

Who teachers call on, who participates, and what teachers attend to matters; for example, whether teachers attend to the ways students share their experiences, or to how students are developing disciplinary identities, matters in who participates (van Es et al., 2017). If students are free to draw on their lived experiences (Suárez, 2020) and to use multiple languages as they share ideas with each other, the teacher, and the class, they are more likely to share what they know rather than trying to fit their ideas into a narrowly defined range of what is acceptable in science classrooms. From this perspective, conducting formative assessment involves developing an awareness of students' understandings. This positions the learning environments we create, the questions

Feedback

we ask, and the ways we invite students to listen and respond to each other as opportunities to understand others' ideas.

For an example of how a teacher can construct a conversation around understanding and making sense of students' ideas, let's turn to a different classroom. Ms. Schafer—who we met in Chapter 6—conducted a whole-class conversation as part of a preplanned, embedded assessment task in which her 6th-grade students were encouraged to relate the findings of science investigations to the big question guiding their unit: "What makes things sink and float?" Students had conducted investigations of the influence of mass on the sinking and floating of objects of the same size, varying the size of objects and their mass before plotting mass and volume in graphs. Now Ms. Schafer invited students to share their developing ideas relevant to the question driving the unit.

What's apparent in this conversation is the priority that Ms. Schafer places on listening to student ideas, their language, and the multiple everyday examples they bring into the conversation. Students' ideas are acknowledged, heard, and taken up into the course of the classroom discussion. The transcript below picks up where students have been working out what they mean when they use the terms "mass" and "density"—one student has suggested that density is like thickness; two other students provide everyday examples of liquids that have different densities.

Student: You know, like saltwater, like fresh water and saltwater. The saltwater is more, has more, like the salt makes it more . . .
Student: [Solidity]
Ms. Schafer: Okay, let's put this up here [hangs paper displaying student idea on board]. Now she's talking about this. You didn't do this experiment. How do you know about this?
Student: My uncle went to Hawaii for his wedding and his honeymoon, and he said that when you lay down in the saltwater the water is so salty there that you just float. Pretty much . . .
Schafer: So the salt water's different. And was he saying that it's easier to float in?
Ms. Schafer: Yes.
Ms. Schafer: How come?
Student: It's way saltier than . . .
Ms. Schafer: What does salt have to do with it?
Student: Salt makes it more dense.
Ms. Schafer: What does that mean? Salt makes it more dense? What's that mean?

> *Student:* Thicker.
>
> *Ms. Schafer:* Thick is kind of, not a science word but, it's a description. Thicker.

In the preceding exchanges, Ms. Schafer listens to the idea Alex is advancing—that saltwater is somehow different from freshwater when it comes to sinking and floating. Ms. Schafer notes this was not something they had investigated in class, leading Alex to share that he was actually basing this example on something his uncle had told him about the saltwater in Hawaii. Then, as Ms. Schafer asks a series of questions that push Alex to explain his thinking, he comes to work out not only that he thinks this has to do with the density of saltwater (the salt makes it more dense) but also that density is kind of like thickness.

A few minutes later, Ms. Schafer makes sure that all students have contributed to the conversation:

> *Ms. Schafer:* All right, who hasn't talked yet? Who wants to? Rosie, and then we'll have Sandy, and then we'll have Charla. And then we'll have Jackie. Okay.
> *Rosie:* Like what Alex was saying, the saltwater is thicker . . .
> *Ms. Schafer:* Can we use the word "thicker"?
> *Rosie:* Yeah.
> *Ms. Schafer:* You want to use the word "thicker"?
> *Rosie:* Yeah.
> *Ms. Schafer:* All right. You want to use the word "thicker." What do you think, thicker?
> *Sandy:* Okay, so the saltwater is thicker because it has more salt.
> *Ms. Schafer:* More salt?
> *Sandy:* No, just salt.
> *Ms. Schafer:* Just salt.
> *Sandy:* And um . . .
> *Ms. Schafer:* Would you say that louder so they can hear you?
> *Sandy:* Okay, so mud and water. You're stuck in the mud, you seem slower than if you're stuck in the water. Because—
> *Ms. Schafer:* Do you agree with that? If you had a mudhole and a waterhole?
> *Sandy:* Mud's thicker.
> *Ms. Schafer:* Mud's thicker.
> *Sandy:* The salt is thicker, and so it makes it easier to float.

Again, the students work out their meaning of the word "thickness" as a proxy for density, relating it to the saltwater example Alex had brought up previously. In addition, Lucy brings in the comparison of mud and water, and how when a person is stuck in the mud, they are slower. By analogy, Lucy brings this idea back to the saltwater, and how the thickness—as with mud—makes it easier to float.

I asked Ms. Schafer to tell me more about her approach to questioning and feedback in class discussions, which she thoughtfully cultivated over her career:

> I think a lot of times what happens to me when I teach science is every year gets better and better and better because I struggle with myself, "what does this mean? How do I get this across to them? And so how can I demonstrate it? How can I show it? How can I prove it? How can I give them evidence?" So in my trying to find a clearer meaning for myself and a way that they can see it, I think that's a process of continual evidence in inquiry and discovery for me. (Furtak, 2006, p. 207)

What's important in Ms. Schafer's example is the way that science and the teacher and students are positioned. We see the teacher engaging in authentic dialogue with students, in conversation with their experiences and ideas, skillfully drawing out and working with their responses.

A Balanced Approach to Constructing Meaning

Clearly, teachers must be able to help students reach particular conclusions in their teaching; what's important is to attend to when, and how, the divergent and convergent approaches are being used to help students to construct meaning (Scott et al., 2006). If we ask questions and give feedback that prioritizes a particular answer, students will not have opportunities to share their diverging ideas; at the same time, if we just draw out their ideas but don't respond to them and help them identify key ideas, students may not come away with the understandings they have come to school to learn (Furtak, 2006).

This means that balancing different functions of classroom discussions and feedback is key to helping students develop meaning in science formative assessment. We need to balance students sharing their ideas with feedback that presses them for more examples and evidence, highlighting key ideas related to science ideas, and helping them make connections between their experiences and science.

As an example, Mr. Riley, in the course of classroom enactment, used different participation structures early in a class to draw out student thinking, and then later in class to help students reflect on their ideas and come to consensus. He also picked up on key student contributions later in the discussion to help students focus on the amount of available oxygen as a key indicator of the rate of cellular respiration.

Mr. Riley started the next phase of the discussion by expanding on the example to emphasize that conditions of what (and when) the football player ate before playing the game were held constant, and then again ask students what they came up with in their responses:

> *Mr. Riley:* Let's assume every week that running back before he plays a game, he eats a big plate of spaghetti and meatballs . . . so the day before, the day of the game at noon the week before the Coliseum. He ate spaghetti and meatballs and then the day of the game in Denver at noon he ate a plate of meatballs and spaghetti. But he was really tired. He got fatigued, he got cramps. He was breathing heavy and his heart was beating faster. Why? What did people come up with? Yeah [student name], what did you think? . . .
> *Student:* Well, I said that his heart, his heart rate, they're not, they're getting less Oxygen per breath than they are in like their home town, so like their heart is working harder to pump blood.
> *Mr. Riley:* Okay, so what's the significance of blood and oxygen?
> *Student:* Your heart needs oxygen to pump blood.
> *Mr. Riley:* Your heart needs Oxygen to pump blood. Okay. And why do we need blood being pumped?
> *Student:* Because that keeps you [alive]?
> *Mr. Riley:* Okay, all right. Yeah, it does. Why does it keep you alive? Can you add to that, [Student]?
> *Student:* It brings oxygen to cells.
> *Mr. Riley:* It brings oxygen to the cells. Okay, so the blood is also helping to carry that oxygen. So I love when you said the heart's gonna beat faster, all right, because it needs more oxygen.
> *Student:* Then you can [take more breaths] 'cause you're getting less oxygen
> *Mr. Riley:* Oh, great. So you, maybe you're taking in more breaths because you're getting less oxygen in every breath that you take in. That's a really good link.

In this exchange, we see Mr. Riley asking students repeatedly to share their thinking, and then using multiple forms of feedback in the form of repeating student ideas, and then using follow-up questions to encourage students to expand on their ideas. Questions like, "Why do we need blood being pumped?" and "Why does it [oxygen] keep you alive?"

help to highlight students' use of particular terms like blood and oxygen, and encourages another student to share their ideas and make connections between breaths and the amount of oxygen available in the air.

Table 7.1 provides examples of different approaches to feedback in the course of classroom conversations; see Chapter 6 for additional examples of how a teacher's talk moves—like those used by Ms. Schafer and Mr. Riley—can support the development of student thinking.

Feedback in Writing

It likely goes without saying that written feedback—where teachers read and provide information to individual learners on their written work—can be time consuming. Sometimes it takes so long to respond to each student's work that feedback arrives later, when the class has moved on and the students' work is "old," as one high school teacher put it. We've known for decades that if teachers provide feedback to students in writing with grades, students often don't look at the feedback at all (Butler, 1987). While written feedback can be helpful to improve students' performance, we know that providing thoughtful, written feedback to individual students—particularly when we think about middle and high school teachers who have more than 100 students—may not always be feasible.

Table 7.1. Examples of Feedback in Classroom Discussion

Type of teacher response/feedback	Description	Example
Convergent approaches: Evaluative or limiting	Teacher response is evaluative, or teacher interrupts student and finishes student thought.	"Yes." "No." "Right." "Good job."
Neutral	Teacher repeats or revoices students' words, other neutral response.	"Okay." "Yeah." "I see." "So you're saying that . . ."
Divergent approaches: Pushing student thinking	Promotes students' thinking by asking them to elaborate their responses or by asking for more information about the previous question; provides descriptive or helpful feedback about quality of student idea.	"What does that mean?" "How do you know that?" "That's an interesting idea, how does that compare to what [student] said?" "I like how you provided evidence to support your claim."

When we do provide feedback to students, it can be done in a way that provides specific information to help students improve their work in the future. One way is to follow a template, such as the one developed by Hondrich and colleagues (2016). This approach can provide information about how well students are doing relative to learning goals and provide strategies/next steps for improvement. Even when provided with stems to guide this type of feedback, though, Hondrich and colleagues found it was quite time-consuming for teachers to provide this type of feedback, and also that it was specific to a lesson (i.e., strategies that might work for teaching one idea or disciplinary domain did not easily abstract to other domains).

Consistent with reframing learning goals as changes or shifts in participation in disciplinary practice, feedback should also be focused beyond knowledge alone, extending to the ways in which students are participating in science practices. Building on Hattie and Timperley's (2007) model of feedback, I've constructed some examples of what helpful feedback on three-dimensional formative assessment tasks could look like when provided at various levels (Table 7.2): Feedback provided at the *task* level focuses on the specifics of the assessment or activity students have at hand, whereas *process* feedback helps with more generalized approaches. *Self-regulation* feedback can provide or refer students to resources that can help them regulate their own learning, and *self* feedback can positively encourage students to bring their ideas, experiences, and resources to the assessment.

Technology

New technologies are emerging that can embed processes of feedback for teachers and students. These rapid-response technologies not only provide faster ways for teachers to aggregate trends in student responses, but they can also provide more specific information to teachers when the response options provided back contain specific information about next steps.

The Diagnoser set of assessment questions, for example, is designed so that students with developing levels of proficiency or understanding can receive more targeted and tailored feedback to support them in their subsequent learning (Minstrell et al., 2008). Teachers can assign sets of questions to students, and then they receive a detailed report back that includes suggested follow-up activities to further support students in their learning. Emerging technologies are using intelligent tutors, with voice and text recognition to analyze student response patterns and provide feedback to students in the moment (Furtak et al., 2019).

Feedback

Table 7.2. Framework for Providing Feedback to Students' Written Work

	Learning goals	Current progress	Next steps
Task	The task is asking you to draw a model about your ideas about [phenomenon]...	Right now, you've got the main components of the model that you can see with your own eyes...	What you can work on next can be to add arrows and label them, and also show zoom-ins to show what you can't see with your own eyes.
Process	We're trying to develop explanations based on evidence	I see that you have a claim here...	Now I suggest you use the sentence starters to help connect that claim with evidence in a sentence.
Self-Regulation	We want to support you in making sure that the explanation you've written is complete...	I can see that you have provided an answer with several pieces to it.	Look at the checklist here—what elements of the explanation have you included, and which ones do you still need to add?
Self	You know that we're trying to figure out this [phenomenon]...	And I know that you've had a lot of personal experiences with this at home.	What similarities or differences can you see between your own experiences and the phenomenon at hand?

During school closures during the COVID-19 pandemic, teachers innovated on the fly to develop ways of using technology to support students with feedback during remote and hybrid learning. I was inspired to see the high school teachers I worked with using familiar and new technologies to provide their students with feedback, such as voice memos to describe to students how they might improve their work. Others used commenting functions and invited students to respond to their suggestions in Google Docs. Apps like Flipgrid created the space for students to record video memos with their ideas, which teachers and fellow students could see and respond to.

Feedback Within and Across Lessons: Short, Medium, and Long Cycles

Many of the examples I've provided in this chapter might be considered "on-the-fly" feedback, where teachers and students listen to and respond to each other as they participate in classroom conversations as a whole class or in small groups. However, feedback can also take place in different timescales. These cycles of feedback are parts of larger systems of assessment, and take place in short, medium, and long cycles (Wiliam, 2007).

Short Cycles

Short cycles of formative assessment are those that take place moment to moment, as teachers move about the classroom and listen to and work with students, and when they support the students in larger class discussions. It also happens when students work with each other, or alone with supports like checklists or rubrics, to help them reflect on the status of their work and make improvements.

Wiliam (2007) made a distinction between this moment-to-moment feedback and that which might influence learning and teaching over a course of a few days; for example, if students create initial models and discuss them in class, teachers might respond in the moment and support students as they work in small groups. In addition, the teacher might look at the models after class, or based on what they heard during the class discussion, they might shift their plans for the following day.

This kind of day-to-day cycle of feedback might also involve teachers looking at student work that wasn't discussed in class, or even preparing a written response to students. Ideally, this would be done on the same day, or within a few days to be maximally effective in supporting students where they are. In my research team, we often ask teachers to sort students' work into several piles that map onto trends or similarities they see in student responses. Our rule is that there must be at least three piles, encouraging us to move beyond looking at what might be considered "right" or "wrong" responses toward viewing a broader range of student thinking. We then work together to consider how to pull out certain students' ideas from their responses and build on them going forward.

MEDIUM CYCLES

Medium-cycle formative assessments take place within and between instructional units. Within units, teachers are always attending to and supporting student thinking, and being reflexive and responsive to student ideas as they plan subsequent lessons and activities. When units are driven by student interests, this means some activities might follow different sequences than prescribed in a unit in order to respond to questions most relevant to students.

In this way, teachers might be aware of and monitoring student progress on elements of learning goals that span a whole year, such as students' engagement in a disciplinary practice like modeling or explanation, and planning individual and class-level supports to help students continue to grow in this practice. It also might be in crosscutting concepts that span multiple units.

Long Cycles

The third category of feedback extends to long cycles of up to an academic year and beyond. In my team's research, we partnered with a school district to develop approaches for tracking the ways that students came to model and understand energy as a crosscutting concept across multiple high school science courses, extending from foundational understandings in 9th-grade physics, to examining energy transfers and transformations in 10th-grade chemistry, to the ways that energy plays a role in cellular respiration, photosynthesis, and ecosystems in 11th-grade biology. Bringing teachers together in cross-disciplinary groups (Furtak et al., 2021) allowed us to examine how long cycles of reflecting on student progress in one grade level could facilitate supporting students in subsequent learning experiences in later science lessons. How would students' understandings of potential and kinetic energy in the context of a skateboarding halfpipe inform the ways they reasoned with energy in the context of explaining how a hot pack could warm up a skier's hands? Through conversations about how students think about and model kinetic and potential energy in one grade level, their teacher for the next course can learn about examples of prior learning to build upon, and language to use, when teaching chemistry. Similarly, building on the language of energy from chemistry and physics classes can help biology teachers support students to bring language like kinetic and potential energy into conversations about respiration and photosynthesis.

We can think about these cycles of feedback as taking place across academic years, not just as students transition from one science course to the next, but also cycles of feedback informing teachers in their own practice as they revise, tailor, and otherwise improve curriculum materials and learning experiences for the next set of students. This is where considering the learning goals as flexible and informed by students is important—we want the learning experiences that we use for students to be informed, as much as possible, by our experiences with students, their interests, and their identities.

A Challenging but Key Practice to Support Student Learning

Feedback is multidirectional not just from teacher to student but among students and in supporting students in advancing their own learning. We can envision how feedback occurs in classroom discussions, through talk moves that help students to advance in their thinking, as well as specific, informational feedback that we provide students in writing. This feedback happens in the moment but also between and across lessons.

If all of this sounds hard to do, you're right—it is. In my postdoctoral research (Furtak & Kunter, 2012), I did a study in which we varied the kinds of feedback we provided to different groups of students. On the days I provided students with simple, evaluative feedback, lessons were shorter and simpler; however, on the days I provided substantive feedback that encouraged students to share and extend their thinking, the lessons took longer and were more challenging to facilitate. It was worth it, however; we found that these lessons—the ones that were longer, and with more substantive feedback responsive to students' ideas—resulted in greater student learning in a follow-up assessment. Feedback is very challenging for teachers, and is perhaps one of the most challenging steps in the formative assessment process as it is highly dependent on teachers' own knowledge of what they are teaching (Heritage et al., 2009; Holmeier et al., 2018).

For the past several years, I've investigated different approaches and resources to support teachers in not only learning how to create space for students to share their thinking, but also to improve the ways in which they respond to students, including the kinds of feedback we've seen. The next section of this book will go into greater detail, with plenty of examples, about the resources that can support teachers in planning for and enacting formative assessment (Chapter 8) and professional learning that helps them learn to do this over time (Chapter 9).

Part III

BEYOND THE CLASSROOM

CHAPTER 8

Tools and Routines for Professional Learning
Collaborative Formative Assessment Design

The structure of the U.S. secondary science teacher's workday typically allows little time for anything outside of lesson planning, grading, and teaching. By making the bulk of a teacher's workday focused on time in classrooms working with students, this model presumes that much of the curriculum and assessment design will happen outside of school, in the hands of professional curriculum and assessment developers. It positions teachers as implementers of formative assessment tasks, not designers of them.

As a first-year graduate student working toward my PhD, I shadowed middle school science teachers as they learned about and enacted formative assessments in their own classrooms to support students' learning about density. I had the chance to travel to schools across the United States to see what these assessments looked like in action, and to spend multiple days with these teachers, joining their classes and conducting in-depth interviews to better understand their practice.

What surprised me was that, even after the study was finished, teachers were still talking about student ideas they had encountered in the course of the project. It wasn't so much the tasks, or even the teaching practices, that had stuck with them; it was orienting frameworks for learning about student ideas, and listening to those ideas. The teachers were clearly learning a lot while they were planning for and enacting formative assessments. These experiences set me on a trajectory to better understand how formative assessment isn't only a mechanism for student learning but also a support for teacher learning through in-depth collaboration focused on better understanding and supporting student thinking.

TEACHER PROFESSIONAL LEARNING THROUGH FORMATIVE ASSESSMENT DESIGN

While we often might consider how tools (such as formative assessment tasks) and routines (that we may use when enacting tasks, such as making initial and revised models) can support student learning (Wertsch, 1998), this chapter and the next will focus on how tools and routines can also support teacher learning. Tools can help teachers map out the curriculum, unpack standards, and identify places to embed formative assessments. Tools can represent elements of quality formative assessment tasks, as we saw in Chapter 5, and ways of providing feedback for students, as in Chapter 6. Tools can structure teachers' interpretation of those ideas, and their planning for subsequent instructional action on the basis of those tools. Finally, tools can support reflection on the role and purposes of formative assessment, students' identities, and teachers' identities (Randall, 2021).

Tools can support routines that teachers engage in together in professional learning settings to develop their use of formative assessment in their science classrooms. Structured routines can engage teachers in routines around looking at student work together, discussing student ideas, and identifying next steps for instruction.

Researchers and teachers have developed approaches for professional learning centered on the design, enactment, and revision of thoughtfully designed tasks; through this process, teachers can study student thinking and improve their classroom practices (e.g., Borko et al., 2008; Horn & Little, 2010; Little, 2003; Whitcomb, 2013; Yoon et al., 2006).

Across a school year, teachers identify ambitious and equitable practices to study and to improve on, repeating particular tasks or concepts to gradually shift their instructional practices (Thompson et al., 2019).

In the course of my team's research, spanning many years and partnerships with teachers, schools, and districts, we have applied these approaches to the process of principled formative assessment design. As in these other studies, we have found that co-designing formative assessment tasks can yield important teacher learning and shifts in classroom practice, and in turn can support student learning. This goes beyond what we might expect from teachers as implementers of assessment and positions them as professionals who are essential and active contributors to the construction of classroom learning environments centered on student ideas.

We have found a number of benefits for teachers engaging in the process of formative assessment co-design. While this takes planning, we've found that taking the space and time to truly dig into its many nuances can support teachers in designing better tasks (Furtak, Kiemer, et al., 2016; Henson, 2019), as well as in providing better feedback to support students in their thinking (Furtak, 2012; Furtak et al., 2018) and in improving their understanding of science (Heredia et al., 2021).

STEPS FOR COLLABORATIVE FORMATIVE ASSESSMENT DESIGN

Over the course of several studies spanning 15 years, my research team has built on these studies to create a process we call the Formative Assessment Design Cycle (FADC), an approach to professional learning that consists of a series of routines, supported by a variety of tools and resources, to aid teachers as they collaboratively design, enact, and reflect on formative assessment tasks to support their students' learning.

Teachers set aside regular time for the meetings, which occur weekly, bimonthly, or monthly. The meetings take 60 to 90 minutes and are convened by a facilitator who brings an agenda and helps to keep the meeting focused and on track. Each meeting typically centers on one phase, so at least five meetings need to be set aside for a complete cycle. Depending on how often teachers meet, then, one cycle could be completed in a few weeks, or across a semester or an academic year. Figure 8.1 provides an overview of the five phases, which I'll describe

Figure 8.1. Formative Assessment Design Cycle

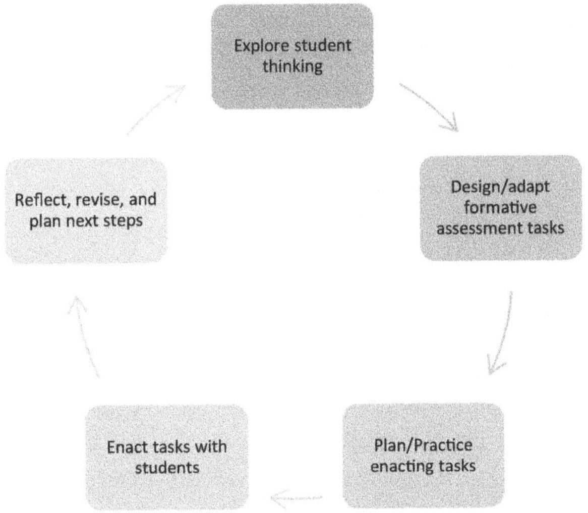

in the following sections in greater detail, with illustrative examples. Table 8.1 provides an overview of the steps of the FADC, common routines within these steps, and a summary of tools we have used in these routines to support teacher learning.

Explore Student Thinking

We begin with a purposeful process of learning about students, their interests, and the goals for the assessment. This starts by investigating student thinking so that students' interests, experiences, and knowledge are at the center of our design process. In some cases, we do this with a pre-assessment to look specifically at examples of student work. In

Table 8.1. Summary of Formative Assessment Design Cycle

Step	Routines	Tools
Explore student thinking	Examine student responses from pre-assessments Map curriculum and identify areas for formative assessment Unpack standards and write learning targets/performances; anticipate & collect information about student thinking	Unit planning tool Unpacking guide Learning progression Standards documents Evidence statements
Design or adapt tasks	Examine existing assessment opportunities within curriculum materials Adapt/revise tasks to align with curriculum & learning targets	Checklists for task quality
Plan for/ practice tasks	Review task and envision the classroom activity structures to put in place Practice eliciting and responding to student thinking	Classroom practices planning tool
Enact tasks with students	Use task as planned with students Collect evidence of student thinking	Note catcher Video-recording device Camera/phone
Reflect, revise, and plan next steps	Sort student responses into multiple piles Review video with colleagues Interpret student response patterns and plan next steps for learning	Learning progression Student responses to assessment task Video

other cases, we have brought a representation of how student understanding can develop in a domain, such as a learning progression (see Chapter 9). Learning progressions can show how student understanding or grasp of science practice might develop over time (Corcoran et al., 2009). The writers of the NGSS also used the approach of learning progressions to show how standards unfold across grade bands for teachers to see examples of how student ideas develop over time, as shown in Figure 8.2.

Tools to support this phase include standards documents, particularly the "Evidence statements" that convey observable learning performances for each of the NGSS performance expectations. It's useful to spend time unpacking the different dimensions of each standard to unwind the disciplinary core idea, crosscutting concept, and science and engineering practices in each standard to make sense of what students will be learning and be assessed on with a given formative assessment.

In this phase of the design process, we can use a variety of approaches to learn more about student interests and cultural resources. For example, we might develop, through online surveys, questions about possible phenomena we can use or issues of concern to students (Edelson et al., 2021). We might create tools that students bring home to complete with their families, inviting these experiences into the

Figure 8.2. Matrix or Learning Progression Showing the Development of the Science and Engineering Practice of Planning and Carrying Out Investigations (adapted from NGSS Lead States, 2013)

Grades K–2	Grades 3–5	Grades 6–8	Grades 9–12
Planning and carrying out investigations to answer questions or test solutions to problems in K–2 builds on prior experiences and progresses to simple investigations, based on fair tests, which provide data to support explanations or design solutions.	Planning and carrying out investigations to answer questions or test solutions to problems in 3–5 builds on K–2 experiences and progresses to include investigations that control variables and provide evidence to support explanations or design solutions.	Planning and carrying out investigations in 6–8 builds on K–5 experiences and progresses to include investigations that use multiple variables and provide evidence to support explanations or solutions.	Planning and carrying out investigations in 9–12 builds on K–8 experiences and progresses to include investigations that provide evidence for and test conceptual, mathematical, physical, and empirical models.

classroom and our processes of design (Tzou et al., 2021). We might also ask students to engage in processes of self-documentation, such as taking and clustering photos of their lives outside of school, to inform our understanding of what they already know and can do (Bell et al., 2015).

Often, as we initiate a new cycle of formative assessment design, investigating student thinking also involves teachers growing in their own understanding of what they will teach and assess. Science teachers, particularly secondary science teachers, often identify as content experts. This makes sense given the preparation and depth of science knowledge required for licensure. This means they are not just disciplinary experts but that they also define themselves by their relationship with a discipline. In my meetings with teachers, it's not unusual for one or more teachers to start talking about the science in more depth, drawing pictures, telling stories—all as a part of the formative assessment design process. This positioning with respect to the content, however, can have a downside. It can mean there's not always space for teachers to share what they're not sure about, and what they don't know, precisely because they're expected to be experts.

Fortunately, engaging in processes of formative assessment co-design can open up spaces in which science teachers can be vulnerable and admit to each other, "I'm not actually sure how this works." And by working together in community with each other and drawing on each other's knowledge and experiences, teachers can learn more about the science they want to teach the students, in essence engaging in their own sensemaking to better support student learning (Heredia et al., 2021).

In 2015, I shadowed two middle school teachers working together to design and enact formative assessments in their science classes. At one of our meetings in early April, the teachers—Sandra and Jack (pseudonyms)—shared with me and another member of the university-based research team how they had enacted a common formative assessment prior to our session. Our efforts to design or adapt a formative assessment task involved searching the internet for readily available tasks, including released items in online assessment item banks, and also flipping through the textbook to consider different questions embedded in the curriculum. After about 15 minutes of intermittent talking and searching, Sandra and I began discussing whether a question or picture from the book might be developed into an assessment in which the students were asked to model relationships between the Earth, moon, and sun. Noting the many images in the textbook, Sandra shared one with the group. Sandra looked closely at the photo for a long time, trying to determine if it was correct or if it contained an error that she recalled being mentioned in a professional development she had attended for the curriculum. For several minutes, she alternately speculated on how the photo might be used as an assessment, for example, "So what if we found a picture like this, and asked students to sketch where the sun would be? Put a picture like this up on the board?" She tried to figure out for herself what the picture was representing, saying, "The sun is over here? If the sun is illuminating the top half of the Earth, the moon is over here?" We ultimately sketched out the figure, shown in Figure 8.3, to discuss it.

The group moved on, looking at more possible images on their computers. But about 6 minutes later, Sandra returned to her interpretation of the picture: "If the sun is on this, shouldn't you be able to see the full moon? Here you shouldn't be able to see the back of the Earth. Now I'm wondering that, because if I can see the whole sun, I should be able to see the whole moon." Jack responded that, in this scenario, the sun would be blocking the whole moon; Sandra replied that you could still see half of the moon and also half of the Earth. Sandra concluded that the scenario being discussed could make a pre-assessment question, building on what they had already learned earlier in the unit, and asking students to draw their own sketch.

In this example, we see an interplay between teachers identifying the goal for their assessment, and in the process of designing the assessment taking time to make sense of the science for themselves, drawing on the differential expertise and interpretations of the other members of the group. The image Sandra was trying to interpret in the textbook represented the Earth, moon, and sun system from a perspective different from how it is usually represented in textbooks; as a result, the

Figure 8.3. Sketch of the Earth–Sun System and List of Learning Goals From "Explore Student Thinking" Meeting

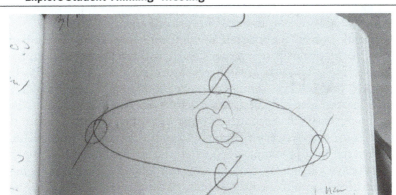

image created productive uncertainty for the teachers as they thought out loud together for several minutes about what the photo was actually representing (Furtak et al., 2021). Through engaging that uncertainty, the teachers made sense of the image for themselves, and then returned to their discussion of how to design the assessment on the basis of the example they had worked out. This instance is one of many I've encountered in the years I've worked with middle and high school teachers. In the course of formative assessment design, we engage deeply with the core science ideas being taught, as well as with how students come to understand them.

Design/Adapt Tasks

The next step is for teachers to collaboratively select, design, and adapt tasks. This usually begins with the mapping of goals and student ideas completed in the first phase, with a particular focus on the major places within a curriculum unit where it makes sense to create space for a deliberate, preplanned opportunity to draw out and work with student thinking and engagement in practice. As mentioned in Chapter 2, we may think of these opportunities as the "joints" or "bends" of a unit (Penuel et al., 2019; Shavelson, Young, et al., 2008), where it's good to know the current state of student learning in order to plan subsequent learning experiences.

As noted, designing tasks from scratch can be time consuming and challenging. To save time, preexisting assessments can sometimes be modified or adapted to align with our goals for formative assessment (Debarger et al., 2017). If teachers are working with a preexisting curriculum, this is the point where the current activities that can be used as formative assessments can be brought out, discussed, and revised, using tools that represent the kinds of design criteria that help students share their ideas, as well as other resources that represent the kinds of questions we want to ask students in three-dimensional science assessments.

Useful tools to support this phase include checklists of criteria for quality formative assessment tasks, such as those shared in Chapter 5. Achieve, Inc., has also created resources such as the "NGSS Task Screener" that teachers can use to guide discussions. Checklists for formative assessment task designs for emergent bilingual learners, such as the one shown in Appendix C (Fine & Furtak, 2020b), ensure that supports for diverse learners are built into the design rather than added on after the task is completed (Lee et al., 2019). Specific prompts to focus the assessments on crosscutting concepts or science and engineering practices can also be useful, such as those presented in Chapter 5 (Penuel & Van Horne, 2018; Van Horne et al., 2016). These tasks should be designed in ways that center students' interests and experiences as we learned in the first phase of the process.

An advantage of engaging multiple times in processes of co-design is that it creates space to repeat and gradually improve on tasks to support ambitious teaching (e.g., Thompson et al., 2019). Over time, teachers can iteratively develop and refine formative assessments to better create space for student thinking in their classrooms (Furtak, Kiemer, et al., 2016; Furtak & Heredia, 2014; Henson, 2019). For example, in one study of high school biology teachers, we found that teachers designed formative assessments more likely to provide space for students to share their ideas, and to make students' thinking visible (Furtak, Kiemer, et al., 2016). This result happens when teachers have a chance to work with a task, to consider how it is structured to draw out student thinking, and then to revise it with the support of their colleagues and sets of tools and resources that represent quality formative assessment task design (Henson, 2019). Figure 8.4 shows two versions of a task that high school physics teachers created: their initial design, and a revised version they developed in a subsequent school year after reflecting on the original task. We can see how the original task shared many features of a quality task, such as being embedded in an everyday, accessible phenomenon of a skateboarder in a halfpipe, and asked students to make both an initial and a revised model after participating in learning experiences in class. The revised version of the task, used in the second year of the project, integrates many more scaffolds to support student thinking in the context of the original task. First, it combines multiple visual representations asking students to model the difference between potential and kinetic energy at different points in a skateboard ramp, scaffolding that helps focus students on the specific relationships at these points in time. The revised version also provides the necessary information about the skater to complete a series of calculations scaffolded by specific questions.

In other studies, we've similarly observed teachers getting more specific about what they want to know about student thinking, and designing simpler tasks with better supports for students to share their thinking (Furtak & Heredia, 2014).

Practice

Once teachers have a good draft of a task, we then move forward with making plans for enactment. This phase can be combined with the "Design Tools" phase, so that as we consider how to use the task with students, we may identify ways to modify the task before putting it to use. Here I emphasize that while we might do our best to anticipate

Figure 8.4. Two Versions of Skateboarder Task

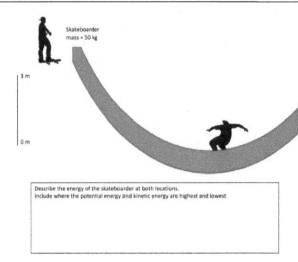

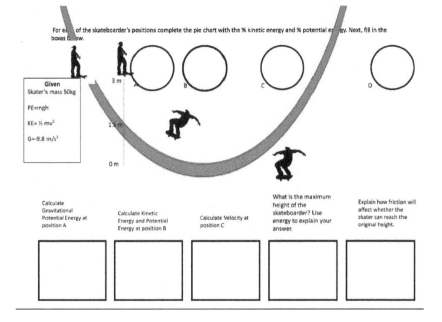

what students will say, we want to avoid essentializing or taking a "glass half-empty" view of students (van der Veen & Furtak, 2017). Instead, we build a plan for enacting the task with students in alignment with the elements of the classroom activity system we've been discussing in this book: What kinds of questions will we ask students? What participation structures will we use—working individually, in pairs, in small groups, or participating in whole-class discussion—to seek more equitable participation? What strategies will we use to ensure that all learners have feedback that will help them to advance in their learning? How will we set norms for student participation, and what kinds of routines will we use to surface student thinking? This plan goes beyond the kind of lesson planning we might typically do for a formative assessment task, and goes into much greater detail for envisioning how the task will go with students and how we will respond to them.

Tools to help unpack learning goals related to standards can support this phase; one version, shown in Figure 8.5, provides space for teachers to list the performance expectation they're assessing, the phenomenon they're using to frame the task, the learning targets or goals from the "Explore Student Thinking" phase, and space to think about the level of grouping, talk strategies, and norms and routines (refer to Chapter 6 for details on these activities). A complete version of the planning tool is included in Appendix G.

Figure 8.5. Formative Assessment Enactment Planning Tool

Performance Expectation/s	
Phenomenon	
Learning Targets	Possible Indicators or Look-fors
	What are students doing? What are you doing?

In the space below, plan for the following:

- **Level of Grouping** *How will students have various opportunities for making sense of the phenomenon/scenario?* (e.g., individual time, small-group collaboration, whole-class discussions)
- **Classroom Talk Strategies** *How will you find out what students know? How will you support students toward figuring out the learning goals?* (e.g., eliciting students' ideas with general prompts, prompts related to science and engineering practices/crosscutting concepts)
- **Norms & Routines** *How will students be supported to share their initial & developing ideas, personal connections? What recurring routines can you use that support student sensemaking and using the science and engineering practices?*

Enact

After completing several meetings in which they have thoughtfully planned for formative assessment, teachers then enact the tasks they have co-designed with their students The focus is to enact the tasks as closely as possible to how they were planned so that teachers have common experiences to reflect upon when they gather again. Teachers might have guides for their facilitation, such as the teacher notes for the High Elevation task in Chapter 5. They might also use small reminders of what they would like to do, or perhaps jot down "back-pocket" questions to ask students as they go around the classroom (Windschitl et al., 2018).

It can be useful to collect multiple sources of data about the lesson and student thinking to inform later reflections. At a minimum, this can involve artifacts of student work, including written responses (either recorded paper or in digital form). If students created a group representation, such as a group model on a whiteboard or poster paper, these can be preserved through snapshots on smartphones before they're wiped clean for the next class. Video or audio recordings can be made with iPads, video cameras, or smartphones to return to for a closer listen to help attend to student participation and the thinking shared in class discussions.

Formative assessment co-design can create space for high school science teachers to coordinate their practice at a more systemic level, with multiple professional learning communities (PLCs) of high school teachers across content areas and schools enacting tasks with similar activity formats across their classrooms (Furtak et al., 2023). As an example, we can look at a PLC of high school chemistry teachers, all of whom co-designed a formative assessment activity in which their students were invited to model energy transfers and transformations in the system of an insulated mug keeping a hot beverage warm (Buell, 2020). Figure 8.6 shows an example of a student-drawn model in response to this activity. In an analysis of multiple teachers' enactment of this modeling task, we saw common themes in the activity formats in which teachers enacted these tasks, showing similar participation structures across classrooms (Furtak et al., 2023). These included teachers introducing the tasks, students taking time to meet to discuss their models in small groups, and then small-group presentations and whole-class discussions.

If videos or audio recordings are not possible, teachers can create a "notecatcher" template to jot down summaries of student ideas during each class period, either when they circulate to small groups or from the whole class. This can be done simply on a sheet of paper with a space for notes from each group.

Figure 8.6. Model of a Cup to Keep a Beverage Warm

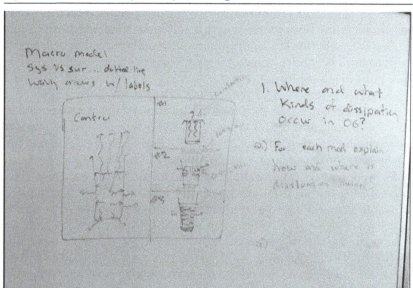

Reflect

Perhaps the most important step in this whole process—one that brings all the previous steps together—is to pause and reflect on what we have learned about student ideas, their engagement in practice, and their application of crosscutting concepts. This helps us then think together about what students know and are able to do, and to think about multiple forms of feedback to inform our subsequent instruction.

Ideally, it's best to reflect on enactment of formative assessment tasks as close as possible to when the task was taught, and certainly within a few days while the task is still fresh, as one of my collaborating teachers once put it. This way we can use what we've learned to plan subsequent steps for our teaching while student learning is still in progress.

In reflecting, teachers should be sure to ask the tough questions that attend to equity. Which students appeared to benefit most from the lesson, and why? In what ways did emergent bilingual learners participate in the task? And of course, what could we improve on next time to better support student learning (Windschitl et al., 2018)?

We should focus intensively on our observations of students—their models, their written explanations, what they said in class—to glean all we can from what they have shared. This can involve working with a whole set of student responses from a class, or from several class periods, and reading through them with a colleague. One approach to this process is to separate student responses into multiple categories, which helps to push beyond a "right or wrong" binary and appreciate the nuance in student responses.

In other instances, and particularly when students have created a complex representation, such as a model, it's useful to preselect a few samples of student work (3–5) and follow a routine called a "student focus session" (Briggs et al., 2015). This approach creates space for teachers to look deeply at the same piece of student work for much more time than we are usually able to when skimming an entire class of responses, and to make inferences not just about what this student knows and can do but to also identify ways to respond to what we see in the student's work to inform our whole-class instruction. There are three main steps in this process:

1. Each teacher reviews the student work independently and jots notes.
2. Each teacher shares their impressions of the student's response.
3. General discussion occurs to reach a consensus.

In our projects, high school science teachers engaged in this process of focusing on small numbers of student responses to a task that invited them to create a model and write an explanation of how energy from the sun is transferred and transformed through solar panels to power appliances in a house (Figure 8.7). Teachers spent time

Figure 8.7. Solar House Task With Student Response

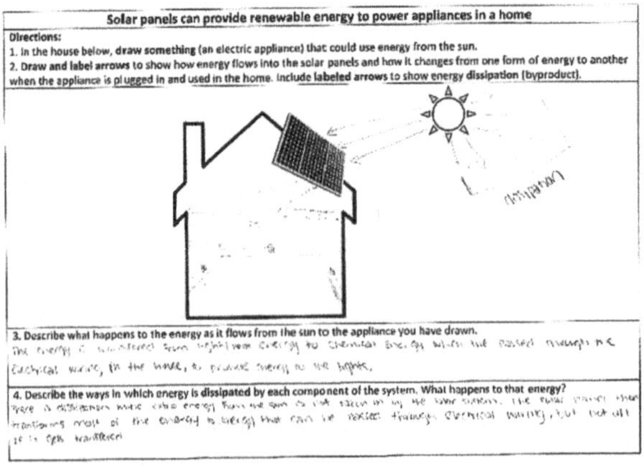

individually reviewing and annotating a copy of the student response, and then, using a rubric, applied a holistic appraisal of the student work (Table 8.2). Each teacher then shared their interpretation of the work, how they interpreted the work with the support of the rubric, and their reasoning for that analysis before engaging in a more general conversation about what they had learned about the student and their thinking. As they worked, they also revised the rubric to better capture student thinking related to learning goals.

Teachers can also watch clips of classroom enactment together so they can base their decisions on what to do next, not just on student work but also on what students have said and how they have participated in the assessment activity. Following established approaches for watching video in professional learning community meetings (Sherin & van Es, 2003), teachers can collectively identify a clip that would be useful to discuss, and invite the teacher whose lesson they are watching to introduce the video. The clip usually can be short—3 to 5 minutes—and watched multiple times to be sure to understand what students and teachers have said before discussion occurs.

To prepare to watch a video together, teachers can spend time talking about the norms they will follow, such as needing to respect the teacher and students, to look past the trivial, to focus on the science content storyline, to look for evidence to support their claims, to consider alternative explanations and teaching strategies, and to look more than once (Borko et al., 2008; Windschitl et al., 2018). They should also focus on main takeaways for each teacher's practice rather than emphasizing what a teacher might perceive would *not* work in a given classroom.

Ultimately, the goal of the reflection phase is not just to identify what students know now but to think together about what can be done to support them in advancing their learning going forward. This invites us to think of the kinds of feedback we could provide students across multiple timescales, as discussed in Chapter 7. How might what we learned inform what we do tomorrow, and next week? If we do the formative assessment task again, how might we revise the task to better meet our goals and to learn about student thinking? Since these steps are meant to be a cycle, this also feeds forward into subsequent steps where teachers set new goals and explore student thinking.

Once teachers have proceeded through the entire cycle, they may choose to move on to another learning goal, assessment task, or curriculum unit, or to look ahead to the next year and plan to complete the same cycle again. Appendix I provides a summary of each phase, activities, resources, and suggested readings for collaborative formative assessment design.

Table 8.2. Solar House Rubric

Level	Modeling	Explanation	Holistic
5	*In addition to the features of Level 4:* • All arrow-label pairs illustrate the relationship between energy transfer and dissipation.	*In addition to the features of Level 4:* • Student's explanation describes at least two examples where dissipation accompanies energy transfer.	• Student provides evidence that dissipation always accompanies any transfer of energy.
4	*In addition to the features of Level 3:* • At least one arrow-label pair illustrating energy transfer also indicates that energy dissipates during that transfer.	*In addition to the features of Level 3:* • Student provides a specific example that energy dissipates in a specific energy transfer.	• Student provides evidence that dissipation occurs during at least one transfer of energy.
3	*In addition to the features of Level 2:* • One or more arrow-label pairs describe energy dissipation.	*In addition to the features of Level 2:* Student describes energy dissipation as a loss of energy through heat. *Note: A Level 3 response does not discuss the relationship between transfer and dissipation.*	• Student describes or illustrates dissipation and transfer of energy as unrelated processes.
2	*In addition to the features of Level 1:* • One or more arrows are clearly labeled to describe energy transfer.	• Student describes that energy is transferred. *Note: A Level 2 response may describe dissipation in terms of a transfer of energy.*	• Student only provides evidence that energy is transferred. • Energy dissipation is missing from the student's response.
1	• The student uses arrows to illustrate the direction of all energy transfers. *Note: A Level 1 response may contain missing labels.*	• Student restates in words the model drawn earlier. • Explanation includes language describing forms of energy. *Note: A Level 1 response does not use verbs to describe energy transfer.*	• Student only provides evidence of knowledge of different forms of energy. • Energy transfer and dissipation are both missing from the student's responses.

(continued)

Level	Modeling	Explanation	Holistic
0	• One or more lines are included instead of arrows, making the direction of transfer ambiguous. • Labels may be provided, but they do not describe energy transfer.	• Off-task or blank response	• Off-task or blank response

INCREASING OPPORTUNITIES FOR TEACHERS TO LEARN THROUGH COLLABORATION AND FORMATIVE ASSESSMENT CO-DESIGN

Formative assessment design doesn't have to happen only outside of schools with curriculum developers, but there is an established benefit for task design, teaching practice, and professional learning when teachers have the time and space to work together.

If sufficient time for ongoing professional development in formative assessment isn't already available, ask administrators for it—and show them the research that supports increased teacher and student learning. We've worked with teachers and their administrators to find space within teachers' instructional days to have these meetings, such as during regular late-start days or during common planning time. At one school where teachers lacked time to collaborate, we shared findings from our collaboration and convinced the principal to shift the school schedule for the following academic year so that all biology teachers could plan together (Furtak, 2012).

While these examples provide evidence that shifting practices in the direction of supporting students' engagement in science is possible, they also are focused on small groups of teachers at individual schools. Teachers can share findings like these with other teachers at their school, or in their district, engaging administrators to support them to further spread local innovations around formative assessment. For example, teachers might identify colleagues at other schools and gather to share ideas with one another, spreading new approaches across school sites (e.g., Thompson et al., 2019). Teachers can also engage with widely available resources, including professional learning modules and summaries of recent research findings, such as collaboratively developed resources for formative assessment design (Penuel et al., 2020).

The bottom line is this: Formative assessment tasks can be developed by teachers who work together over time to create resources that center their own students' experiences and interests. They need not start from scratch but can use existing resources to create better tasks and to organize their teaching in ways that promote more equitable participation. Research shows that doing this over time can support teacher learning, lead to better tasks, and better support student learning.

CHAPTER 9

Learning Progressions
Tools for Formative Assessment

Throughout the book, I've built on the connections among curriculum, instruction, and assessment, and broadened our focus to consider many elements of classroom activity systems and how they support student learning through formative assessment. Something we haven't discussed in as much detail is how and when to embed formative assessments in units of learning, how to navigate the kinds of ideas students are likely to share in formative assessment, and how to plan subsequent steps for instruction.

This is where learning progressions come in. I mentioned learning progressions briefly in Chapter 8 as one of many tools that can be used to support teachers' design and enactment of formative assessment (Alonzo et al., 2022; Furtak & Heredia, 2014). This chapter will go into much greater detail about learning progressions, including three key ways that they can support formative assessment in science classrooms.

DEFINING LEARNING PROGRESSIONS

Learning progressions are representations of how student learning might develop in a given domain (Corcoran et al., 2009). They are defined by having upper anchors, or top levels, that represent the culminating ideas, practices, and understandings students can develop in a period of time, such as an instructional unit, a school year, a grade band, or even through their entire K–12 education. At the lower anchor, or entry point, learning progressions represent the beginning understandings students are likely to exhibit at the start of that period. In the middle of the progression are various intermediate levels that students may progress through as they learn.

Figure 9.1 provides an annotated example of a learning progression for the NGSS crosscutting concept of Stability and Change. The lower anchor begins in the early elementary grades, the upper anchor at the end of high school, and intermediate understandings are represented for upper elementary and middle school. The lower anchor ideas are much simpler, such as the idea that some things stay the same while other things change. Once students reach high school, these ideas are more complex, including how change can be quantified and modeled and the role of feedback in systems.

Learning progressions came into prominence in the mid-2000s as scaffolds for curriculum and assessment design (Corcoran et al., 2009). They are *hypothesized*, meaning they represent the ways in which particular student ideas *could* develop when students have opportunities to participate in particular learning experiences such as sequences of curriculum materials (Alonzo & Gotwals, 2012). That said, student learning is complex and not always linear (Furtak et al., 2014), and students often provide responses that might be at different levels of a learning progression (Alonzo et al., 2022).

Looking back over the past 15 years or so, a large number of efforts have occurred to create learning progressions with different design features in science education, and for many different purposes (Alonzo & Gotwals, 2012; Duschl et al., 2011). Some progressions have been created as underlying frameworks for curriculum and assessment design (Jin et al., 2009), whereas others were made to help teachers trace their growth in ambitious teaching (Thompson et al., 2013). Some focus more on disciplinary core ideas, others on science practices, and some combine both.

Learning progressions can be well-suited to support formative assessment design and enactment classrooms (Bennett, 2011). In this sense, a learning progression is a kind of map that represents the complex terrain of student thinking within a domain (Furtak, 2012). They can help teachers to map out where and when they want to embed assessments, provide an interpretive framework for the ideas students

Figure 9.1. Sample Learning Progression for Systems and System Models; adapted from National Science Teachers Association, n.d.

K-2	3-5	6-8	9-12
Stability and Change: For both designed and natural systems, conditions that affect stability and change and factors that control rates of change are critical elements to consider and understand.			
• Some things stay the same while other things change. • Things may change slowly or rapidly.	• Change is measured in terms of differences over time and may occur at different rates. • Some systems appear stable, but over long periods of time will eventually change.	• Explanations of stability and change in natural or designed systems can be constructed by examining the changes over time and forces at different scales, including the atomic scale. • Small changes in one part of a system might cause large changes in another part. • Stability might be disturbed either by sudden events or gradual changes that accumulate over time • Systems in dynamic equilibrium are stable due to a balance of feedback mechanisms.	• Much of science deals with constructing explanations of how things change and how they remain stable. • Change and rates of change can be quantified and modeled over very short or very long periods of time. Some system changes are irreversible. • Feedback (negative or positive) can stabilize or destabilize a system. • Systems can be designed for greater or lesser stability.
↑ Lower anchor	←———— Intermediate levels ————→		↑ Upper anchor

share on those assessments, and also help teachers determine the next steps for instruction on the basis of what students know now. Learning progressions can serve as foundations for assessment design, and can inform the interpretation of responses to trace students' learning progress over time (Briggs et al., 2006).

LEARNING PROGRESSIONS FOR THREE-DIMENSIONAL ASSESSMENT

Learning progressions can have many different designs, cover different spans of time, and have many different features. Learning progressions can represent sequences for units of instruction, such as those that look at the development of understanding across grade bands or the entire K–12 spectrum. These progressions differ from those derived from empirical research and modeling of student response patterns, and thus may start with the everyday ideas students bring to school, and then build to more sophisticated ideas over time (Duschl et al., 2011; Shavelson, 2009).

When the NGSS were being developed, a committee of science and education leaders developed learning progressions that mapped the development of increasingly sophisticated ideas and engagement in practice over time (Board on Science Education, 2012). These progressions created for the NGSS represent how disciplinary core ideas, science and engineering practices, and crosscutting concepts unfold over time, so they are *unidimensional*, representing the progression of a single construct or idea at a time (Wilson, 2009). These kinds of learning progressions cover core ideas such as force and motion (Alonzo & Steedle, 2009), carbon cycling (Jin et al., 2009), and celestial motion (Plummer & Krajcik, 2010). Learning progressions can also trace the development of student participation in science practices. For example, progressions have been developed for scientific argumentation (Berland & McNeill, 2010) and modeling (Pierson et al., 2017; Schwarz et al., 2009). Finally, learning progressions can trace the development of how students apply crosscutting concepts to novel phenomena, such as energy and matter cycling in systems (Buell et al., 2019a). Several progressions have combined multiple dimensions, creating sets of learning goals better aligned with multidimensional (2D or 3D) instruction. For example, there are progressions that combine argumentation with students' understanding of biodiversity (Songer et al., 2009) and the interrelationship between students' developing understandings of models and evolution (Lehrer & Schauble, 2012).

THREE FUNCTIONS FOR LEARNING PROGRESSIONS IN FORMATIVE ASSESSMENT

Learning progressions have three key functions when it comes to formative assessment (Alonzo et al., 2022; Covitt et al., 2018). First, the progressions can help to map a curriculum and to plan formative assessments that will draw out student thinking at key points in a sequence of learning. Second, learning progressions can be a guide to help teachers parse and interpret student responses on assessments. Third, they can create space to anticipate and plan feedback for students, and to identify possible next steps for instruction. Let's dig into each of these and explore some examples.

Embedding Formative Assessments in Instructional Units

All of the different kinds of learning progressions can serve as the foundations for embedding formative assessments in units of instruction. Learning progressions can help to define sequences of learning experiences that correspond to shifts between different levels of the progression. Teachers can use learning progressions along with curriculum materials to better understand when we might want to know, as teachers, how students are progressing in their learning through the unit, how they are applying their learning back to the central questions driving the unit, and to design questions that can create space for students to share their thinking.

Planning guides help teachers create different learning targets or performances that would lead up to the performance expectation, a kind of "staircase" that helps us envision how different assessment opportunities build on each other to support students as they approach learning goals (Figure 9.2). These tools include "look fors," or the kinds of things that students might do or say while they are learning—that is, we want to look or listen for anything related to the different levels of the learning progression. A blank version of the planning tool is provided in Appendix J.

This tool involves multiple kinds of representations to help teachers identify what to assess, and to think about that in the context of their unit plan. In the example in Figure 9.2, the first two boxes at the top of the planning tool show a two-dimensional learning progression—in this case, a progression for modeling (science and engineering practice) and energy (crosscutting concept)—and then leaves space for teachers to migrate that progression into a particular disciplinary core idea, such as force and motion or cellular respiration. Below these progressions is space for teachers to list the different performance expectations they will be helping students learn in the unit.

Figure 9.2. Planning Tool for Formative Assessment With Example of Energy Learning Progression

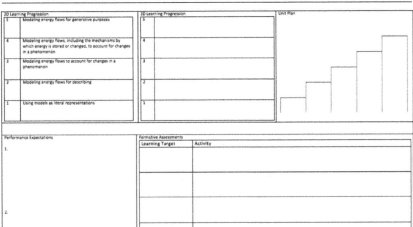

At the top right of the tool is a representation called the staircase model, which represents the main ideas and practices students will be gradually building through the unit as steps. Teachers can think through what these steps might be, and then identify what students would need to know and be able to do as they advance up each step; these become the points in the unit where we can embed formative assessments, which can then be listed in the space at the bottom of the page. This tool can be used not just to plan a new unit of learning but also to unpack standards and an existing curriculum to better understand where and why formative assessments are—or could be—embedded within a unit. In addition, we can then use these particular points as opportunities to create formative assessment tasks that create space for students to share their thinking related to the specific learning progression (Alonzo et al., 2022; Covitt et al., 2018; Furtak, 2012).

As an example, we can explore the Carbon Time learning progression, which focuses on the role of carbon in socioecological systems (Gunckel et al., 2012; Mohan et al., 2009). Instructional materials based on the learning progression include assessments and activities embedded in everyday phenomena such as soda water fizzing and ethanol burning. The learning progression helps to define the ways that these units and assessments build on each other; in my own research, we have also investigated how this progression can serve as a framework for teachers as they design assessments and interpret student responses (Furtak & Tayne, 2019). An adapted version of this learning progression is shown in Table 9.1.

This progression shows how students' ideas can develop from lower-level anchors based on their everyday experiences, becoming increasingly scientific and articulated at the molecular level as they move toward understandings of higher anchors. Exploring how student ideas can develop with the support of this type of progression can create space for teachers to unpack how these ideas are taught in their own curriculum materials, and to consider how formative assessments might be embedded to support students as they learn. Figure 9.3 shows a teacher-drawn outline of the progression of ideas within their own unit, which they created when discussing the progression shown in Table 9.1.

When it comes to designing formative assessments, we can use the learning progression to design specific questions and tasks in ways that are open-ended and invite students to apply these ideas to novel or familiar contexts. For example, we might ask students, "Where does the new material for a plant growing in the sunlight come from as it grows?" Similarly, we could ask a question about the surroundings of

Table 9.1. Learning Progression Excerpt (adapted from Mohan, Chen & Anderson [2009])

			Sample student responses
Upper Anchor	Carbon-transforming processes	Generating organic carbon	"The plants increase in weight comes from CO2 in the air. The carbon in that molecule is used to create glucose, and several polysaccharides which are used for support" (p. 690).
	Scientific accounts	Photosynthesis	"The weight comes mostly from H2O it receives, which it uses in its light reactions to eventually produce glucose to provide itself with energy" (p. 688).
	Macroscopic events	Plant growth	"I think their weight comes from the soil and fertilizer because as it grows it increases in weight, and fertilizer and soil are the things that make a plant grow" (p. 686).
Lower Anchor	Informal accounts	Natural processes in plants (e.g., it is enabled by water, sunlight, air, etc.)	"I think it's leaves. Leaves comes from trees; the weight comes from when a plant grows, the weight also grows bigger" (p. 685).

Learning Progressions

Figure 9.3. Teacher Notes for Planning Progression of Student Ideas in Unit

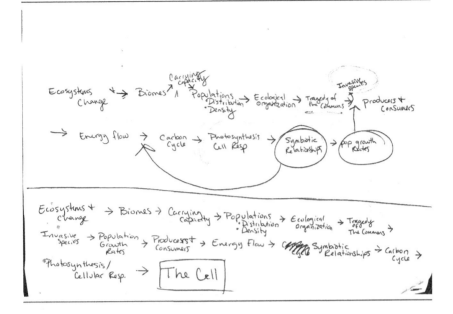

the plant, such as "Does the plant growing in the sunlight change the air? How?" Students could be invited to draw models of these relationships. The phrasing of the learning progression can help us identify elements that we could prompt students to show in their models (e.g., air, sunlight, carbon, etc.), and which we might look at as we interpret their models. Each of these possible prompts illustrates how the learning progression can help us design formative assessment tasks that we can then use to interpret student thinking.

An 11th-grade biology teacher who used this learning progression to help plan her unit and formative assessments embedded within it reflected, "I think it's useful to know where the students should be and then where we can take them with that work, the learning progression like, what, how do they follow that and where should they be at the end so that we can go back and see what we need to know from them in the beginning and then base our curriculum on that, or what we're going to teach on that."

Interpreting Student Thinking

When we're creating learning environments in which we're asking students to share their ideas and asking authentic questions that draw out their experiences, it can be helpful to have an interpretive framework.

This is the next place where learning progressions can be very useful: They provide maps on which we can locate particular student understandings, provide examples of what those understandings might look and sound like in student work and student talk, and help us "look for" particular scientific connections with students' ideas.

Learning progressions are also key tools to support us in the unstructured conversations that occur when we ask students about their thinking—once they share their ideas, how might we interpret them? The different ideas and levels can help us place students' thinking into the context of larger processes of learning, and to help us think about how best to support students as they move forward.

As an example, we can see how a professional learning community (PLC) of 9th-grade physics teachers used a learning progression to interpret student ideas over two school years (Henson, 2019). The teachers worked with a learning progression that then allowed them to describe specific "look fors" intended to guide them to identify student thinking at particular levels of the learning progression relevant to that performance expectation (Figure 9.4):

> **HS-PS-3-2.** Develop and use models to illustrate that energy at the macroscopic scale can be accounted for as a combination of energy associated with the motions of particles (objects) and energy associated with the relative positions of particles (objects).

For her dissertation research, Kate Henson worked with these teachers and traced the ways they used the learning progression to inform their planning. She documented how, in early meetings, teachers had mostly general interpretations of student thinking on a formative assessment task asking students to model kinetic and potential energy at different points on a halfpipe in a skate park and to explain how this relates to whether the skateboarder will get back to their initial height (see Appendix H for the full task).

Teachers looked carefully at two student work samples using the learning progression as an interpretive framework. In the conversation of the first student's work sample, the teachers focused more explicitly on what the student had written down:

> *Chris:* . . . if we're just looking at the KE and PE stuff, they're spot on.
> *Andy:* What was it that you called . . . ?
> *Chris:* So I would give that a level 3.
> *Kate:* The mechanisms?

Figure 9.4. Learning Progression for Energy (Buell et al., 2019a)

	A learning progression for modeling energy flows	What to look for in student work related to HS-PS-3-2
5	• Students are able to *generalize their model* to unknown or multiple phenomena, and can *explain limitations of applying the model* to a new phenomenon.	
4	• Students *develop a model* that illustrates a mechanism that can explain or predict the phenomenon, AND *use* the model to make predictions about how changing one part of the model would influence energy flows elsewhere in the system. • Students can explain how the total energy of the system constrains the magnitude of change possible. • Students can *describe limitations of the model* in explaining or predicting the phenomenon.	• Explanation of mechanism • Explanation of what would happen if . . . • Total energy constraints— • Limitations—
3	• Students *use* or *develop* a model that relates changes in the phenomenon directly to changes in energy through transfers/transformations by identifying specific indicators. • Students begin to show evidence that their model is accounting for conservation and dissipation. • Model includes energy flows into, within, and out of the system.	• Indicators of transfer/transformation • Indicators of dissipation
2	• Students *use* or *develop* a model to illustrate a relationship or pattern between the increase in one form of energy and the decrease in another form, or transferred from one location or object to another. • Students identify the most relevant components and relationships in the model *and* distinguish between the system and surroundings • Model focuses on energy flows within the system only.	• Evidence of transfer/transformation
1	• Students *use* or *develop* a model that shows, through drawings or labels, the components involved in a phenomenon, some (but not necessarily all relevant) energy forms, transfers, or transformations.	• General labels or drawings

> *Andy:* Yeah, the mechanisms. I don't see anything about mechanism on here, but we also didn't ask them—
> *Kate:* Right, that's . . .
> *Chris:* We didn't ask them.
> *Avery:* Yeah. That's a problem. . . .
> *Chris:* However, they do talk about a mechanism at the bottom where they are going through total energy being the sum of potential and kinetic (Henson, 2019, pp. 138–139).

Chris had identified a particular student response, "Because once they hit the middle of the ramp, then they become equal (PE and KE) to total energy," and related it to the learning progression, using the "look fors" as ways to hone in on specific elements of the student response. After an extended conversation about what this student understood, the group of teachers ultimately interpreted the response as the student understanding that KE and PE were not equal to each other, but together they equaled total energy. In discussing a second student example, the teachers dug into greater depth about how modifications of the task would be necessary to better understand students' understanding of energy conservation and dissipation, which were located at level 3 of the learning progression.

This example helps us to see the ways in which teachers can be supported to dig more deeply into student work with the support of a learning progression linked to the task. At the same time, when using learning progressions to interpret student thinking, we don't want to oversimplify or overgeneralize. We can only make inferences about where a particular piece of student work, at a moment in time, might be located on that progression (and more pieces of student work are better), rather than trying to say a student is *at* a particular level at a particular moment (Alonzo et al., 2022). We hope to use the progressions just to guide our support for students in their learning, not to assign particular ways of knowing or being to them. This has important implications for equity—if we label students as having particular understandings, we can limit their capacity for growth. If learning progressions primarily contain what "most" student learning looks like, they could further privilege dominant ideas and exclude students whose identities and experiences are different from those presented in—or used to develop—the learning progression. As such, interpreting ideas relative to the progression, and finding students lacking, could further identify the ways in which students don't "measure up."

While progressions can aid interpreting student ideas, then, we want to avoid focusing on what students lack, or seeking to simply correct or replace their ideas (Furtak, 2012). Instead, we should seek to use progressions in ways that explicitly honor the resources and ideas that learners bring, and build on them. The levels of the progression allow us to give targeted feedback to improve the quality of student work from one level to the next. But making inferences about student thinking with a learning progression should always be done cautiously because there is also the possibility that a student's work can be located at multiple levels (Alonzo et al., 2022; Furtak et al., 2014).

Planning Next Steps for Instruction

Learning progressions can also embed suggestions for instructional next steps, going beyond frameworks for planning instructional experiences and assessment tasks and interpreting ideas to suggest feedback at different levels. This can be phrased as "things to work on," giving teachers a progression, sample student ideas, activities that students could do next, and subsequent instructional steps to support student learning (Minstrell et al., 2008). For example, Table 9.2 shows the next steps for students, and for instruction, that my team designed with teachers to support their students in a project about natural selection and evolution (Furtak et al., 2014). We developed this version of the learning progression to support teachers in feeling better prepared to modify their instruction on the basis of student responses, following studies indicating that feedback can be the most challenging step in formative assessment (Heritage et al., 2009). Each of the middle and lower anchor levels includes features of student responses, illustrating what students understand and are still working on, as well as suggested next steps for learning.

Carrie, one of the high school biology teachers we worked with in this project, led a conversation with her students based on the ideas in this progression. She was seeking to better understand student responses to a formative assessment task, in which students modeled data similar to that of Darwin's finches on the Galapagos Islands; students then used that model to develop evidence-based explanations about the likelihood of particular beak types surviving to reproduce given environmental changes (Furtak & Heredia, 2016).

After students had completed their written responses on the formative assessment, Carrie asked the whole class, "If the environmental conditions select for the elimination of a certain beak type and the environment changes back to its original conditions, would the eliminated or extinct beak type make a return? Give me thumbs up if you think yes."

Table 9.2. Sample Learning Progression for Component of Natural Selection, With Feedback Suggestions (adapted from Furtak et al., 2014)

Learning progression level	Features of student responses	Next steps for instruction
Genetic changes happen through random genetic processes.		
Genetic change occurs with no specific mechanism.	Students acknowledge that changes in traits are based in genes, but do not specify what that is or how it happens.	Students explore mechanisms for genetic change (e.g., crossing over, recombination of genes, mutations, etc.) and relate those changes in genotype to changes in phenotype.
Environment causes genetic changes.	Response indicates that changes in traits have a genetic basis, but that change is caused by the environment and can be passed on to offspring.	Students explore how DNA can change due to environmental factors, but these changes are not necessarily inherited; in addition, selection is based on genetic differences occurring over generations.
Changes in traits have no genetic basis.	Describe how trait changes might be observed at the macro-level—not yet related to genes.	Review DNA-RNA-protein phenotype link with students, helping them see that phenotypes are controlled by genes.

Carrie paused for a few moments as a handful of students gave a thumbs-up. She then continued, "Give me a thumb down if you think no." The majority of students in the class gave a thumbs-down.

Carrie: A lot of us said yes. If you said yes, can you explain why?
Andrea: Because that's how that beak came to be in the first place. To get the food each finch, after several centuries grows a beak to help them get the most food possible.
Carrie: Hold on. Do they grow that beak to help them get, they're like I want this kind of beak so they grow that to help them get it? What do you mean by that?

Learning Progressions 173

> *Andrea:* Their genes kind of change.
> *Darby:* Evolve
> *Andrea:* Yeah, evolve after several generations.
> *Carrie:* Can anyone help Andrea. Yeah, Anna.
> *Anna:* I said maybe. Because the beak would like, evolve back again to that beak size.
> *Carrie:* Okay. Here's the answer. The big, big glaring answer to number 5 is no. So here's the deal. Now hold on—so thank you for being a brave underdog and being like "uh, I thought no." Here's the deal. Could that beak type return? Well there's one way you could say yes, um, but it's not very likely. So why is the answer no? Could someone explain it to me? Keira, yeah?
> *Keira:* If they, if they go extinct once they really can't come back 'cause they're all dead.
> *Carrie:* Okay? So if they go extinct, they can't come back 'cause they're all gone. But why did we think that they could come back?
> *Keira:* Because it's a variation.
> *Carrie:* Variation. Because we say, well if it becomes the wet years again, maybe it's that variation, but that variation is now out of the DNA and out of the gene pool. And so unless that same random variation happens to show up again, which isn't all that likely 'cause it's a random variation out of like billions of DNA codes, right? So unless that random variation, um, occurs again . . . it's most likely that that's not just going to show up again in the population a few years later. Does that make sense?

Carrie paused for a moment, and then asked students to give "thumbs up if that makes sense." She then asked students to discuss their new answers with their neighbors, and then to write down how their answers might have shifted based on the class discussion:

> Okay, so now I want you to explain the new answer to your neighbor for number five. And right below your, your answer, I want you to draw a line and draw, like just draw a little line there. And then I want you to give me a new idea. I wanna see if you actually understand how I explained that that actually wouldn't happen. Okay? Now if you got it right, or if you feel like you kind of gave that ideal answer in the beginning, put it away, then go ahead and put a little star next to it and then that'll help me know that that's why you didn't like rewrite it.

Carrie used a variety of participation structures—individuals writing and revising responses, partner talk, and whole-class discussion—to support students in developing explanations for how particular variations could go extinct in the population. As she did so, she drew on ideas from the learning progression that encouraged students to consider how genes contributed new genetic variations to populations, and how particular variations were not likely to reoccur in populations as a result of random molecular processes.

FEATURES OF LEARNING PROGRESSIONS THAT SUPPORT FORMATIVE ASSESSMENT

Looking across these three uses of learning progressions for formative assessment, we can identify which features of learning progressions can be most useful to teachers as they design and enact formative assessment with their students. While more complex versions of learning progressions are clearly important for measurement, assessment, and curriculum design, simpler "on-the-ground" versions of the progressions can help teachers navigate classroom conversations and interpret students' work more easily (Furtak, 2012; Furtak & Tayne, 2019). These features are summarized in Table 9.3.

Table 9.3. Features of Learning Progressions That Support Their Use as Resources for Formative Assessment

Features to support formative assessment	Description *Learning Progression . . .*
Aligned with the curriculum	Serves as foundation for curriculum, instruction and assessment
Smaller grain size	Includes levels that students may progress through within one instructional unit/academic year
Accompanied by other tools	Is accompanied by other resources to support its use in sorting and responding to student ideas and in planning formative assessment tasks
Phrased in simple terms	Not overly filled with jargon; easy to skim and interpret
Sample responses	Includes sample student work/responses from the curriculum to guide teacher interpretation of students' oral and written work
Next steps for teaching	Includes information on how to support the continued development of student ideas and engagement in practice at each level

If we view learning progressions as part of a larger classroom activity system, it's important to use the same progression underlying curriculum and instruction for assessment. The majority of the progressions above involve instances where curriculum, instruction, and assessment were developed together around a common progression. This allows instruction to proceed in ways consistent with the progress for learning represented in the progression. In contrast, a system out of alignment—where the curriculum doesn't follow the same underlying structure as the learning progression—will lead to tensions between what students are learning and what they are assessed on, making the representation less useful for supporting instruction.

When compared with the kinds of learning progressions that appear in the NGSS that span an entire academic career from kindergarten through 12th grade, teachers found it more useful to have progressions at a small grain size—those that could be used within one academic year, or even within a single instructional unit. That said, we recognize that interpreting student ideas in a curriculum unit might be facilitated by a progression that is specifically designed for that unit, and that doesn't span more sophisticated understandings that might not be addressed in the curriculum for several more years. It is also helpful to teachers when learning progressions are accompanied by other tools, such as those included in Chapter 8, that help them to unpack standards, plan where assessments might be used, and design assessment tasks that can draw out student ideas.

Teachers can add examples of how student ideas look and sound when they are mapped onto the learning progression. It helps if the progression itself is stated in simple language, and not made so complex that it takes a while to understand what each level might be. When developing these progressions, we always pull examples from student writing, models, drawings, and verbal responses to help teachers match the more technical language in the learning progression with what they might be seeing and hearing in their classroom. Another way of doing this can be to include "look fors," or specific elements of student ideas or indicators that teachers can watch for while teaching. An example of this from our project with energy is that a "look for" when students are reasoning about respiration might be oxygen, glucose, or other elements of the equation for cellular respiration. Examples of how these might come out in students' everyday talk could be speaking about air, sugar, food, or other observable, everyday experiences. Finally, we have found that providing specific steps to support student learning—as shown in Table 9.2—can help teachers not only interpret student ideas but also to have ways of responding both in the moment and later through adaptations to instructional tasks.

POTENTIAL TO GUIDE FORMATIVE ASSESSMENT, WITH CAUTION

In this chapter, we've seen how there are multiple forms of learning progressions with design features that can support the process of planning, enacting, and taking action on student responses to formative assessment. In less-structured science learning environments, it can be tremendously helpful to have well-articulated guides for how we want to support student learning through a unit, or across a school year, or multiple school years. These progressions can inform where we plan to engage students with formative assessment, and to plan tasks that will draw out their ideas. We can use the progressions to interpret the ideas students share, and to provide feedback tailored to their ideas and that help them move forward.

In addition to these affordances, however, learning progressions have several constraints. As described above, whenever we try to put something in writing, and represent it in a linear way, it implies that this is the "right" way of learning, or that student learning "should" follow this particular path (Alonzo et al., 2022). Unfortunately, in my own research, I've seen how lower-level ideas in some learning progressions have reinforced the idea that some student ideas are "wrong," and that they should be replaced by the ideas at higher levels in the progression (Furtak, 2012). Instead, we should think about the progressions as representing possible pathways, or even as underlying structures for curriculum and assessment design. This is a key contrast with how learning actually unfolds in real time, in ways that can be nonlinear, iterative, or on paths not represented by the progressions (Furtak et al., 2014).

To best support student learning through formative assessment, we should continue to develop resources that document students' many assets, as well as ways to use these to support instruction. An alternative approach to learning progressions could be tools that guide teachers in noticing how student thinking shows up in descriptions of everyday and home experiences (Tzou et al., 2021), rather than articulating what students might have wrong, or be missing. In addition, these representations can be used in community with other teachers, supporting us as we look deeply at student work to truly understand and center students' ideas in our teaching.

CHAPTER 10

Conclusion
Formative Assessment for Ambitious and Equitable Science Learning: Toward a New Horizon

J. Myron (Mike) Atkin, a former New York teacher, science education professor, and dean of the Stanford Graduate School of Education, was an early and important mentor in my journey to becoming a science education researcher. He often used the metaphor of a horizon to describe shifts in practice and his long view on educational reform.

When we think of a horizon, it's the edge of what we can see, where the land meets the sky, based on where we are and our point of view. As we move forward and change our current position, that horizon shifts. Mike emphasized that we never actually get to the horizon, as it recedes from us as we move. He used this metaphor to help us see how we need an orienting goal to move toward, but that goal will shift and change as we learn and make progress.

It's with this idea of a horizon that I will close the book.

MAIN ARGUMENTS

I've brought together three intersecting and overlapping conversations that create an urgent need to change what formative assessment looks like in science, and how we enact it with students. Students should have ample opportunities to engage in science practices and apply crosscutting concepts as they learn about the big ideas in science, and we need to broaden how we conceptualize learning so we are looking at shifts in practice over time, not just the knowledge students accumulate. We seek to design learning experiences that engage students in these practices to learn the main ideas of science. These learning experiences are designed to recenter expertise in the classroom around students, their interests, and their strengths.

Formative assessment must similarly shift for us to achieve this vision. We need tasks that build on students' interests and experiences and invite them to bring those into the classroom. Tasks that center the identities of learners who aren't used to seeing themselves in the science they are learning. Tasks that have design features that help students show what they know, and to draw on all their linguistic resources to do so. Then, we seek to use these tasks to organize student participation in learning that is interactive, that challenges students to share their ideas and support them with evidence, and to listen and respond to each other.

Throughout the book, I've used the idea of classroom activity systems to help us see how formative assessment tasks are part of a larger ecology in support of student learning. We need to think much more broadly than designing better formative assessment tasks embedded in curricula: We need to consider how these tasks are part of a larger activity system for ambitious teaching, including structures within the classroom; routines that organize classroom activity; as well as the multiple identities and experiences that teachers and learners bring to school.

While we are on the journey toward this new horizon of three-dimensional formative assessment that supports ambitious and equitable instruction, we also need to acknowledge what lies beyond. Educational researchers and practitioners are partnering with students and communities to re-vision how assessment aligns with larger goals that sustain students' interests and communities, yet we are still building examples of what this can look like (Likely, 2022; Randall, 2021). We also seek to better understand how assessments can link up with larger movements in education toward joy and thriving (Love, 2019).

WHAT CAN WE DO?

While individual teachers will take away benefits from the pages of this book, sustainable changes in teaching are supported through long-term work with colleagues. If you've read the book and want to do more, I suggest that you reach out to other teachers on your team, or at your school, who are also interested in broadening student participation in science learning through formative assessment. If you're teaching the same class, try planning for and enacting a task together, and then coming back to look at student responses and to plan next steps. If you're working in different classes or content areas, think about how similar instructional approaches—such as asking students to make initial and revised models—can support learning across different units. Even teachers working in isolated settings such as at small or rural schools need not do this alone—they can link up online to learn with colleagues. You can also draw upon ongoing efforts happening at larger scales to support the journey toward more equitable science formative assessment.

CLOSING

Ultimately, I hope this book not only provides new frameworks for planning for and enacting formative assessments in science but also allows us to step back to view the larger systems influencing what is possible in assessment, as well as mechanisms to both interrogate and change the current state of practice. This means looking beyond the science, and beyond our own classrooms, to identify—and to question—the ways in which larger structural factors are influencing our ability to realize the potential of formative assessment in our classrooms.

As we move forward toward this horizon, the path may shift, or become unclear. But I encourage us to look up and keep moving toward that vision. I'm not calling upon this metaphor to suggest that true reform will never be possible; instead, I hope to use it to describe how we are moving toward a future that will always be shifting and changing, and although we may not be there yet, it's a worthy goal to keep moving ahead, and to keep trying.

APPENDIX A

Phenomenon Planner

	Same	Close	Proximal	Distal
Phenomenon				
When will it be embedded in unit?				
Considerations	Observable Interesting Relevant Sustaining knowledge and practices	Observable Interesting Relevant Sustaining knowledge and practices	Observable Interesting Relevant Sustaining knowledge and practices	Observable Interesting Relevant Sustaining knowledge and practices
Tradeoffs				

APPENDIX B

Heated Cup Task

Directions: Read the story below and use it to draw and explain a model about energy. You may use all your linguistic resources to do so, and write your response in any language.

Instrucciones: Lea la historia a continuación y úsela para dibujar y explicar un modelo sobre la energía. Puede utilizar todos sus recursos lingüísticos para hacerlo y escribir su respuesta en cualquier idioma.

Imagine you are heating a cup of water in the microwave to make a warm drink. You het the water for just about a minute, so it doesn't start steaming or boiling.

1. What kind of warm drink are you making?

2. Draw a model that shows what is happening to the molecules in the liquid before and after it is heated.

- ❏ Model Checklist
- ❏ Show what's visible and invisible
- ❏ Label your drawing
- ❏ Make a key
- ❏ Explain ideas that we've been talking about:
  - ❏ Molecules
  - ❏ Thermal energy
  - ❏ Kinetic energy

Before   After

3. In the space below, explain what is happening when the liquid in the mug is heated. In your explanation, you need to include:
- ❏ How the molecules are moving before and after the cup is put in the microwave
- ❏ How the motion of the molecules is related to the temperature before and after heating
- ❏ How the motion of the molecules relates to kinetic and thermal energy

Adapted from "Heated Cup of Water" at the NGSS Task Annotation Project, original task available at https://www.achieve.org/files/sites/default/files/18-126%20Heated%20Cup%20of%20Water_Annotations.pdf

APPENDIX C

Formative Assessment Task Design Checklist

Adapted from Fine & Furtak (2020a, 2020b)

Culture and Language	Present/ Not Present	Notes
Questions explicitly create space for students to share their own cultural understandings, lived experiences, and practices.		
Task, task instructions, objectives, and/or scoring tools are written in at least one language in addition to English.		
Task instructions encourage students to use all their linguistic resources to help them make sense of the task and/or communicate their thinking.		
Task Components		
Contains open-ended components.		
Contains multiple components.		
Allows for multiple points of entry; that is, students do not need to answer questions in a set order to be successful.		
Students are asked to create diagrams/graphics/models to accompany their written explanations.		
Scaffolds support contextualization, metacognition, and/or understanding the text.		
Scaffolds		
Support contextualization of the task		
Help students engage with challenging elements of the task		

Culture and Language	Present/ Not Present	Notes
Alignment and Rigor		
Task assesses grade-level appropriate disciplinary core ideas, science and engineering practices, and crosscutting concepts		
Academic vocabulary is grade-level; vocabulary can include some definitions to provide students with more context to help them understand what is being asked.		
Includes questions with high cognitive demand		
Clear Objectives and Scoring Criteria		
The learning objective/s of the task is/are clearly stated at the beginning of the task.		
Task supports student self-assessment such as a rubric or checklist to help students understand elements of quality work.		

APPENDIX D

Weather in Three Places Task

Rafa called his grandmother in **Santiago**, Chile, on FaceTime last week, and saw it was warm and sunny there, but here in **Denver** it was snowing. Later, Rafa's friend Chi told him that in **Lagos**, Nigeria, the weather is more or less the same all year.

Why is the weather so different in these three places?

1. Draw four Earths that show *what causes* each of these three locations to experience:
   a. Winter   b. Spring   c. Summer   d. Fall

2. Label each Earth with the season.

3. Label the location of the three cities at each Earth:

4. Write a claim to answer the question, *Why is the weather so different in these three places?*

Adapted from Kang, H., Thompson, J., & Windschitl, M. (2014). Creating opportunities for students to show what they know: The role of scaffolding in assessment tasks. *Science Education*, 98(4), 674–704.

5. Use evidence from what you've learned in class to support your claim.

6. What are some possible limitations of the model and explanation you've provided?

7. The table below provides average temperatures, by month, at the three locations (Santiago, Denver, Lagos).

Ask students to organize, represent, and analyze the data in at least two ways. Ask students to use tools (digital tools, if appropriate), technologies, or models and to apply concepts of statistics and probability (e.g., functions that fit the data, slope, intercept, and correlation coefficient) to analyze the data.
Ask students to compare how the representations and analyses help them to identify patterns in the data.
Ask students to make a valid and reliable scientific claim using their analyses as evidence.
Ask students to consider the limitations of their data analysis.

Average Monthly High/Low Temperatures, by Location

high/low temp (C)		Jan	Feb	Mar	Apr	May	Jun	Jul	Aug	Sep	Oct	Nov	Dec
Denver, Colorado	high	49	49	58	65	73	86	92	90	82	68	57	47
	low	20	21	29	35	45	55	61	59	50	37	27	19
Santiago, Chile	high	86	85	82	75	67	61	60	63	67	73	79	84
	low	53	52	49	44	40	37	36	37	41	44	48	51
Lagos, Nigeria	high	92	93	93	91	89	86	84	84	85	87	90	92
	low	74	77	78	77	76	74	74	74	74	74	75	75

APPENDIX E

Snowmelt Task

It makes a big difference which side of the street you're on after a snowstorm in Colorado. As the picture below shows, one side of the street can be completely melted out, while the other side of the street is still covered in snow. How might this happen?

Draw a model that shows how the snow might melt faster on one side of the street than the other. Label your drawing and symbols. Use a key to show what colors and symbols mean.

Model checklist
Include ideas about the Sun and solar energy that we've been working on together:
- ❏ How does sunny versus shady matter?
- ❏ How does angle of sunlight matter?
- ❏ How does the amount of direct sunlight matter?
- ❏ Is there a pattern of East, West, North, or South sidewalks? Why or why not?
- ❏ Other ideas from our class's explanation checklist.

In your written explanation, explain why the snow melts faster on one side of the street than the other. Remember to use evidence and reasons to back up your ideas so that other people can see your thinking.

After discussing your model in a small group, draw a revised version of your model here.

APPENDIX F

High-Elevation Task

TEACHER GUIDE

Elevation 5280 Cellular Respiration Task Overview

Evidence statement: HS LS 1–7 Evidence Statements

INTRODUCTION

Show video

Elevation 5280: Altitude Sickness Broncos Stadium video
www.youtube.com/watch?v=GmHStBrb4yI
Read: "Since 1975, the Denver Broncos have the best home record in the NFL. Since 2007, the Colorado Rockies have the 14th-best home record in the MLB—yet rank dead last in their away-game record during that same span. Since 2003 (the longest data set I could find), the Denver Nuggets have the fourth-best home record in the NBA yet rank 13th in their away-game record. Coincidence? I wouldn't count on it."
Prompt for discussion: Why might visiting teams struggle more when it comes to playing at the Broncos' stadium or another Denver sport stadium?
Students talk with their table groups about the prompt.
Come back together as a full class and discuss.
[Students will likely come up with elevation, air is thin—may not know what that means exactly; students may bring up altitude sickness; they might talk about the oxygen masks on the sideline.]
Questions to guide whole-class discussion:

- *What does it mean that the air is thin?*
- *Why does it matter that the air is thin? How might that impact visiting teams' athletic performance?*
- *Why might they have oxygen masks on the sideline?*

PART 1

Hand out part 1

Students independently answer questions 1–3 and model.
Come together as a full class and discuss questions 1–3 and model.
Share out ideas—volunteers from each table

- *Where does the energy come from?*
- *Discuss oxygen as a limiting factor.*

Look for the breakdown of sugar and the breaking of bonds of sugar.
Prompt students to consider oxygen, glucose, carbon dioxide, water, and energy.

PART 2

Hand out part 2

Students work with a partner to revise their model; encourage students to include inputs and outputs, oxygen, glucose, carbon dioxide, water, and energy. If time allows, students work with a partner to trace energy back to the sun.

STUDENT HANDOUT

Part 1

Scenario: The Oakland Raiders are at Mile High Stadium this weekend. They have had a good season overall, but at this game they aren't playing as well as usual. Team members experience increased heart rate, increased breathing rate, and **overall fatigue** (tiredness, low energy). The Broncos win by a large margin.
Cellular Respiration Equation

PART 1

Including matter and energy from the cellular respiration equation, draw a model (picture, chart, diagram, etc.) to show how the Oakland Raiders running back gets and uses energy to play the game against the Denver Broncos.

Show things that you can see, and things that you cannot see. *Use arrows and labels to show the flow of energy and cycling of matter.*

Use your model to respond to the following three questions:
(1) In two to three sentences, describe how the running back gets and uses his energy to play football.

_____
_____
_____
_____

(2) Assuming the Raiders players eat exactly the same food before the game as they usually do, explain what is different for the Raiders players when they play at Mile High Stadium compared to the Coliseum (their home stadium) and other stadiums at sea level?

_____
_____
_____
_____

(3) Hypothesize why the Raiders experience greater fatigue in Denver, using increased heart rate and breathing rate as evidence to support your explanation.

_____
_____
_____
_____
_____

PART 2

Revise your model from part 1. Including matter and energy from the cellular respiration equation, draw a model (picture, chart, diagram, etc.) to show how the Oakland Raiders running back gets and uses energy to play the game against the Denver Broncos. Show things that you can see, and things that you cannot see.

Work with a partner to discuss how the running back's energy can be traced back to the sun. Write a few sentences to explain your thinking **OR** draw a model.

_____
_____
_____
_____
_____

APPENDIX G

Enactment Planning Guide

Performance Expectation/s

Phenomenon

Learning Targets   Possible Indicators or Look-fors
What are students doing? What are you doing?

In the space below, plan for the following:
- **Level of Grouping** *How will students have varying opportunities for making sense of the phenomenon/scenario?* (e.g., individual time, small-group collaboration, whole-class discussions)
- **Classroom Talk Strategies** *How will you find out what students know? How will you support students toward figuring out the learning goals?* (e.g., eliciting students' ideas with general prompts, prompts related to science and engineering practices/crosscutting concepts?)
- **Norms & Routines** *How will students be supported to share their initial and developing ideas? Personal connections? What recurring routines can you use that support student sensemaking and using the science and engineering practices?*

Lesson Time	Level of Grouping	Talk Strategies	Norms & Routines
0:05			
0:10			
0:15			
0:20			
0:25			
0:30			
0:35			

Lesson Time	Level of Grouping	Talk Strategies	Norms & Routines
0:40			
0:45			
0:50			
0:55			
1:00			
1:05			
1:10			
1:15			
1:20			

APPENDIX H

Skateboarder Modeling Task

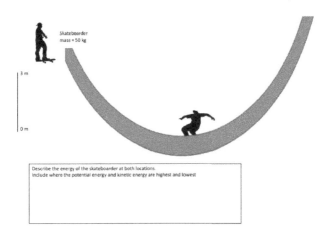

Describe the energy of the skateboarder at both locations.
Include where the potential energy and kinetic energy are highest and lowest

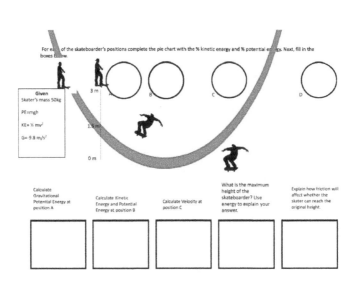

For each of the skateboarder's positions complete the pie chart with the % kinetic energy and % potential energy. Next, fill in the boxes below.

Given
Skater's mass 50kg

PE=mgh
KE= ½ mv²
G= 9.8 m/s²

| Calculate Gravitational Potential Energy at position A | Calculate Kinetic Energy and Potential Energy at position B | Calculate Velocity at position C | What is the maximum height of the skateboarder? Use energy to explain your answer. | Explain how friction will affect whether the skater can reach the original height. |

APPENDIX I

Sample Meeting Agendas for Collaborative Formative Assessment Design

Phase	Goals	Possible Activities	Resources	Suggested Readings
Introduction and overview	Learn about the design process Set a learning goal Establish norms for working together in PLC	Select & unpack one or more performance expectations	NGSS	Chapter 1 "A Virtuous Cycle" (Furtak & Heredia, 2016)
Explore student thinking	Discuss student ideas and identify possible learning targets	Examine student ideas Identify possible phenomena of interest to learners Discuss possible placement of formative assessment task in instructional unit	Student initial models Curriculum materials	Chapters 3 & 9

Phase	Goals	Possible Activities	Resources	Suggested Readings
Design/adapt formative assessment tasks	Design activities and practices that will surface range of student ideas and engagement in practice	Co-design or revise a formative assessment task Select & refine phenomenon to frame task	Curriculum materials Sample assessment tasks Appendix A Appendix C	Chapters 4 & 5
Plan/practice enacting tasks	Decide on teacher practices to go with the task. Anticipate student responses. Revise and finalize task.		Talk moves Enactment planner (Appendix F)	Chapters 6 & 7
Enact tasks with students	Enact the formative assessment task with students and collect data	Device to record audio/video Photos of students	Notecatcher Back-pocket questions	Chapters 6 & 7
Reflect, revise, and plan next steps	Reflect on student ideas that surfaced and how well the design of the activity met the intended goal	Video reflection Sorting activity	Classroom video/audio Student work samples Data analysis protocols	Chapters 7 & 8

APPENDIX J

Learning Progression Unit Planner

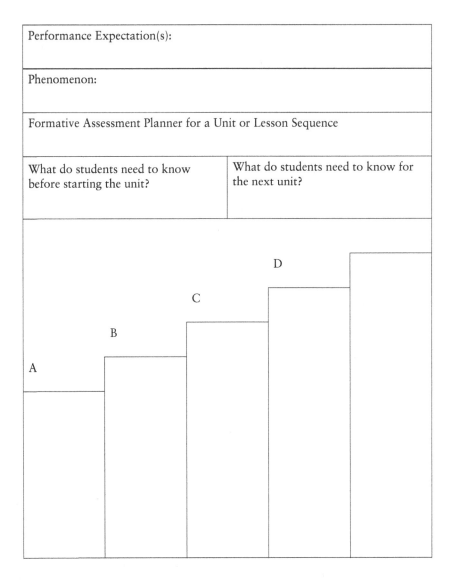

Learning Targets	Possible Indicators or Look-fors	Formative Assessments
		A—
		B—
		C—
		D—

References

Achieve, Inc. (2014). *NGSS/CCSS-M sample classroom assessment tasks*. Retrieved from www.nextgenscience.org/classroom-sample-assessment-tasks

Achieve, Inc. (2018). *Task annotation project in science*. www.achieve.org/our-initiatives/equip/toolssubject/science/task-annotation-project-science

Affolter, R., McNeill, K. L., & Brinza, G. (2022). Supporting trust, risk taking, and equity in your classroom. *Science Scope, 45*(5), 26–34.

Aikenhead, G. S., & Ogawa, M. (2007). Indigenous knowledge and science revisited. *Cultural Studies of Science Education, 2*(3), 539–620. https://doi.org/10.1007/s11422-007-9067-8

Alonzo, A. C., & Gotwals, A. W. (Eds.) (2012). *Learning progressions in science*. Sense Publishing.

Alonzo, A. C., & Steedle, J. T. (2009). Developing and assessing a force and motion learning progression. *Science Education, 93*(3), 389–421.

Alonzo, A. C., Wooten, M. M., & Christensen, J. (2022). Learning progressions as a simplified model: Examining teachers' reported uses to inform classroom assessment practices. *Science Education, 106*(4), 852–889. https://doi.org/10.1002/sce.21713

Ambitious Science Teaching. (n.d.). *High School • Gas Laws • Legacy Series*. https://ambitiousscienceteaching.org/high-school-%E2%80%A2-gas-laws-%E2%80%A2-legacy-series

American Educational Research Association, American Psychological Association, & National Council on Measurement in Education. (2014). *Standards for educational and psychological testing*. American Educational Research Association.

Andrade, H. G. (1999). *Student self-assessment: At the intersection of metacognition and authentic assessment*. http://ovidsp.ovid.com/ovidweb.cgi?T=JS&CSC=Y&NEWS=N&PAGE=fulltext&D=eric3&AN=ED431030

Au, W. (2009). *Unequal by design: High-stakes testing and the standardization of inequality*. Routledge.

Ayala, C. C., Shavelson, R. J., Ruiz-Primo, M. A., Brandon, P., Yin, Y., Furtak, E. M., Young, D. B., & Tomita, M. (2008). From formal embedded assessments to reflective lessons: The development of formative assessment suites. *Applied Measurement in Education, 21*(4), 315–334.

Bang, M. (2019, September 19). *Making assessment responsive to culturally and linguistically diverse students, families, and communities*. NCME Special

Conference on Classroom Assessment, Boulder, CO. https://youtu.be/NFKRrGcHzZk

Bang, M., & Medin, D. (2010). Cultural processes in science education: Supporting the navigation of multiple epistemologies. *Science Education*, 94(6), 1008–1026. https://doi.org/10.1002/sce.20392

Bang, M., Warren, B., Rosebery, A. S., & Medin, D. (2012). Desettling expectations in science education. *Human Development*, 55(5–6), 302–318. https://doi.org/10.1159/000345322

Banilower, E. R., Smith, P. S., Malzahn, K. A., Plumley, C. L., Gordon, E. M., & Hayes, M. L. (2018). *Report of the 2018 NSSME+*. Horizon Research Inc.

Beatty, I. D., & Gerace, W. J. (2009). Technology-enhanced formative assessment: A research-based pedagogy for teaching science with classroom response technology. *Educational Technology*, 18, 146–162. https://doi.org/10.1007/s10956-008-9140-4

Belczewski, A. (2009). Decolonizing science education and the science teacher: A white teacher's perspective. *Canadian Journal of Science, Mathematics and Technology Education*, 9(3), 191–202. https://doi.org/10.1080/14926150903118326

Bell, B., & Cowie, B. (2001). *Formative assessment and science education*. Kluwer Academic Publishers.

Bell, P., Morrison, D., & DeBarger, A. H. (2015). *How to launch STEM investigations that build on student and community interests and expertise* (No. 31). University of Washington. https://stemteachingtools.org/brief/31

Bennett, R. E. (2011). Formative assessment: A critical review. *Assessment in Education: Principles, Policy & Practice*, 18(1), 5–25. https://doi.org/10.1080/0969594X.2010.513678

Berland, L. K., & McNeill, K. L. (2010). A learning progression for scientific argumentation: Understanding student work and designing supportive instructional contexts. *Science Education*, 94(5), 765–793. https://doi.org/10.1002/sce.20402

Bernstein, B. (1996). *Pedagogy, symbolic control and identify*. Taylor & Francis.

Black, P., & Wiliam, D. (1998). Assessment and classroom learning. *Assessment in Education*, 5(1), 7–74.

Black, P., Wilson, M., & Yao, S.-Y. (2011). Road maps for learning: A guide to the navigation of learning progressions. *Measurement: Interdisciplinary Research & Perspective*, 9(2–3), 71–123. https://doi.org/10.1080/15366367.2011.591654

Board on Science Education. (2012). *A framework for K–12 science education: Practices, crosscutting concepts, and core ideas*.

Borko, H., Jacobs, J., Eiteljorg, E., & Pittman, M. (2008). Video as a tool for fostering productive discussions in mathematics professional development. *Teaching and Teacher Education*, 24(2), 417–436. https://doi.org/10.1016/j.tate.2006.11.012

Braaten, M., Bradford, C., Kirchgasler, K. L., & Barocas, S. F. (2017). How data use for accountability undermines equitable science education. *Journal of Educational Administration*, 55(4), 427–446. https://doi.org/10.1108/JEA-09-2016-0099

Briggs, D. C., Alonzo, A. C., Schwab, C., & Wilson, M. (2006). Diagnostic assessment with multiple-choice items. *Educational Assessment*, *11*(1), 33–63.

Briggs, D.C., Diaz-Bilello, E., Peck, F., Alzen, J., Chattergoon, R., & Johnson, R. (2015). Using a learning progression framework to assess and evaluate student growth. Boulder, CO: Center for Assessment, Design, Research and Evaluation (CADRE) and National Center for the Improvement of Educational Assessment.

Brown, B. (2019). *Science in the city: Culturally relevant STEM education*. Routledge.

Buell, J. Y. (2020). *Designing for relational science practices*. University of Colorado Boulder.

Buell, J. Y., Briggs, D. C., Burkhardt, A., Chattergoon, R., Fine, C.G.M., Furtak, E. M., Henson, K., Mahr, B., & Tayne, K. (2019a). *A learning progression for modeling energy flows in systems*. www.colorado.edu/cadre/sites/default/files/attached-files/report_-_a_learning_progression_for_modeling_energy_flows_in_systems.pdf

Buell, J., Furtak, E.M., Deverel-Rico, C. & Henson, K. (2019b, April 2). *Toward a framework for selecting phenomena at the intersection of curriculum and assessment*. [Paper presentation]. Association of Research in Science Teaching, Baltimore, MD.

Burgess, T., & Patterson Williams, A. (2022). Utilizing theory to elucidate the work of creating equity for transformation within the science classroom. *Science Education*, *106*(5), 1071–1083. https://doi.org/10.1002/sce.21721

Butler, R. (1987). Task-involving and ego-involving properties of evaluation: Effects of different feedback conditions on motivational perceptions, interest, and performance. *Journal of Educational Psychology*, *79*(4), 474–482.

Cazden, C. B. (2001). *Classroom discourse: The language of teaching and learning*. Heinemann.

Coffey, J. (2003). Involving students in assessment. In J. M. Atkin & J. E. Coffey (Eds.), *Everyday assessment in the science classroom* (pp. 75–87). NSTA Press.

Cohen, E. G. (1994). *Designing groupwork* (2nd ed.). Teachers College Press.

Collins, A. (1998). National science education standards: A political document. *Journal of Research in Science Teaching*, *35*(7), 711–727.

Corcoran, T., Mosher, F. A., & Rogat, A. (2009). Learning Progressions in Science: An Evidence-Based Approach to Reform. *CPRE Research Reports*. https://repository.upenn.edu/cpre_researchreports/53

Council, N. R. (1996). *National science education standards*. National Academy Press.

Council, N. R. (2014). *Developing assessments for the Next Generation Science Standards*. National Academies Press.

Covitt, B. A., Gunckel, K. L., Caplan, B., & Syswerda, S. (2018). Teachers' use of learning progression-based formative assessment in water instruction. *Applied Measurement in Education*, *31*(2), 128–142. https://doi.org/10.1080/08957347.2017.1408627

Cowie, B., Jones, A., & Otrel-Cass, K. (2011). Re-engaging students in science: Issues of assessment, funds of knowledge and sites for learning. *International Journal of Science and Mathematics Education*, *9*(2), 347–366. https://doi.org/10.1007/s10763-010-9229-0

Debarger, A. H., Penuel, W. R., Moorthy, S., Beauvineau, Y., Kennedy, C. A., & Boscardin, C. (2017). Investigating purposeful science curriculum adaptation as a strategy to improve teaching and learning. *Science Education, 101*(1), 66–98. https://doi.org/10.1002/sce.21249

Deverel-Rico, C. & Furtak, E.M. (2022). *Students' differential opportunities for sensemaking in two teachers' enactments of a co-designed formative assessment task*. [Paper presentation]. Annual Meeting of the American Educational Research Association, San Diego, CA.

Dini, V., Sevian, H., Caushi, K., & Picón, R. O. (2020). Characterizing the formative assessment enactment of experienced science teachers. *Science Education, 104*(2), 290–325. https://doi.org/10.1002/sce.21559

Donovan, B. M. (2014). Playing with fire? The impact of the hidden curriculum in school genetics on essentialist conceptions of race. *Journal of Research in Science Teaching, 51*(4), 462–496. https://doi.org/10.1002/tea.21138

Dunn, K. E., & Mulvenon, S. W. (2009). A critical review of research on formative assessment: The limited scientific evidence of the impact of formative assessment in education. *Practical Assessment, Research and Evaluation, 14*(7), 1–11.

Duschl, R. A., & Gitomer, D. H. (1997). Strategies and challenges to changing the focus of assessment and instruction in science classrooms. *Educational Assessment, 4*(1), 37–73. https://doi.org/10.1207/s15326977ea0401

Duschl, R., Maeng, S., & Sezen, A. (2011). Learning progressions and teaching sequences: A review and analysis. *Studies in Science Education, 47*(2), 123–182. https://doi.org/10.1080/03057267.2011.604476

Edelson, D. C., Reiser, B. J., McNeill, K. L., Mohan, A., Novak, M., Mohan, L., Affolter, R., . . . & Suárez, E. (2021). Developing research-based instructional materials to support large-scale transformation of science teaching and learning: The approach of the OpenSciEd middle school program. *Journal of Science Teacher Education, 32*(7), 780–804. https://doi.org/10.1080/1046560X.2021.1877457

Engeström, Y. (1987). *Learning by expanding: An activity-theoretical approach to developmental research* (2nd ed.). Cambridge University Press. https://lchc.ucsd.edu/mca/Paper/Engestrom/Learning-by-Expanding.pdf

Engeström, Y. (1999). Expansive visibilization of work: An activity-theoretical perspective. *Computer-Supported Cooperative Work, 8*, 63–93.

Engeström, Y. (2001). Expansive learning at work: Toward an activity theoretical reconceptualization. *Journal of Education and Work, 14*(1), 133–156. https://doi.org/10.1080/13639080020028747

Engle, R. A., & Conant, F. R. (2002). Guiding principles for fostering productive disciplinary engagement: Explaining an emergent argument in a community of learners classroom. *Cognition and Instruction, 20*(4), 399–483. https://doi.org/10.1207/S1532690XCI2004_1

Filsecker, M., & Kerres, M. (2012). Repositioning formative assessment from an educational assessment perspective: A response to Dunn & Mulvenon (2009). *Practical Assessment, Research, and Evaluation, 17*(16), 1–9.

Fine, C. (2021). *Co-designing for translanguaging in middle school science formative assessment*. Doctoral dissertation, University of Colorado Boulder.

Fine, C. G. (2022). Translanguaging interpretive power in formative assessment co-design: A catalyst for science teacher agentive shifts. *Journal of Language, Identity & Education*, 21(3), 191–211. https://doi.org/10.1080/15348458.2022.2058858

Fine, C., & Furtak, E. M. (2020a). A framework for science classroom assessment task design for emergent bilingual learners. *Science Education*, 104(3), 393–420. https://doi.org/10.1002/sce.21565

Fine, C., & Furtak, E. M. (2020b). Science classroom assessments that work for emergent bilingual learners. *The Science Teacher*, 87(9), 38–48.

Flores, N., & García, E. S. (2022). Power, language, and bilingual learners. In N. S. Nasir, C. D. Lee, R. Pea, & M. McKinney de Royston (Eds.), *Handbook of the cultural foundations of learning* (pp. 178–192). Taylor & Francis.

Ford, M. J., & Forman, E. A. (2006). Chapter 1: Redefining disciplinary learning in classroom contexts. *Review of Research in Education*, 30(1), 1–32. https://doi.org/10.3102/0091732X030001001

Freire, P. (1968). *Pedagogy of the oppressed*. Continuum.

Furtak, E. M. (2006). *The dilemma of guidance in scientific inquiry teaching*. Stanford University Press.

Furtak, E. M. (2012). Linking a learning progression for natural selection to teachers' enactment of formative assessment. *Journal of Research in Science Teaching*, 49(9), 1181–1210. https://doi.org/10.1002/tea.21054

Furtak, E. M., Badrinarayan, A., Penuel, W. R., Duwe, S., & Patrick-Stuart, R. (2021). *Assessment of crosscutting concepts: Creating opportunities for sensemaking*. National Science Teachers' Association Press.

Furtak, E. M., Bakeman, R., & Buell, J. Y. (2018). Developing knowledge-in-action with a learning progression: Sequential analysis of teachers' questions and responses to student ideas. *Teaching and Teacher Education*, 76, 267–282. https://doi.org/10.1016/j.tate.2018.06.001

Furtak, E. M., & Deverel-Rico, C. (2021). *Two paradigms for formative assessment and their consequences for opportunity to participate in science learning* [Paper presentation]. American Educational Research Association Annual Meeting, April 11, 2021 [Virtual conference].

Furtak, E. M., Deverel-Rico, C., Student, S. R., & Burkhardt, A. (2023). How can crosscutting concepts organize formative assessments across science classrooms? Results of a video study. Annual Meeting of the American Educational Research Association, Chicago, IL.

Furtak, E. M., Glasser, H., & Wolfe, Z. (2016). *The feedback loop: Using formative assessment data to inform science teaching and learning*. NSTA Press.

Furtak, E. M., & Heredia, S. (2014). Exploring the influence of learning progressions in two teacher communities. *Journal of Research in Science Teaching*, 51(8), 982–1020.

Furtak, E. M., & Heredia, S. C. (2016). A virtuous cycle: Using the formative assessment design cycle to support the NGSS. *The Science Teacher*, 83(2), 36–42.

Furtak, E. M., Heredia, S. C., & Morrison, D. (2019). Formative assessment in science education: Mapping a shifting terrain. In H. Andrade, R. Bennett, & G. Cizek (Eds.), *Handbook of Formative Assessment in the Disciplines* (pp. 97–125). Taylor & Francis.

Furtak, E. M., Kiemer, K., Circi, R. K., Swanson, R., León, V. de, Morrison, D., & Heredia, S. C. (2016). Teachers' formative assessment abilities and their relationship to student learning: Findings from a four-year intervention study. *Instructional Science*, *44*(3), 267–291. https://doi.org/10.1007/s11251-016-9371-3

Furtak, E. M., & Kunter, M. (2012). Effects of autonomy-supportive teaching on student learning and motivation. *The Journal of Experimental Education*, *80*(3), 284–316. https://doi.org/10.1080/00220973.2011.573019

Furtak, E. M., & Lee, O. (In Press). *Equity and justice in classroom assessment of STEM subjects*. Community for Advancing Discovery Research in Education (CADRE).

Furtak, E. M., Morrison, D. L., & Kroog, H. (2014). Investigating the link between learning progressions and classroom assessment. *Science Education*, *98*, 640–673.

Furtak, E. M., Ruiz-Primo, M. A., Shemwell, J. T., Ayala, C. C., Brandon, P. R., Shavelson, R. J., & Yin, Y. (2008). On the fidelity of implementing embedded formative assessments and its relation to student learning. *Applied Measurement in Education*, *21*(4). https://doi.org/10.1080/08957340802347852

Furtak, E. M., & Tayne, K. (2019). Affordances and constraints of learning progression designs in supporting formative assessment. In *Bridging research and practice in science education: Selected papers from the ESERA 2017 conference*. Springer.

Garner, B., Thorne, J. K., & Horn, I. S. (2017). Teachers interpreting data for instructional decisions: Where does equity come in? *Journal of Educational Administration*, *55*(4), 407–426. https://doi.org/10.1108/JEA-09-2016-0106

Gee, J. P. (2001). Identity as an analytic lens for research. *Review of Research in Education*, *25*, 99–125.

Gee, J. P. (2008a). A sociocultural perspective on opportunity to learn. In P. A. Moss, D. C. Pullin, J. P. Gee, E. H. Haertel, & L. J. Young (Eds.), *Assessment, equity, and opportunity to learn* (pp. 76–108). Cambridge University Press.

Gee, J. P. (2008b). What is academic language? In A. S. Rosebery & B. Warren (Eds.), *Teaching science to English language learners: Building on students' strengths* (pp. 57–70). VANSTA.

Gipps, C. (1999). Chapter 10: Socio-cultural aspects of assessment. *Review of Research in Education*, *24*(1), 355–392. https://doi.org/10.3102/0091732x024001355

Gitomer, D. H., & Duschl, R. A. (1998). Emerging issues and practices in science assessment. In B. J. Fraser & K. G. Tobin (Eds.), *International handbook of science education* (pp. 791–810). Kluwer Academic Publishers.

González, N., & Moll, L. C. (2002). Cruzando el Puente: Building bridges to funds of knowledge. *Educational Policy*, *16*(4), 623–641. https://doi.org/10.1177/0895904802016004009

Gould, S. J. (1981). *The mismeasure of man*. W. W. Norton & Company.

Grapin, S. E., Llosa, L., Haas, A., & Lee, O. (2021). Rethinking instructional strategies with English learners in the content areas. *TESOL Journal*, *12*(2). https://doi.org/10.1002/tesj.557

Gravel, B. E., Wright, C. G., Tucker-Raymond, E., Milner, A., Fair, S., & Alvarado, A. (2022). "They know, but they don't know": Expanding relationality

through hip hop making. Annual Meeting of the American Educational Research Association.
Gunckel, K. L., Covitt, B. Salinas, I., & Anderson, C. W. (2012). A learning progression for water in socio-ecological systems. *Journal of Research in Science Teaching, 49*(7), 843–868. https://doi.org/10.1002/tea.21024
Gutiérrez, R. (2008). A "gap-gazing" fetish in mathematics education? Problematizing research on the achievement gap. *Journal for Research in Mathematics Education, 39*(4), 357–364. https://doi.org/10.2307/40539302
Gutiérrez, K., & Rogoff, B. (2003). Cultural ways of learning: Individual traits or repertoires of practice. *Educational Researcher, 32*(5), 19–25.
Harding, S. (2008). *Sciences from below: Feminisms, postcolonialities, and modernities*. Duke University Press.
Hattie, J., & Timperley, H. (2007). The power of feedback. *Review of Educational Research, 77*(1), 81–112.
Henson, K. (2019). Designing tools to support teacher activity focused on student thinking to inform instruction. Doctoral dissertation, University of Colorado Boulder.
Heredia, S.C., Furtak, E.M., Morrison, D.L. & Gröschner, A. (2021). The disciplinary nature of science teachers' talk in the process of formative assessment design. In de E. Vries, Y. Hod, & J. Ahn (Eds.), Proceedings of the 15th International Conference of the Learning Sciences—ICLS 2021 (pp. 729–732). International Society of the Learning Sciences.
Heritage, M., Kim, J., Vendlinski, T., & Herman, J. (2009). From evidence to action: A seamless process in formative assessment? *Educational Measurement: Issues and Practice, 28*(3), 24–31. https://doi.org/10.1111/j.1745-3992.2009.00151.x
Hickey, D. T. (2015). A situative response to the conundrum of formative assessment. *Assessment in Education: Principles, Policy & Practice, 22*(2), 202–223. https://doi.org/10.1080/0969594X.2015.1015404
Holmeier, M., Grob, R., Nielsen, J. A., Rönnebeck, S., & Ropohl, M. (2018). Written teacher feedback: Aspects of quality, benefits and challenges. In *Transforming assessment: contributions from science education research* (Vol. 4, pp. 175–208). Springer International Publishing. https://doi.org/10.1007/978-3-319-63248-3
Hondrich, A. L., Hertel, S., Adl-Amini, K., & Klieme, E. (2016). Implementing curriculum-embedded formative assessment in primary school science classrooms. *Assessment in Education: Principles, Policy & Practice, 23*(3), 353–376. https://doi.org/10.1080/0969594X.2015.1049113
Horn, I. S., & Little, J. W. (2010). Attending to problems of practice: Routines and resources for professional learning in teachers' workplace interactions. *American Educational Research Journal, 47*(1), 181–217. https://doi.org/10.3102/0002831209345158
Jin, H., Choi, J., & Anderson, C. W. (2009). Development and validation of assessments for a learning progression on carbon cycling in socio-ecological systems. *Journal of Research in Science Teaching, 46*(6), 675–698.
Jordan, B., & Putz, P. (2004). Assessment as practice: Notes on measures, tests, and targets. *Human Organization, 63*(3), 346–358. https://doi.org/10.17730/humo.63.3.yj2w5y9tmblc422k

Kang, H. (2022). Teacher responsiveness that promotes equity in secondary science classrooms. *Cognition and Instruction*, *40*(2), 206–232. https://doi.org/10.1080/07370008.2021.1972423

Kang, H., & Furtak, E. M. (2021). Learning theory, classroom assessment, and equity. *Educational Measurement: Issues and Practice*, *40*(3), 73–82. https://doi.org/10.1111/emip.12423

Kang, H., Talafian, H., & Tschida, P. (2022). Expanding opportunities to learn in secondary science classrooms using unconventional forms of classroom assessments. *Journal of Research in Science Teaching*. https://doi.org/10.1002/tea.21824

Kang, H., Thompson, J., & Windschitl, M. (2014). Creating opportunities for students to show what they know: The role of scaffolding in assessment tasks. *Science Education*, *98*(4), 674–704. https://doi.org/10.1002/sce.21123

Kang, H., Windschitl, M., Stroupe, D., & Thompson, J. (2016). Designing, launching, and implementing high-quality learning opportunities for students that advance scientific thinking. *Journal of Research in Science Teaching*, *53*(9), 1316–1340. https://doi.org/10.1002/tea.21329

Kimmerer, R. W. (2013). *Braiding sweetgrass*. Milkweed Editions.

Kluger, A. N., & DeNisi, A. (1996). The effects of feedback interventions on performance: A historical review, a meta-analysis, and a preliminary feedback intervention theory. *Psychological Bulletin*, *119*, 254–284.

Kumashiro, K. K. (2000). Toward a theory of anti-oppressive education. *Review of Educational Research, 70*(I), 25–53.

Lampert, M., Franke, M. L., Kazemi, E., Ghousseini, H., Turrou, A. C., Beasley, H., Cunard, A., & Crowe, K. (2013). Keeping it complex: Using rehearsals to support novice teacher learning of ambitious teaching. *Journal of Teacher Education*, *64*(3), 226–243. https://doi.org/10.1177/0022487112473837

Latour, B. (2018). *Down to Earth: Politics in the new climatic regime*. Polity Press.

Latour, B., & Woolgar, S. (1979). *Laboratory life: The construction of scientific facts*. Princeton University Press.

Lave, J., & Wenger, E. (1991). *Situated learning: Legitimate peripheral participation*. University of Cambridge Press.

Learning in Places Collaborative. (2021). *Educator frameworks and storylines*. http://learninginplaces.org/

Lee, O., & Grapin, S. E. (2022). The role of phenomena and problems in science and STEM education: Traditional, contemporary, and future approaches. *Journal of Research in Science Teaching*, *59*(7), 1301–1309. https://doi.org/10.1002/tea.21776

Lee, O., Llosa, L., Grapin, S., Haas, A., & Goggins, M. (2019). Science and language integration with English learners: A conceptual framework guiding instructional materials development. *Science Education*, *103*(2), 317–337. https://doi.org/10.1002/sce.21498

Lee, O., Llosa, L., Jiang, F., Haas, A., O'Connor, C., & Booven, C. (2016). Elementary teachers' science knowledge and instructional practices: Impact of an intervention focused on English language learners. *Journal of Research in Science Teaching*, *53*(4), 579–597. https://doi.org/10.1002/tea.21314

Lee, O., Quinn, H., & Valdes, G. (2013). Science and language for English language learners in relation to Next Generation Science Standards and with implications for Common Core State Standards for English language arts and mathematics. *Educational Researcher*, 42(4), 223–233. https://doi.org/10.3102/0013189X13480524

Lehrer, R., & Schauble, L. (2012). Seeding evolutionary thinking by engaging children in modeling its foundations. *Science Education*, 96(4), 701–724. https://doi.org/10.1002/sce.20475

Lemke, J. L. (1990). *Talking science: Language, learning, and values*. Ablex Publishing Corporation.

Likely, R. (2022). Learning through the curls: How hair culture can expand science and social studies. *Black History Bulletin*, 85(2), 30–32. https://doi.org/10.1353/bhb.2022.0010

Likely, R., & Wright, C. (2022). The journey of decolonization as a scientist and science education researcher. In A. J. Rodriguez & R. L. Suriel (Eds.), *Equity in STEM education research* (Vol. 26, pp. 147–167). Springer International Publishing. https://doi.org/10.1007/978-3-031-08150-7_8

Little, J. W. (2003). Inside teacher community: Representations of classroom practice. *Teachers College Record*, 105(6), 913–945. https://doi.org/10.1111/1467-9620.00273

Looney, A., Cumming, J., Kleij, F. van D., & Harris, K. (2018). Reconceptualising the role of teachers as assessors: Teacher assessment identity. *Assessment in Education: Principles, Policy and Practice*, 25(5), 442–467. https://doi.org/10.1080/0969594X.2016.1268090

Love, B. L. (2019). *We want to do more than survive*. Beacon.

Lowell, B. R., Cherbow, K., & McNeill, K. L. (2022). Considering discussion types to support collective sensemaking during a storyline unit. *Journal of Research in Science Teaching*, 59(2), 195–222. https://doi.org/10.1002/tea.21725

Luehmann, A. (2007). Identity development as a lens to science teacher preparation. *Science Education*, 91(5), 822–839. https://doi.org/10.1002/sce

Madkins, T. C., & McKinney de Royston, M. (2019). Illuminating political clarity in culturally relevant science instruction. *Science Education*, 103(6), 1319–1346. https://doi.org/10.1002/sce.21542

Marin, A., & Bang, M. (2018). "Look it, this is how you know:" Family forest walks as a context for knowledge-building about the natural world. *Cognition and Instruction*, 36(2), 89–118. https://doi.org/10.1080/07370008.2018.1429443

McNeill, K. L., Lizotte, D. J., Krajcik, J., & Marx, R. W. (2006). Supporting students' construction of scientific explanations by fading scaffolds in instructional materials. *The Journal of the Learning Sciences*, 15(2), 153–191.

Menken, K. (2006). Teaching to the test: How No Child Left Behind impacts language policy, curriculum, and instruction for English language learners. *Bilingual Research Journal*, 30(2), 521–546. https://doi.org/10.1080/15235882.2006.10162888

Michaels, S., O'Connor, M.C., Hall, M. W., & Resnick, L. B. (2010). *Accountable talk sourcebook: For classroom conversation that works*. University of Pittsburgh, Learning Research and Development Center.

Minstrell, J., Anderson, R., Kraus, P., & Minstrell, J. (2008). From practice to research and back: Perspectives and tools in assessing for learning. In *Assessing science learning: Perspectives from research and practice* (pp. 37–68). National Science Teachers' Association Press.

Mohan, L., Chen, J., & Anderson, C. W. (2009). Developing a multi-year learning progression for carbon cycling in socio-ecological systems. *Journal of Research in Science Teaching, 46*(6), 675–698. https://doi.org/10.1002/tea.20314

Morales-Doyle, D. (2017). Justice-centered science pedagogy: A catalyst for academic achievement and social transformation. *Science Education, 101*(6), 1034–1060. https://doi.org/10.1002/sce.21305

Morrison, D. L. (2015). Formative assessment and equity: An exploration of opportunities for eliciting, recognizing, and responding within science classroom conversations. Doctoral dissertation, University of Colorado Boulder.

Moss, P. A. (2008). Sociocultural implications for assessment I. In *Assessment, equity, and opportunity to learn*. Cambridge University Press.

Moss, P. A., Girard, B. J., & Greeno, J. G. (2008). Sociocultural implications for assessment II: Professional learning, evaluation, and accountability. In *Assessment, Equity, and Opportunity to Learn*. Cambridge University Press.

Nasir, N. S., Lee, C. D., Pea, R., & McKinney de Royston, M. (2022). *Handbook of the cultural foundations of learning*. Taylor and Francis.

National Academies of Science, Engineering and Medicine. (2018). *How people learn II: Learners, contexts and cultures*. National Academies Press.

National Academies of Science, Engineering and Medicine. (2019). *Science and engineering for grades 6–12: Investigation and design at the center* (p. 25216). National Academies Press. https://doi.org/10.17226/25216

National Academies of Sciences, Engineering, and Medicine. (2022). *Science and engineering in preschool through elementary grades: The brilliance of children and the strengths of educators* (E. A. Davis & A. Stephens, Eds.; p. 26215). National Academies Press. https://doi.org/10.17226/26215

National Research Council. (2014). *Developing assessments for the next generation Science standards*. National Academies Press.

National Science Teachers Association. (n.d). *Matrix of crosscutting concepts in NGSS*. https://static.nsta.org/ngss/MatrixOfCrosscuttingConcepts.pdf

Next Generation Storylines & iHub. (2019). *Why don't antibiotics work like they used to?* www.nextgenscience.org

NGSS Lead States. 2013. *Next generation science standards: For states, by states*. Washington, DC: The National Academies Press.

Noble, T., Suarez, C., Rosebery, A., O'Connor, M. C., Warren, B., & Hudicourt-Barnes, J. (2012). "I never thought of it as freezing": How students answer questions on large-scale science tests and what they know about science. *Journal of Research in Science Teaching, 49*(6), 778–803. https://doi.org/10.1002/tea.21026

Odden, T.O.B., & Russ, R. S. (2019). Defining sensemaking: Bringing clarity to a fragmented theoretical construct. *Science Education, 103*(1), 187–205. https://doi.org/10.1002/sce.21452

OpenSciEd. (2020a). *OpenSciEd teacher handbook, Version 3.0*. OpenSciEd.org

OpenSciEd. (2020b). *OpenSciEd unit 6.2: Thermal energy: How can containers keep stuff from warming up or cooling down?* Openscied.org

OpenSciEd. (2021). *Covid-19 & health equity unit, grades K–2: What can we do to keep our community healthy?* Openscied.org

OpenSciEd. (2022a). *OpenSciEd unit 6.6: Cells & systems: How do living things heal?* Openscied.org

OpenSciEd. (2022b). *OpenSciEd unit 7.6: Earth's resources and human impact: How do changes in Earth's system impact our communities and what can we do about it?* Openscied.org

OpenSciEd. (n.d.). *Intentional use of classroom routines.* www.openscied.org/intentional-use-of-classroom-routines

Otero, V., & Nathan, M. J. (2008). Preservice elementary teachers' views of their students' prior knowledge of science. *Journal of Research in Science Teaching, 45*(4), 497–523.

Paris, D. (2012). Culturally sustaining pedagogy. *Educational Researcher, 41*(3), 93–97. https://doi.org/10.3102/0013189x12441244

Paris, D., & Alim, H. S. (2017). *Culturally sustaining pedagogies: Teaching and learning for justice in a changing world.* Teachers College Press.

Patterson Williams, A. D., Athanases, S. Z., Higgs, J., & Martinez, D. C. (2020). Developing an inner witness to notice for equity in the fleeting moments of talk for content learning. *Equity & Excellence in Education 53*(4), 504–517.

Pellegrino, J. W., Chudowsky, N., & Glaser, R. (2001). *Knowing what students know: The science and design of educational assessment.* National Academies Press.

Penuel, W. R., Bell, P., & Neill, T. (2020). Creating a system of professional learning that meets teachers' needs. *Phi Delta Kappan, 101*(8), 37–41. https://doi.org/10.1177/0031721720923520

Penuel, W. R., Van Horne, K., Turner, M. L., Jacobs, J. K., & Sumner, T. (2019). Developing tasks to assess phenomenon-based science learning: Challenges and lessons learned from building proximal transfer tasks. *Science Education, 103*(6), 1367–1395. https://doi.org/10.1002/sce.21544

Penuel, W. R., & Shepard, L. A. (2016). Assessment and teaching. In D. H. Gitomer & C. Bell (Eds.), *Handbook of research on teaching* (5th ed., pp. 787–850). American Educational Research Association.

Penuel, W. R., & Van Horne, K. (2018). *Practice brief 41: Prompts for integrating crosscutting concepts into assessment and instruction* (STEM Teaching Tools Initiative, Institute for Science + Math Education). University of Washington. https://stemteachingtools.org/brief/41

Philip, T. M., & Azevedo, F. S. (2017). Everyday science learning and equity: Mapping the contested terrain. *Science Education, 101*(4), 526–532. https://doi.org/10.1002/sce.21286

Pickering, A. (1995). *The mangle of practice: Time, agency, and science.* University of Chicago Press.

Pierson, A. E., Clark, D. B., & Sherard, M. K. (2017). Learning progressions in context: Tensions and insights from a semester-long middle school modeling curriculum. *Science Education, 101*(6), 1061–1088. https://doi.org/10.1002/sce.21314

Plummer, J. D., & Krajcik, J. (2010). Building a learning progression for celestial motion: Elementary levels from an earth-based perspective. *Journal of Research in Science Teaching, 47*(7), 768–787. https://doi.org/10.1002/tea.20355

Posner, G., Strike, K. A., Hewson, P., & Gertzog, W. (1982). Accommodation of a scientific conception: Toward a theory of conceptual change. *Science Education, 66*(2), 211–227.

Pryor, J., & Crossouard, B. (2008). A socio-cultural theorisation of formative assessment. *Oxford Review of Education, 34*(1), 1–20. https://doi.org/10.1080/03054980701476386

Pryor, J., & Crossouard, B. (2010). Challenging formative assessment: Disciplinary spaces and identities. *Assessment and Evaluation in Higher Education, 35*(3), 265–276. https://doi.org/10.1080/02602930903512891

Randall, J. (2021). Color neutral is not a thing. *Educational Measurement: Issues and Practice, 40*(4), 82–90.

Randall, J., Poe, M., & Slomp, D. (2021). Ain't oughta be in the dictionary: Getting to justice by dismantling anti-black literacy assessment practices. *Journal of Adolescent and Adult Literacy, 64*(5), 594–599. https://doi.org/10.1002/jaal.1142

Robertson, A. D., Atkins, L. J., Levin, D. M., & Richards, J. (2016). What is responsive teaching? In A. D. Robertson, R. Scherr, and D. Hammer (Eds.), *Responsive Teaching in Science and Mathematics* (pp. 1–25). Routledge.

Rosebery, A. S., Ogonowski, M., DiSchino, M., & Warren, B. (2010). "The coat traps all your body heat": Heterogeneity as fundamental to learning. *Journal of the Learning Sciences, 19*(3), 322–357. https://doi.org/10.1080/10508406.2010.491752

Rudolph, J. L. (2002). *Scientists in the classroom: The cold reconstruction of American science education*. Palgrave.

Ruiz-Primo, M. A., Briggs, D. C., Iverson, H., Talbot, R. M., & Shepard, L. (2011). Impact of undergraduate science course innovations on learning. *Science, 331*(6022), 1269–1270.

Ruiz-Primo, M. A., & Furtak, E. M. (2006). Informal formative assessment and scientific inquiry: Exploring teachers' practices and student learning. *Educational Assessment, 11*(3–4), 237–263.

Ruiz-Primo, M. A., & Furtak, E. M. (2007). Exploring teachers' informal formative assessment practices and students' understanding in the context of scientific inquiry. *Journal of Research in Science Teaching, 44*(1), 57–84.

Ruiz-Primo, M. A., & Li, M. (2004). On the use of students' science notebooks as an assessment tool. *Studies in Educational Evaluations in Educational Evaluation, 30*, 61–85. https://doi.org/10.1016/j.stueduc.2004.03.004

Sadler, D. R. (1989). Formative assessment and the design of instructional systems. *Instructional Science, 18*, 119–144.

Schmidt, W. H., McKnight, C. C., & Raizen, S. A. (1997). *A splintered vision: An investigation of U.S. science and mathematics education*. Kluwer Academic Publishers.

Schwarz, C. V., Reiser, B. J., Davis, E., Kenyon, L., Achér, A., Fortus, D., Shwartz, Y., Hug, B., & Krajcik, J. (2009). Developing a learning progression for scientific modeling: Making scientific modeling accessible and meaningful for learners. *Journal of Research in Science Teaching, 46*(6), 632–654. https://doi.org/10.1002/tea.20311

Scott, P., Mortimer, E. F., & Aguiar, Or. G. (2006). The tension between authoritative and dialogic discourse: A fundamental characteristic of meaning making interactions in high school science lessons. *Science Education, 90*(4), 605–631.

Shavelson, R. J. (2009). Reflections on learning progressions. In *Proceedings of Learning Progressions in Science Conference*: https://education.msu.edu/projects/leaps/proceedings/Shavelson.pdf

Shavelson, R. J., Yin, Y., Furtak, E. M., Ruiz-Primo, M. A., Ayala, C. C., Young, D. B., Tomita, . . . & Pottenger, F. M. (2008). On the role and impact of formative assessment on science inquiry teaching and learning. In J. Coffey, R. Douglas, & C. Stearns (Eds.), *Assessing science learning* (pp. 21–36). NSTA Press.

Shavelson, R. J., Young, D. B., Ayala, C. C., Brandon, P. R., Furtak, E. M., Ruiz-Primo, M. A., Tomita, M., & Yin, Y. (2008). On the impact of curriculum-embedded formative assessment on learning: A collaboration between curriculum and assessment developers. *Applied Measurement in Education*, 21(4), 295–314.

Shepard, L. A. (2021). Ambitious teaching and equitable assessment. *American Educator, Fall*, 1–10. https://www.aft.org/ae/fall2021/shepard

Shepard, L. A. (2000). The role of assessment in a learning culture. *Educational Researcher*, 29(7), 4–14. https://doi.org/10.3102/0013189X029007004

Shepard, L. A. (2009). Commentary: Evaluating the validity of formative and interim assessment. *Educational Measurement: Issues and Practice*, 28(3), 32–37. https://doi.org/10.1111/j.1745-3992.2009.00152.x

Shepard, L. A., Penuel, W. R., & Pellegrino, J. W. (2018). Using learning and motivation theories to coherently link formative assessment, grading practices, and large-scale assessment. *Educational Measurement: Issues and Practice*, 37(1), 21–34.

Sherin, M., & van Es, E. (2003). A new lens on teaching: Learning to notice. *Mathematics Teaching in the Middle School*, 9(2), 92–95.

Smith, J. B., Lee, V. E., & Newmann, F. M. (2001). *Achievement in Chicago elementary schools*. Consortium on Chicago School Research.

Smylie, M. A., & Wenzel, S. A. (2006). *Promoting instructional improvement*. Consortium on Chicago School Research.

Songer, N. B., Kelcey, B., & Gotwals, A. W. (2009). How and when does complex reasoning occur? Empirically driven development of a learning progression focused on complex reasoning about biodiversity. *Journal of Research in Science Teaching*, 46(6), 610–633.

Spencer, M. B., Offidani-Bertrand, C., Harris, K., & Velez, G. (2022). Examining links between culture, identity, and learning. In N. Nasir, C. Lee, R. Pea, & M. McKinney de Royston (Eds.), *Handbook of the Cultural Foundations of Learning* (pp. 44–61). Taylor & Francis.

Suárez, E. (2020). "Estoy Explorando Science": Emergent bilingual students problematizing electrical phenomena through translanguaging. *Science Education*, 104(5), 791–826. https://doi.org/10.1002/sce.21588

Taylor, C. S. (2022). *Culturally and socially responsible assessment: Theory, research, and practice*. Teachers College Press.

Tekkumru-Kisa, M., & Stein, M. K. (2015). Learning to see teaching in new ways: A foundation for maintaining cognitive demand. *American Educational Research Journal*, 52(1), 105–136. https://doi.org/10.3102/0002831214549452

Tekkumru-Kisa, M., Stein, M. K., & Doyle, W. (2020a). Theory and research on tasks revisited: Task as a context for students' thinking in the era of ambitious reforms in mathematics and Science. *Educational Researcher, X49*(8), 606–617. https://doi.org/10.3102/0013189X20932480

Tekkumru-Kisa, M., Kisa, Z., & Hiester, H. (2020b). Intellectual work required of students in science classrooms: Students' opportunities to learn science. *Research in Science Education*. https://doi.org/10.1007/s11165-020-09924-y

TERC. (2011). *The inquiry project: Seeing the world through a scientist's eyes.* https://inquiryproject.terc.edu

Thompson, J. J., Hagenah, S., McDonald, S., & Barchenger, C. (2019). Toward a practice-based theory for how professional learning communities engage in the improvement of tools and practices for scientific modeling. *Science Education, 103*(6), 1423–1455. https://doi.org/10.1002/sce.21547

Thompson, J., Richards, J., Shim, S.-Y., Lohwasser, K., Esch, K. S. V., Chew, C., Sjoberg, B., & Morris, A. (2019). Launching networked PLCs: Footholds into creating and improving knowledge of ambitious and equitable teaching practices in an RPP. *AERA Open, 5*(3). https://doi.org/10.1177/2332858419875718

Thompson, J., Windschitl, M., & Braaten, M. (2013). Developing a theory of ambitious early-career teacher practice. *American Educational Research Journal, 50*(3), 574–615. https://doi.org/10.3102/0002831213476334

Tzou, C., Bang, M., & Bricker, L. (2021). Commentary: Designing science instructional materials that contribute to more just, equitable, and culturally thriving learning and teaching in science education. *Journal of Science Teacher Education, 32*(7), 858–864. https://doi.org/10.1080/1046560X.2021.1964786

Tzou, C., Meixi, Suárez, E., Bell, P., LaBonte, D., Starks, E., & Bang, M. (2019). Storywork in STEM-art: Making, materiality and robotics within everyday acts of Indigenous presence and resurgence. *Cognition and Instruction, 37*(3), 306–326. https://doi.org/10.1080/07370008.2019.1624547

van der Veen, S., & Furtak, E. M. (2017). What's wrong with imagining you're a 5th grader? *Phi Delta Kappan, 98*(8), 80.

van Es, E. A., Hand, V., & Mercado, J. (2017). Teacher noticing: Bridging and broadening perspectives, contexts, and frameworks. https://doi.org/10.1007/978-3-319-46753-5

Van Horne, K., Penuel, W. R., & Bell, P. (2016). *Practice brief 30: Integrating science practices into assessment tasks.* STEM Teaching Tools Initiative, Institute for Science + Math Education. University of Washington. https://stemteachingtools.org/brief/30

vanZee, E., & Minstrell, J. (1997). Using questioning to guide student thinking. *The Journal of the Learning Sciences, 6*(2), 227–269.

Vossoughi, S., Hooper, P.A.K., & Escudé, M. (2016). Making through the lens of culture visions for educational equity. *Harvard Educational Review, 86*(2), 206–232. https://doi.org/10.17763/0017-8055.86.2.206

Wenger, E. (1998). *Communities of practice: Learning, meaning, and identity.* Cambridge University Press.

Wertsch, J. V. (1998). *Mind as action.* Oxford University Press.

Whitcomb, J. A. (2013). Learning and pedagogy in initial teacher preparation. In I. B. Weiner (Ed.), *Handbook of psychology* (2nd ed., pp. 441–463). John Wiley & Sons.

White, B. Y., & Frederiksen, J. R. (1998). Inquiry, modeling, and metacognition: Making science accessible to all students. *Cognition and Instruction*, *16*(1), 3–118.
White, R., & Gunstone, R. (1992). *Probing understanding*. Falmer.
Wiliam, D. (2007). Keeping learning on track: Classroom assessment and the regulation of learning. In F. K. Lester (Ed.), *Second handbook of mathematics teaching and learning* (pp. 1053–1098). Information Age Publishing.
Wilson, M. (2009). Measuring progressions: Assessment structures underlying a learning progression. *Journal of Research in Science Teaching*, *46*(6), 716–730. https://doi.org/10.1002/tea.20318
Wilson, M. (2018). Making measurement important for education: The crucial role of classroom assessment. *Educational Measurement: Issues and Practice*, *37*(1), 5–20. https://doi.org/10.1111/emip.12188
Wilson-Lopez, A., Sias, C., Smithee, A., & Hasbún, I. M. (2018). Forms of science capital mobilized in adolescents' engineering projects. *Journal of Research in Science Teaching*, *55*(2), 246–270. https://doi.org/10.1002/tea.21418
Windschitl, M. (2004). Folk theories of "inquiry:" How preservice teachers reproduce the discourse and practices of an atheoretical scientific method. *Journal of Research in Science Teaching*, *41*(5), 481–512.
Windschitl, M., & Thompson, J. (2011). Ambitious pedagogy by novice teachers: Who benefits from tool-supported collaborative inquiry into practice and why? *Teachers College Record*, *113*(7), 1311–1360.
Windschitl, M., Thompson, J., & Braaten, M. (2018). *Ambitious science teaching*. Harvard Education Press.
Wisniewski, B., Zierer, K., & Hattie, J. (2020). The power of feedback revisited: A meta-analysis of educational feedback research. *Frontiers in Psychology*, *10*, 3087. https://doi.org/10.3389/fpsyg.2019.03087
Wright, C., & Riley, A. (2021). Mitigating the need for resiliency for Black girls: Reimagining the cultural brokering through a lens of science as white property. *Cultural Studies of Science Education*, *16*(2), 495–500. https://doi.org/10.1007/s11422-020-10005-9
Yoon, K. S., Garet, M. S., Birman, B., & Jacobson, R. (2006, December). Examining the effects of mathematics and science professional development on teachers' instructional practice: Using professional development activity log. http://www.ccsso.org/publications/
Zembal-Saul, C., McNeill, K. L., & Hershberger, K. (2012). *What's your evidence? Engaging K–5 children in constructing explanations in science*. Pearson.

Index

Accountability and assessment, 41–43
Achieve, Inc., 60
Activity systems
   formative assessment as activity system, 23–32
   formative assessment in practice, 33–38
Activity theory, 21–23, 41
Activity triangle, 22–23, 24
Affolter, R., 109
Aikenhead, G. S., 40
Alim, H. S., 10
Alonzo, A. C., 161, 162, 163, 164, 165, 170, 171, 176
"Ambitious instruction", 9, 11–13, 47–49, 144, 177–179
Ambitious Science Teaching, 64, 73–74, 98
American Educational Research Association, 42
American Psychological Association, 42
Andrade, H. G., 92, 127
Atkin, J. Myron "Mike", 177
Au, W., 42
Ayala, C. C., 117
Azevedo, F. S., 10, 45

Bang, M., xv, 36, 40, 46, 47, 51
Banilower, E. R., 41
Beatty, I. D., 101
Belczewski, A., 47
Bell, B., 30
Bell, P., 148
Bennett, R. E., 21, 24, 162
Berland, L. K., 163

Bernstein, B., 44
Black, P., 5, 30, 117, 125
Board on Science Education, xv, xix, 4, 7, 10, 163
Borko, H., 144, 157
Braaten, Melissa, 44, 98–99
Braiding Sweetgrass (Kimmerer), 47
Briggs, D. C., 156, 163
Brown, B., 46, 87, 91, 130
Buell, Jason, 63, 64, 154, 163
Burgess, T., 11, 13
Butler, R., 135

Cazden, C. B., 119
Claim-evidence-reasoning, 4
Clarification Statements, 76–77, 96
Classroom setting
   high school biology class case study, 119–124, 128–129
   norms and routines, 111–117
   participation structures, 106–111
   talk moves, 118–119
Coffey, J., 24, 92, 115
Cohen, E. G., 109
Collaborative design
   increasing opportunities for, 159–160
   and professional education for teachers, 144–145
   sample meeting agendas, 201–202
   steps in design process, 145–159
Collins, A., 40
Conant, F. R., 74, 108
Constraints on formative assessment, 43–45, 176
Conversations, classroom, 119–124, 129–133

Corcoran, T., 147, 161, 162
Council, N. R., 7
COVID-19 sample unit, 13–16
Covitt, B. A., 164, 165
Cowie, B., 28, 30, 73, 77, 90
Crosscutting concepts, 7–8, 12, 27–28, 78–81, 161–162, 163. *See also* Three-dimensional learning
Crossouard, B., 7, 129, 130
Culture and language, context of, xvi–xvii, 61, 83–87, 100
Cycles, short, medium and long, 137–140

Debarger, A. H., 150
DeNisi, A., 125
Design process
  Formative Assessment Design Cycle, 145–159
  task design checklist, 185–186
Deverel-Rico, Clarissa, 111, 119, 130
Digital technology, 100–103
Dini, V., 43, 44
Disciplinary knowledge/core ideas, 7–8, 12, 27, 76–77. *See also* Three-dimensional learning
  science learning, 126–127, 148, 163
Donovan, B. M., 42
Dunn, K. E., 30
Duschl, R. A., 23, 110, 129, 162, 163

Edelson, D. C., 9, 69, 147
Enactment, 105–106
  case study, 119–124
  planning guide, 197–198
Engeström, Y., xviii, 7, 21, 24, 33
Engle, R. A., 74, 108
Equity and justice, 9–11, 13, 39
  constraints, 43–45
  examples, 49–53
  formative assessment as vehicle, 45–47
  self-reflection, 47–49
  structural influences, 40–43
Eurocentrism, 40, 42

Feedback
  cycles of, 137–140
  model of, 127–138
  overview, 125–126
  and science learning, 126–127
  in writing, 135–136
Filsecker, M., 30
Fine, Caitlin, 29, 36, 39, 83, 116, 150
Flipgrid software, 101
Flores, N., 39
Ford, M. J., xv, 6, 7
Forman, E. A., xv, 6, 7
Formative assessment
  as activity system, 23–32
  broadening views of, 19–21
  context of classroom activity, 21–23
  feedback, 30–31
  formal contrasted with informal, 32
  formative assessment tasks, 28–29
  guiding questions, 24–32
  historical and accountability functions, 41–43
  overview, 4–5
  routines and interactions, 29–30
  vehicle for equity and justice, 45–47
Formative Assessment Design Cycle (FADC), 145–159
Framework for K-12 Science Education, 7, 12, 58
Framework-aligned learning, 37
Frederiksen, J. R., 118
Freire, Paulo, 41
Furtak, E. M., xvii, xix, 4, 13, 24, 26, 28, 29, 30, 36, 45, 46, 49, 58, 78, 81, 83, 100, 105, 111, 115, 119, 130, 133, 136, 139, 140, 145, 150, 151, 153, 154, 159, 161, 162, 165, 171, 174, 176

García, E. S., 39
Garner, Brette, 44
Gee, J. P., xix, 7
Gerace, W. J., 101
Gipps, C., 42, 44, 45
Gitomer, D. H., 23, 110, 129

Index

Glasser, H., 115
González, N., 7, 39
Gotwals, A. W., 162
Gould, S. J., 42
Grapin, S. E., 10, 11
Gravel, Bryan, 100
Gunckel, K. L., 165
Gunstone, R., 60
Gutiérrez, K., 129
Gutiérrez, R., 126

Harding, S., 40
Hattie, J., 125, 136
Heated Cup Task, 183–184
Henson, Kate, 145, 151, 168
Heredia, Sara, xvii, 100, 145, 148, 151, 161, 171
Heritage, M., 140, 171
Hickey, D. T., 127
High-Elevation Task, 191–195
Historicity, 35–36, 52
History of assessment, 41–43
Holmeier, M., 140
Hondrich, A. L., 136
Horn, I. S., 144

Intentional engagement, 35

Jin, H., 162, 163
Jordan, B., 23
Justice, 46–47. *See also* Equity and justice

Kahoot (kahoot.com), 100, 102
Kang, H., xix, 3, 4, 12, 13, 29, 46, 48, 64, 83, 91, 96, 97, 105, 114
Kerres, M., 30
Kiemer, K., xvii, 46, 105, 145, 151
Kimmerer, Robin Wall, 40, 47
Kluger, A. N., 125
Krajcik, J., 163
Kumashiro, K. K., 10, 23, 45
Kunter, M., 140

Lampert, M., 9
Language and culture, context of, 83–87

Latour, B., 10, 40
Lave, J., 7
Learning in Places Collaborative, 47, 48, 51–53
Learning progressions
 functions of, 164–174
 limitations of, 176
 overview, 161–163
 in support of formative assessment, 174–175
 unit planner, 203–204
Lee, O., 10, 11, 13, 45, 46, 49, 58, 83, 150
Lehrer, R., 163
Lemke, J. L., 106
Li, M., 63, 65
Likely, R., 47, 49, 50, 51, 178
Little, J. W., 144
Looney, A., 48
"Lotions and Potions" curriculum, 49–51
Love, B. L., 178
Lowell, B. R., 116
Luehmann, A., 7

Madkins, T. C., 39
Marin, A., 40
McKinney de Royston, M., 39
McNeill, K. L., 91, 163
Mediated activity, formal assessment as, 33–34, 126, 127
Medin, D., 36
Meeting agendas for collaborative design, 201–202
Menken, K., 116
Minstrell, J., 136, 171
Mohan, L., 165
Moll, L. C., 7, 39
Morales-Doyle, D., 10
Morrison, Deb, 36, 100
Moss, P. A., xviii, xix, 4, 23, 24, 27, 46
Multidimensional instruction, 163. *See also* Three-dimensional learning
Multiple voices, 21, 34–35
Mulvenon, S. W., 30

Nasir, N. S., 12
Nathan, M. J., 43
National Academies of Science, Engineering and Medicine (NASEM), xv, xix, 4, 10, 37, 39, 41, 45, 47, 57, 58, 116, 118
National Council on Measurement in Education, 42
National Research Council (NRC), 12, 58, 59, 88
Next Generation Science Standards (NGSS), 7, 65
  Evidence Statements, 88
  Lead States, 8, 40, 76, 77, 81, 96
  and learning progressions, 163
  performance expectations, 147
Next Generation Storylines, 66
Noble, T., 33
No Child Left Behind (NCLB) Act, 42

Odden, T. O. B., 28, 59, 78, 130
Ogawa, M., 40
OpenSciEd, 13, 30, 66, 78, 80, 92, 109, 117
Otero, V., 43

Paris, D., 10, 39, 61
Participation structures in classroom, 106–111
Patterson Williams, A. D., 11, 13, 48
Pellegrino, J. W., 5, 43, 63
Penuel, W. R., 26, 32, 43, 60, 65, 66, 69, 81, 150, 159
Phenomena
  phenomenon planner, 181
  resources, 69
  role of, 57–62
  support of formative assessment, 66–69
  types of phenomena, 63–66
Philip, T. M., 10, 45
Pickering, A., 40
Pierson, A. E., 163
Plummer, J. D., 163
POGIL (Process-Oriented Guided Inquiry Learning), 101

Posner, G., 60
Pre-assessments, 146–150
Predict-Observe-Explain assessments, 60
Professional education and collaborative design, 144–145
Pryor, J., 7, 129, 130
Putz, P., 23

Quinn, Helen, 27–28, 78

Randall, J., xix, 44, 45, 46, 48, 58, 61, 83, 130, 144, 178
Riley, A., 44, 45
Robertson, A. D., 130
Rogoff, B., 129
Rosebery, A. S., 35
Rudolph, J. L., 6
Ruiz-Primo, M. A., 30, 63, 65, 100
Russ, R. S., 28, 59, 78, 130

Sadler, D. R., 24, 92
SAIL (Science and Integrated Language) curriculum, 11
Scaffolds, 74, 90–91, 96, 102–103, 109, 115, 151, 162
Schauble, L., 163
Schmidt, W. H., 40
Schwarz, C. V., 65, 77, 163
Science and Engineering in Preschool Through Elementary Grades (NASEM), 45, 46
Science and engineering practices, 7, 12, 77–78, 163. *See also* Three-dimensional learning
Science education, 7–9
Scientist circles, 109
Scott, P., 133
Self-reflection, 47–49, 52
"Settled science", 40–41
Shavelson, R. J., 31, 32, 150, 163
Shepard, L. A., xix, 5, 9, 26, 43
Sherin, M., 157
Skateboarder Modeling Task, 199
Smith, J. B., xv, 9
Smylie, M. A., xv, 9
Snowmelt Task, 189

Sociocultural theory, 6–7, 9
Songer, N. B., 163
Spencer, M. B., 39
Staircase model, 164–165
Steedle, J. T., 163
Stein, M. K., 28, 29
STEM Teaching Tools, 81
Suárez, E., 36, 37, 116, 130
summative assessment, 5, 68, 69, 71

"Talk moves", 118–121, 140
Tasks
 defined, 72–73
 integration of three dimensions, 75–81
 multicomponent formative assessment tasks, 92–99
 role of, 73–75
 task design, 81–92, 185–186
 technology-assisted tasks, 100–103
Taylor, C. S., 61, 84, 92
Tayne, K., 165, 174
Technology
 and feedback, 136–137
 and task design, 100–103
Tekkumru-Kisa, M., 28, 29, 72, 73, 75, 81, 82
TERC, 116
Thompson, J., 9, 116, 144, 151, 159, 162
Three-dimensional learning, 7–9
 shift to, 11–13
 and task design, 75–81
Timperley, H., 125, 136

Tzou, C., xv, 4, 11, 12, 34, 47, 51, 130, 148, 176

unlearning, 23

van der Veen, Stacey, 153
van Es, E., 130, 157
Van Horne, Katie, 78, 81, 150
Vossoughi, S., 10

Watson, Mandy, 87–88
Weather in Three Places Task, 187–188
Wenger, E., 7
Wenzel, S. A., xv, 9
Wertsch, J. V., 7, 33
Whitcomb, J. A., 144
White, B. Y., 118
White, R., 60
Wiliam, D., 5, 30, 43, 117, 125, 138
Wilson, M., 5, 163
Wilson-Lopez, A., 10, 46
Windschitl, M., xv, xix, 9, 12, 32, 36, 64, 65, 73, 74, 110, 117, 128, 154, 155, 157
Wisniewski, B., 30, 125
Woolgar, S., 40
Wright, Christopher, 44, 45, 47, 49, 100

Yoon, K. S., 144
Young, D. B., 31, 32, 150

Zembal-Saul, C., 92, 100

About the Author

Erin Marie Furtak is professor of STEM Education at the University of Colorado Boulder. A former public high school biology and Earth science teacher, she studies how science formative assessment can broaden student participation in science learning, and how formative assessment co-design supports teacher learning. Her research partnerships with teachers and school districts have been supported by numerous national and international fellowships and grants. She writes for multiple venues, including scholarly and practitioner-facing journals, edited volumes, blogs, and higher education websites. She received the 2011 Presidential Early Career Award for Scientists and Engineers from the White House Office of Science and Technology Policy. She lives in small-town Colorado with her husband, two children, and two dogs.